IMAGES
of America

Indian Trail and Edgemont Amusement Parks

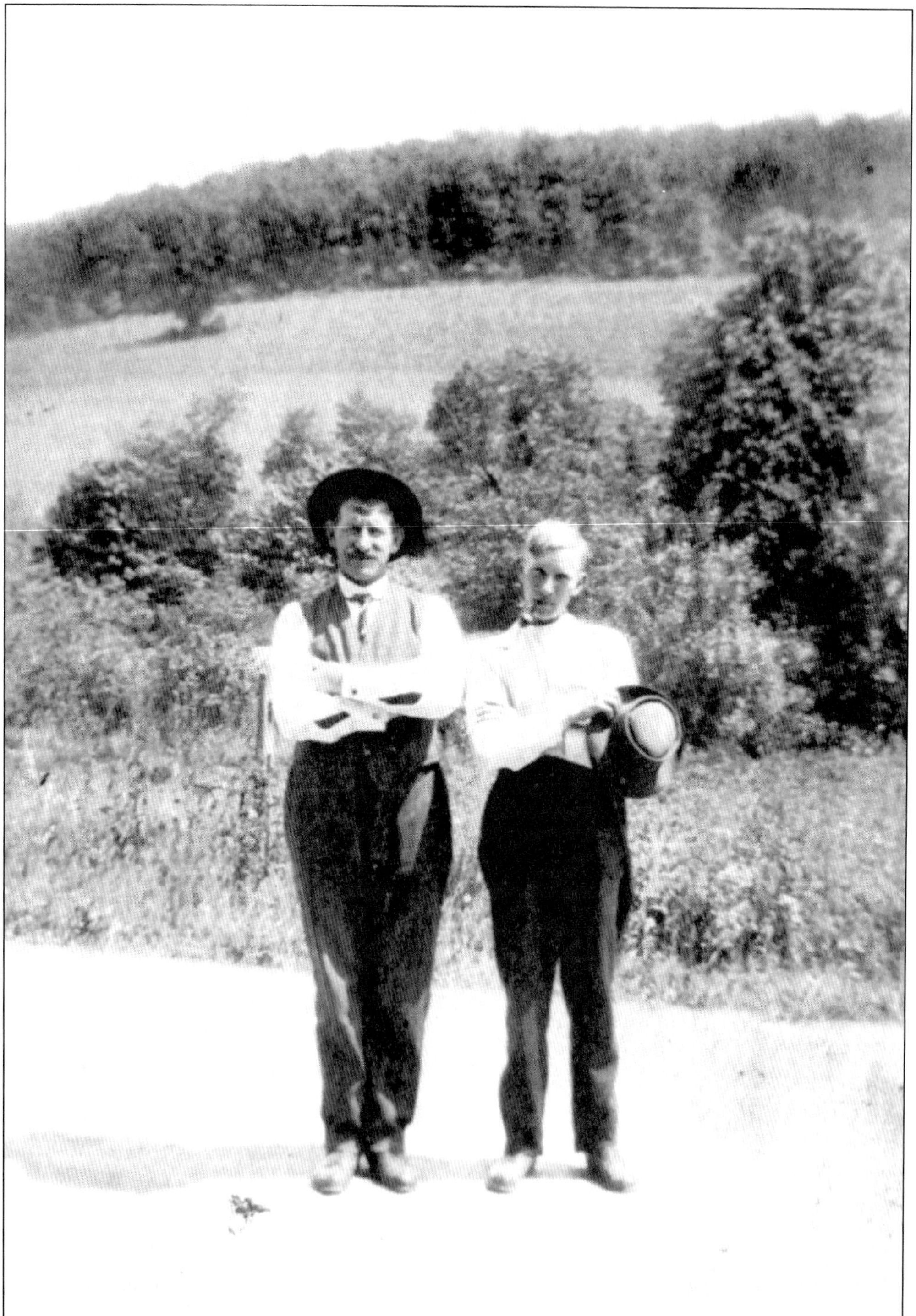

Amandes and Sam Jacoby stand on the dirt road that will become Route 248, in the area where Indian Trail Park will be built. At the park, Amandes will run the arcade and then the concessions with his wife, Sarah. (Courtesy Elda Miller.)

IMAGES
of America

INDIAN TRAIL AND EDGEMONT AMUSEMENT PARKS

Sean and Johanna S. Billings for the
Lehigh Township Historical Society

ARCADIA
PUBLISHING

ISBN 0-7385-3707-1

First published 2005

Published by Arcadia Publishing,
Charleston, SC

Library of Congress Catalog Card Number: 2004111642

For all general information, contact Arcadia Publishing:
Telephone 843-853-2070
Fax 843-853-0044
E-mail sales@arcadiapublishing.com
For customer service and orders:
Toll-free 1-888-313-2665

Visit us on the Internet at www.arcadiapublishing.com

To our daughter Kayleigh, who puts up with her father's obsession with history and her mother's obsession with stuffed soccer balls.

CONTENTS

ACKNOWLEDGMENTS

Special thanks go to the following individuals who provided photographs and information for this book: the William Beck family, Hilda Gaugler, Leslie Greffe, Larry Hillborn, Alverta Jones, Emily Jones, Blaine Kahle, Dale Miller, Elda Miller, Rollin Minnich Jr., Belle Minnich, Kenneth Moyer, Kristine Moyer, Adam Newhard, Gloria Newhard, Laura E. Scheirer, Julia Smith, Shirley Szoke, Stephen Unger, and Alyce Unger.

The authors are also grateful to the hardworking volunteers who keep the Lehigh Township Historical Society going: Daniel Hummel, Ken Marsh, Franklin Mummey, Sarah Pagotto, Peter Pagotto, Beverly Putt, Wilson Putt, Chris Satow, and Nancy Thatcher.

The Lehigh Township Historical Society thanks those who contributed to the rebuilding of the Trading Post at Indian Trail Park. Among them are Atas International, Alcoa, and Quality Roofing Supply of Allentown. David Costa and Frank Guerra of Costa Construction worked tirelessly on this reconstruction project. The society also thanks the many individuals and local businesses, far too many too list, who made monetary donations.

INTRODUCTION

Most communities are thrilled to have one amusement park within their town borders. Lehigh Township, however, was lucky enough to have not one, but two.

Edgemont Park opened in the first decade of the 20th century as a trolley stop for the Blue Ridge Traction Company on its route from Walnutport to Danielsville. By the time the Great Depression hit in 1929, Edgemont had already been operating for decades. That same year, Samuel and William Solliday built Indian Trail Park just five miles away. Despite the difficulties of the 1930s, both parks survived and prospered into the 1940s and beyond.

Edgemont and Indian Trail featured swimming, food, and entertainment. Both eventually had rides and dance halls, though they were nothing like modern-day amusement parks. They were a part of the community. Rather than being owned by some out-of-state corporation, they were run by families. In both cases, the families lived on the park grounds. Family members operated rides, served food, and landscaped. They were the ones who decided what attractions to add as the years passed.

Although separate, the two parks had a relationship with each other. The Minniches, who were involved with Indian Trail, for example, went on to own Edgemont. Joseph Cerrone, who operated Edgemont during its later years, served as a pall bearer for Leroy Kahle, who had owned Indian Trail. Both parks were situated in wooded areas, allowing the incorporation of nature into activities such as swimming, picnicking, and playing. Because the parks provided an inexpensive day out, many families held their reunions there.

Though they had a lot in common, the parks developed their own personalities. Indian Trail had a cement-bottom pool, while Edgemont's pool had a dirt bottom. Indian Trail featured a roller coaster, while Edgemont did not. Edgemont had an auction and a farmers' market, both absent at Indian Trail.

Today, little remains of what existed at each location. Indian Trail's playground and pavilion still stand, though the rides, games, and entertainments are long gone, except when special events are held there. Edgemont is no longer a park but is privately owned by several businesses. Even though their heydays are over, Edgemont and Indian Trail remain vivid in the memories of residents.

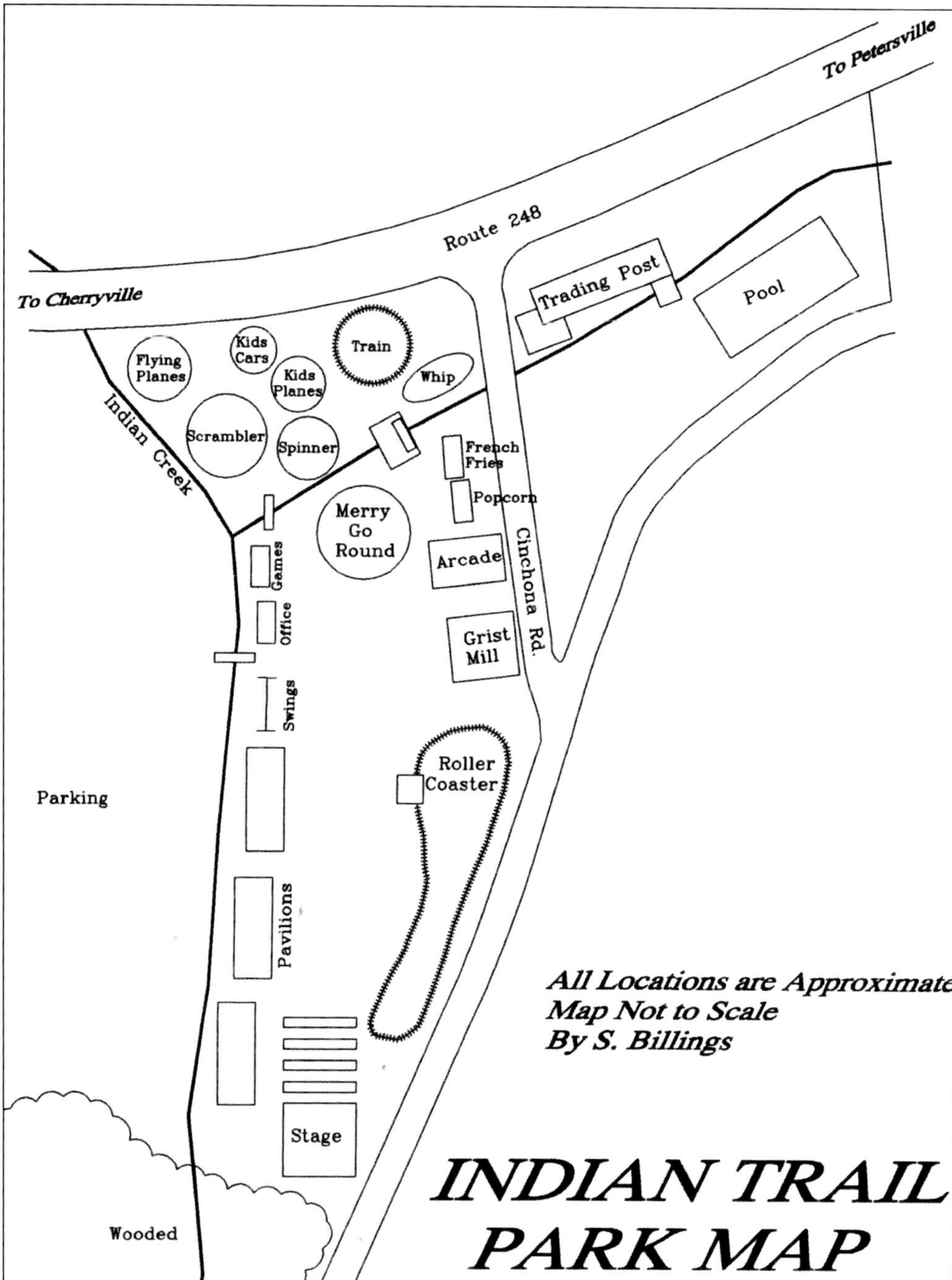

This map of Indian Trail Park shows the approximate locations of the rides and buildings. Note that the rides changed and were moved over the years.

One

Indian Trail Park
The Beginning

Indian Trail Park is situated on the banks of the Indian Creek in the town of Pennsville, located in Lehigh Township, Northampton County. The property is part of the original Indianland Tract set aside in 1735 by Thomas Penn as a place for local tribes displaced by early settlers. The Native Americans never used the reservation, and in 1803, Adam Dreisbach obtained 155 acres of the tract, including the area now known as Indian Trail Park. In 1804, Dreisbach sold the land to John Royer. John Applebach then purchased the 30 acres that would become Indian Trail Park. In 1818, the property, listed as a gristmill with 23 acres, was sold at sheriff's sale to Christian Hagenbuch. In 1819, he sold the land to Daniel Kleckner. The cornerstone on the building, which has since been torn down, read, "1849 Daniel Kleckner." In 1884, the land was sold to John H. Beck, then to Howard H. and Estelle N. Laubach, and then to James O. and Mary J. Hower.

Allentown building contractor Samuel Solliday and his brother William purchased the property on May 15, 1929, from the Howers. The brothers formed Indian Trail Park Inc. to build and operate the park on the land along the Indian Creek. The land was deeded over to the corporation on August 10, 1929. Samuel Solliday was the corporation's president, and his wife, Lillie, was the secretary.

The Sollidays promoted the park as a picnic ground and "Cool Retreat from the Summer's Heat." The grounds offered a natural setting with shade, shelter, tables, benches, fountains, and campsites. Picnic areas covered about five acres along the creek. One of the park's big attractions was the concrete swimming pool, graded from two to nine feet in depth. The pool had lifeguards and a modern dressing room with steel lockers. Benches and umbrellas surrounded the perimeter of the pool for use by patrons. The entire park was beautifully landscaped with fish ponds, fountains, and stone walls surrounding the gardens.

The park also contained a penny arcade, run by Amandes Jacoby in the early days. One machine created aluminum circles customized with a person's name on them. Other machines offered postcards featuring photographs of movie stars. The penny arcade also included moving picture machines and a crane that scooped candy and dumped it into a shoot.

If a picnic was not in a patron's plans, soda, popcorn, candy, and hot dogs could be purchased at concession stands, or meals could be purchased at the restaurant. Amandes and Sarah Jacoby ran the concession stand in the early 1930s for the Sollidays. As a child, Elda Jacoby would be sent from the concession stand to the restaurant to stock up on popsicles when the stand ran out.

Burro rides, another popular attraction, were given by six burros brought in from Texas and cared for by a man named Harry Trexler. Four of them were named Ginger, Clara, Jack, and Bill. The names of the other two are unknown.

The first rides at the park included a roller coaster and merry-go-round. The roller coaster, though small by today's standards, was fast and exciting with small individual cars, rather than a train of cars, going around the circuit. The merry-go-round was an Illions machine with Dentzel horses. The two inner rows traveled up and down, and the outer row remained stationary. A long arm sticking out contained metal rings made of steel and brass. If you could grab a brass ring on the way around, you won a free ride. One of the horses from Indian Trail's merry-go-round ended up at Knoebel's Amusement Resort's carousel museum in Elysburg.

Indian Trail Park Inc. also offered land for sale on the hillside overlooking the park. Twenty summer bungalows were built there on lots 50 to 60 feet wide. In the early 1930s, the lot prices ranged from $275 to $400, according to the brochure.

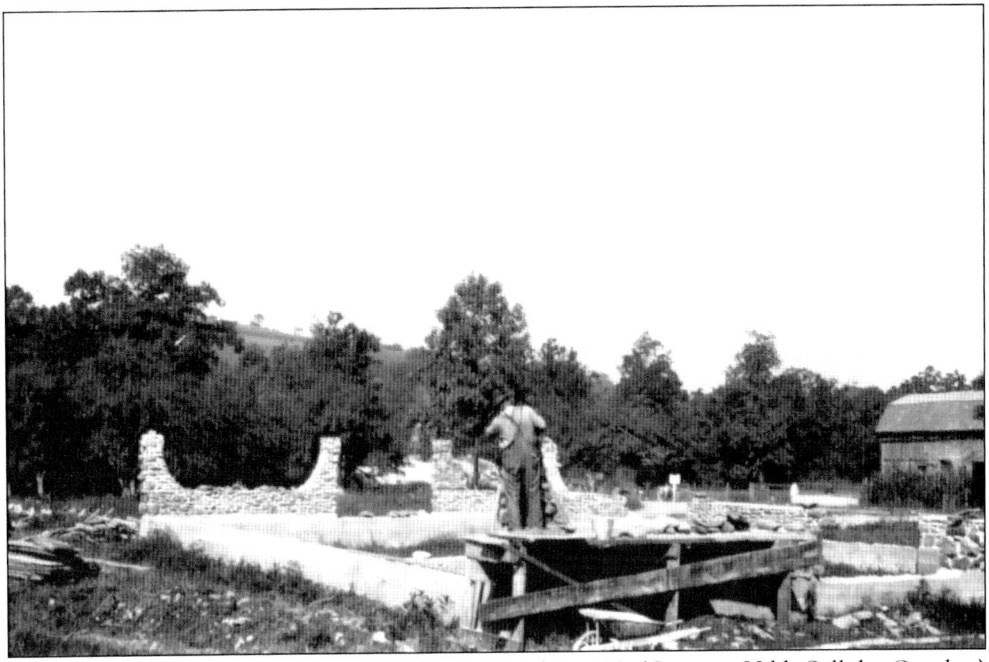

The Trading Post at Indian Trail Park was constructed in 1929. (Courtesy Hilda Solliday Gaugler.)

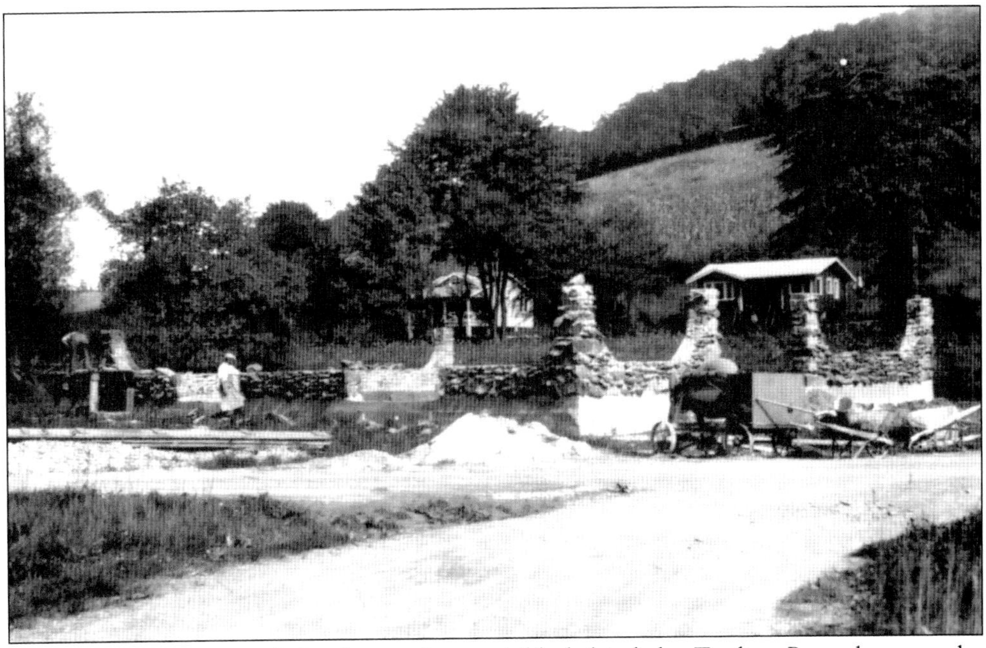

Some of the cottages and the dirt roads are visible behind the Trading Post, shown under construction in 1929. (Courtesy Hilda Solliday Gaugler.)

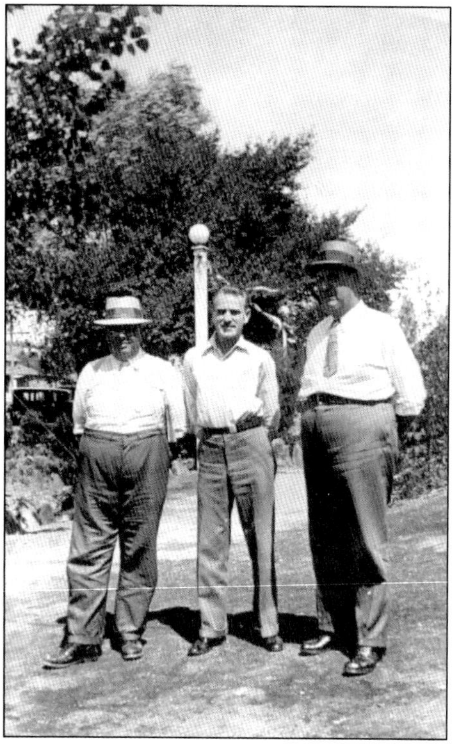

William (left) and Samuel Solliday (right) started the park in 1929. Shown with them is a man named Bill Beitler. (Courtesy Hilda Solliday Gaugler.)

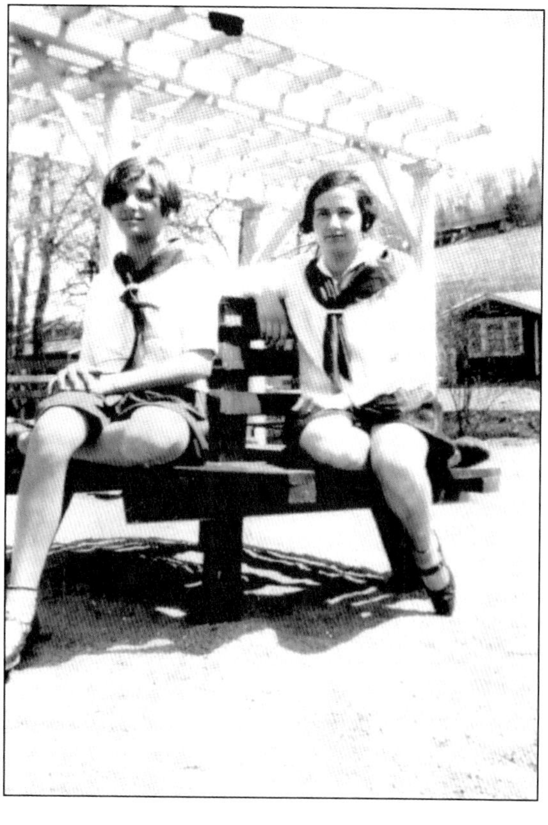

Samuel and Lillie Solliday had two daughters, Hilda (left) and Irene, seated at a table near the pool. (Courtesy Hilda Solliday Gaugler.)

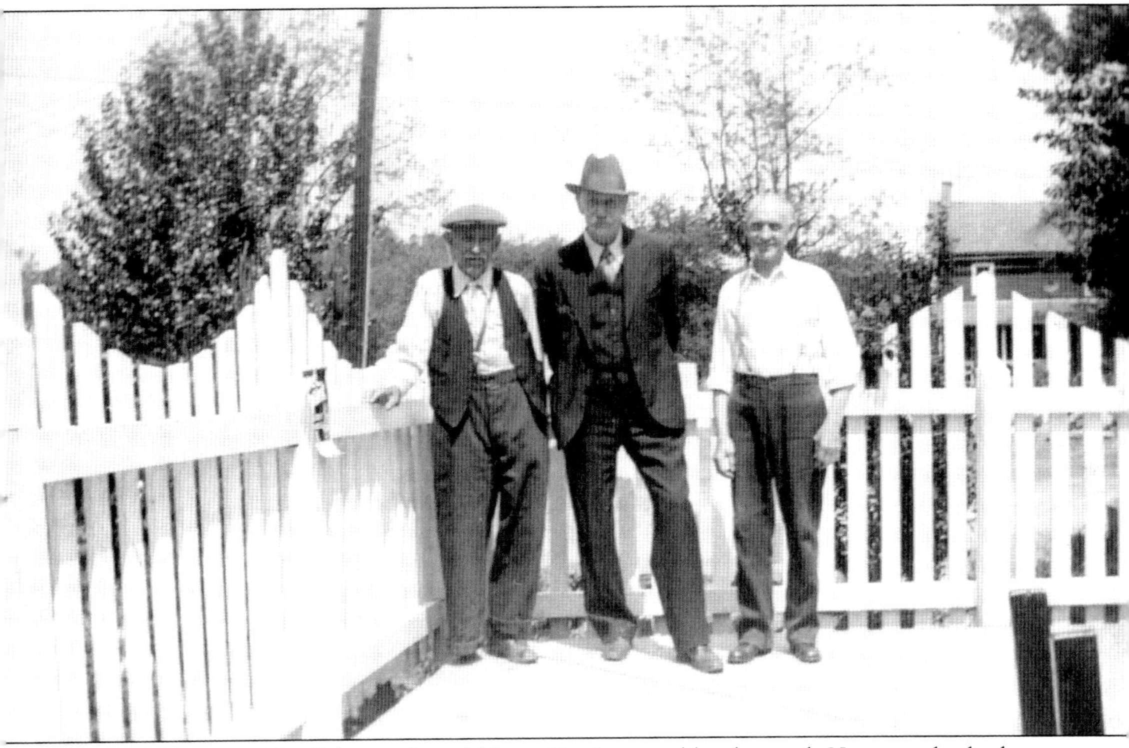

Harvey (left), Pappy Knoll (center), and Harry Trexler stand by the pool. Harvey, who had a wooden leg, made baskets that were sold at the park. Pappy Knoll was Lillie Solliday's father, and Harry Trexler took care of the burros while his wife cooked at the restaurant. (Courtesy Hilda Solliday Gaugler.)

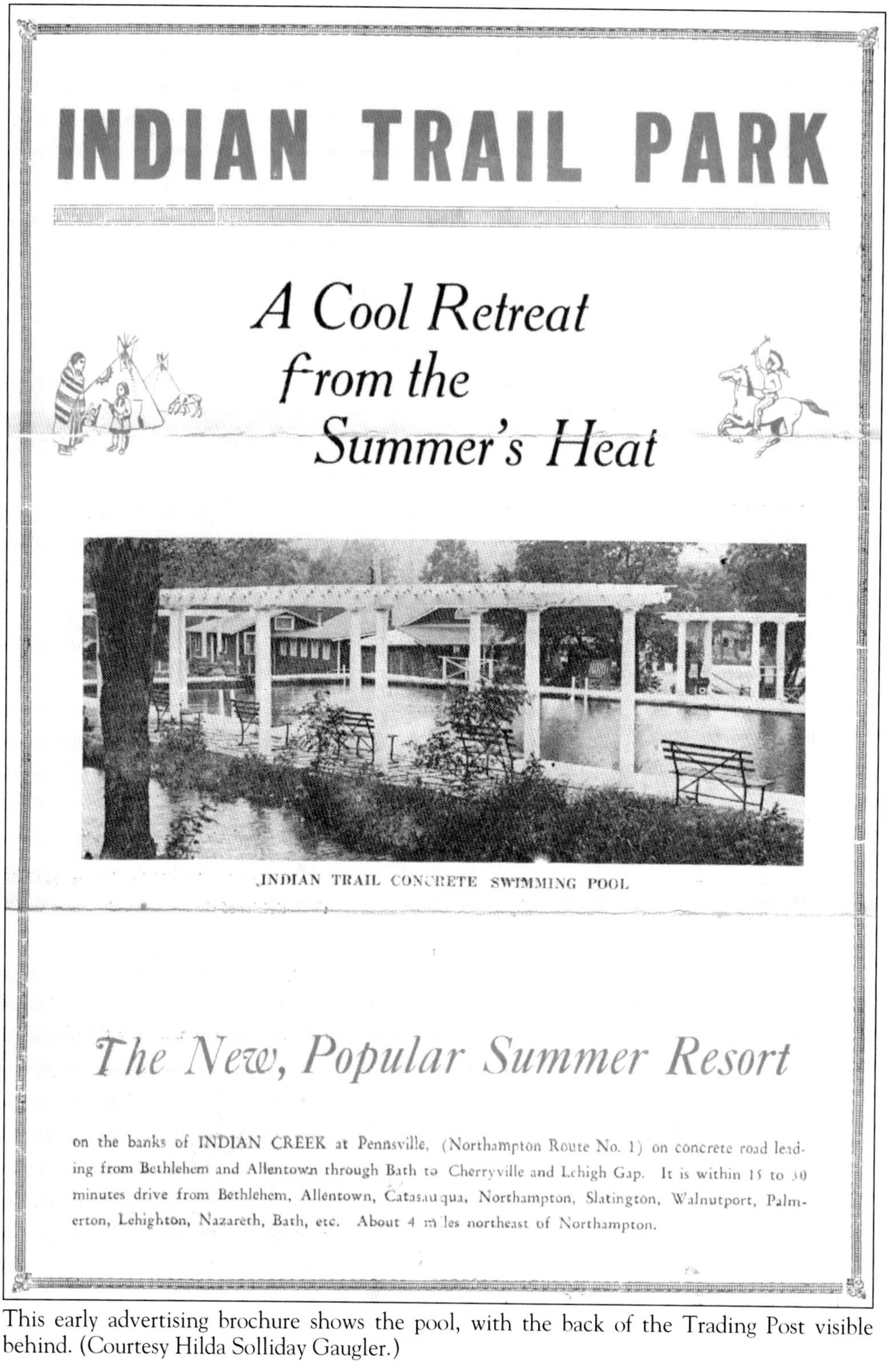

INDIAN TRAIL PARK

A Cool Retreat from the Summer's Heat

INDIAN TRAIL CONCRETE SWIMMING POOL

The New, Popular Summer Resort

on the banks of INDIAN CREEK at Pennsville, (Northampton Route No. 1) on concrete road leading from Bethlehem and Allentown through Bath to Cherryville and Lehigh Gap. It is within 15 to 30 minutes drive from Bethlehem, Allentown, Catasauqua, Northampton, Slatington, Walnutport, Palmerton, Lehighton, Nazareth, Bath, etc. About 4 miles northeast of Northampton.

This early advertising brochure shows the pool, with the back of the Trading Post visible behind. (Courtesy Hilda Solliday Gaugler.)

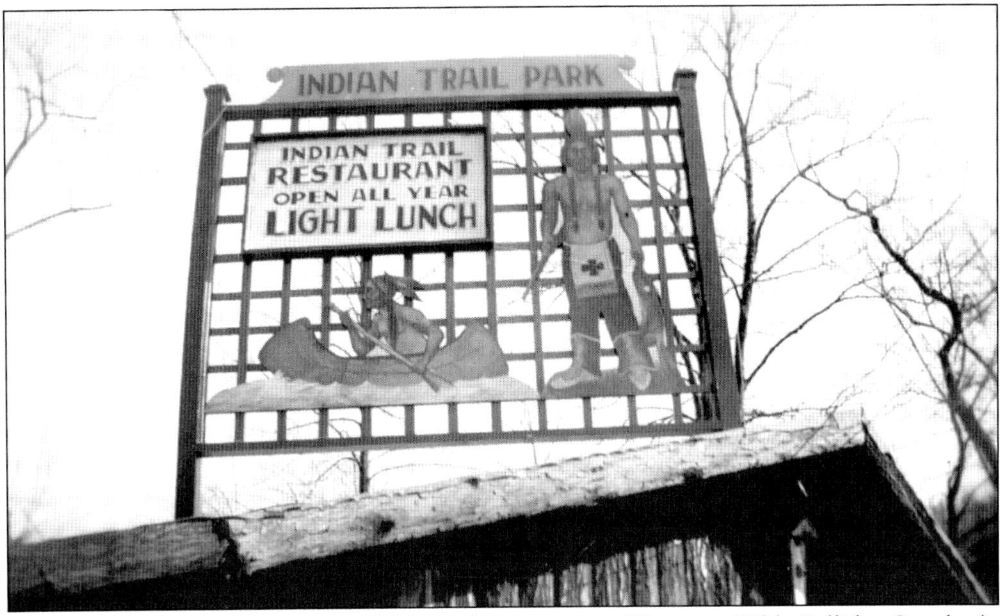

This early Indian Trail Park sign advertises the restaurant. (Courtesy Hilda Solliday Gaugler.)

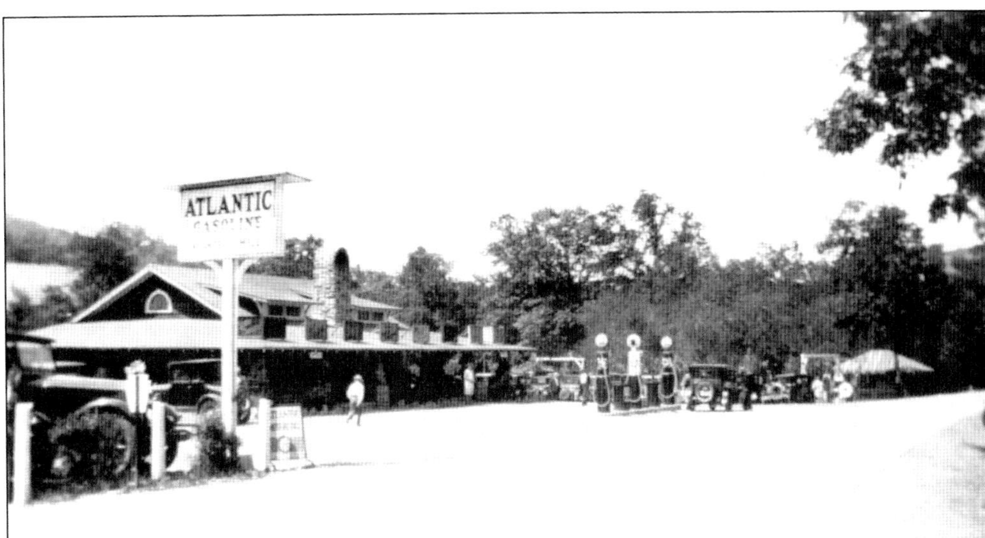

The Trading Post is displayed in this 1930s view, looking toward Cherryville on what is now Route 248. At this time, the Trading Post contained a soda fountain and restaurant and sold Atlantic gas. Three pumps are visible in front of the building. (Courtesy Hilda Solliday Gaugler.)

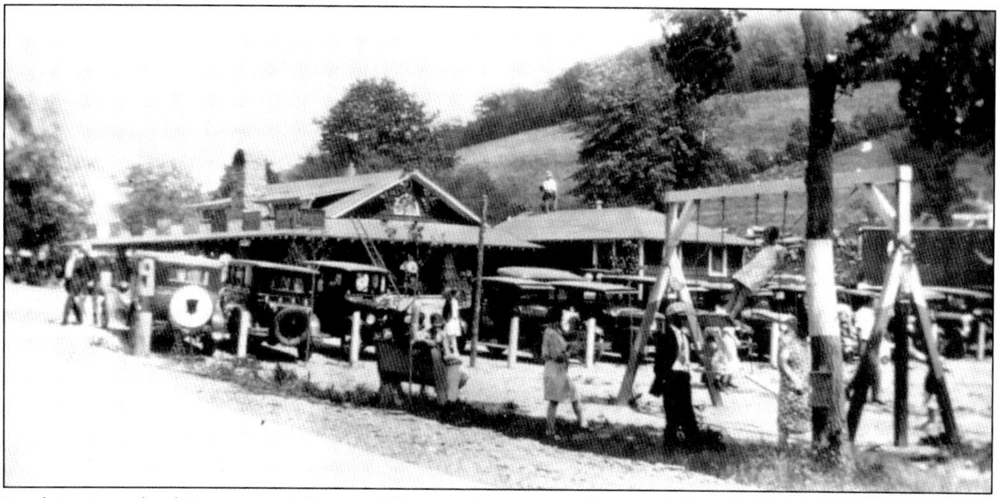

In this view, looking toward Petersville on what is now Route 248, playground equipment can be seen to the right. (Courtesy Hilda Solliday Gaugler.)

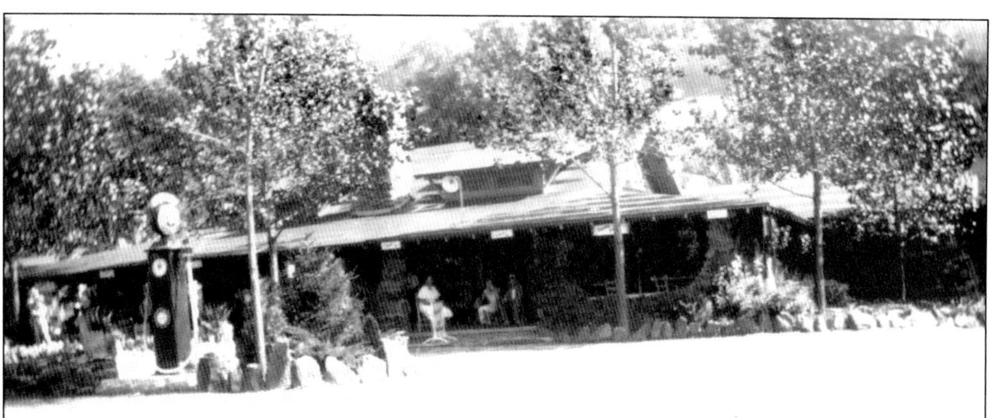

The trees in front of the Trading Post have grown considerably. Only one gas pump remains. (Courtesy Hilda Solliday Gaugler.)

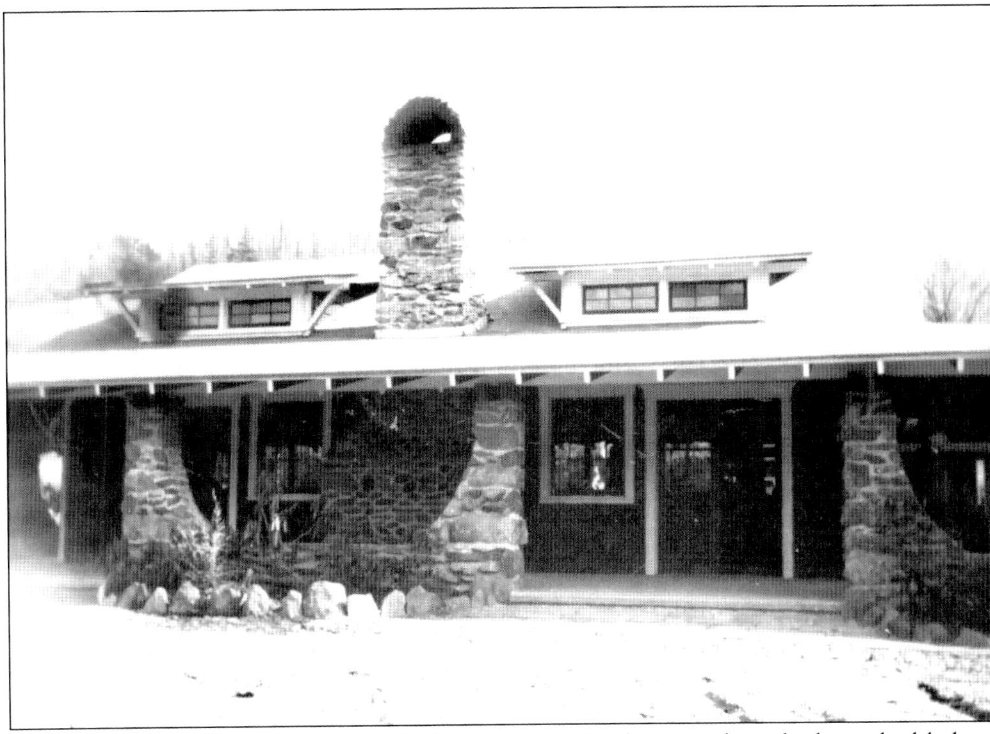

The original natural wood siding on the building gave it a brown color, which was highlighted with white trim. Later, the siding was painted white, and the trim was first painted green and then red. (Courtesy Hilda Solliday Gaugler.)

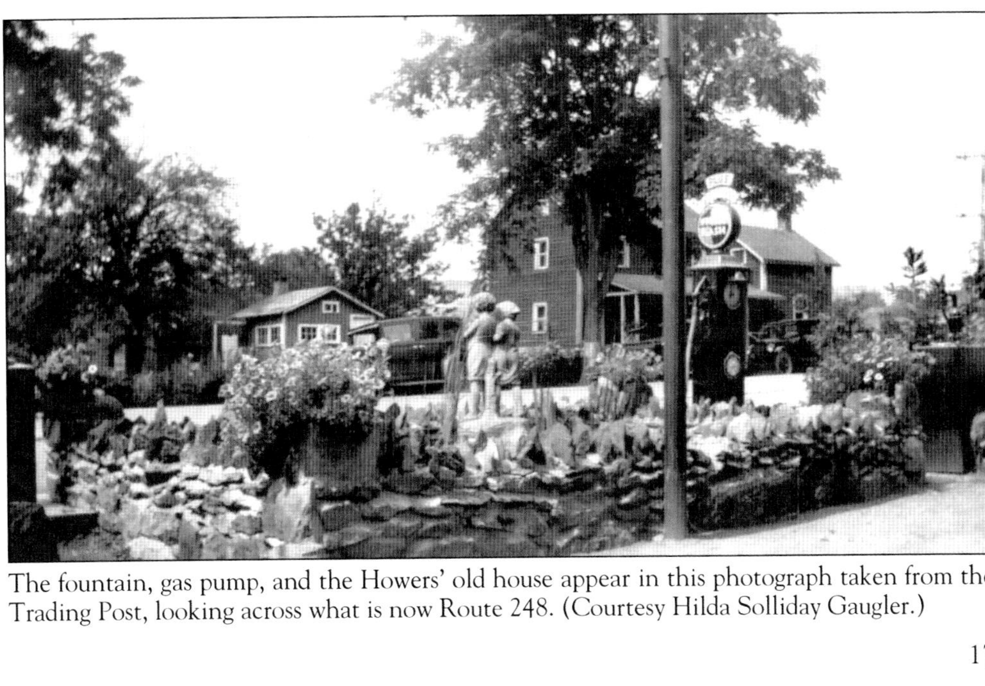

The fountain, gas pump, and the Howers' old house appear in this photograph taken from the Trading Post, looking across what is now Route 248. (Courtesy Hilda Solliday Gaugler.)

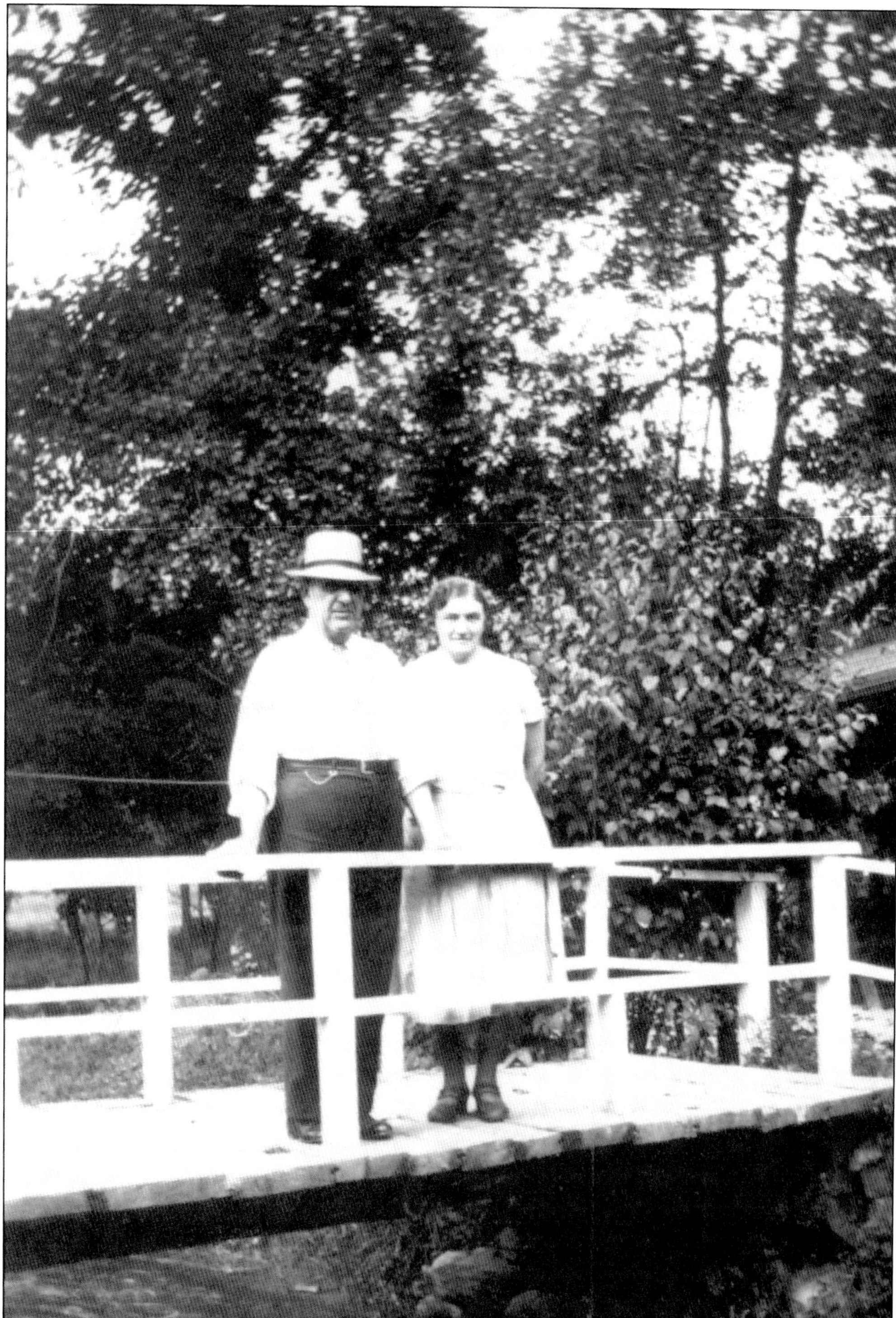

Samuel and Lillie Solliday stand on the bridge that crossed the creek between the Trading Post and the pool. (Courtesy Hilda Solliday Gaugler.)

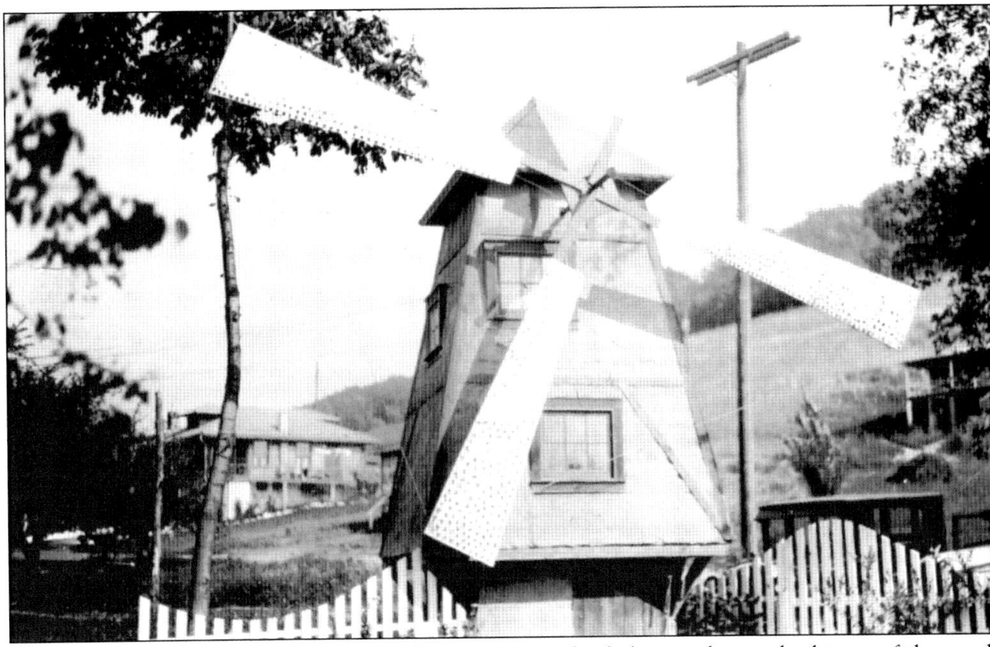

The windmill shown here stood at the eastern end of the pool, overlooking a fish pond. (Courtesy Larry Hillborn.)

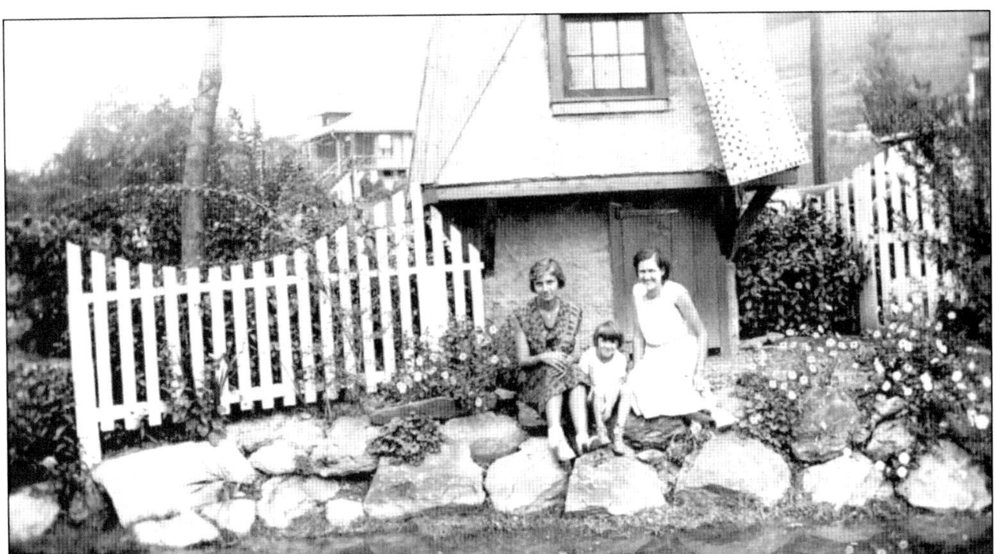

Hilda Solliday (left), Mary Jane Beitler (center), and Irene Solliday sit at the base of the windmill. (Courtesy Hilda Solliday Gaugler.)

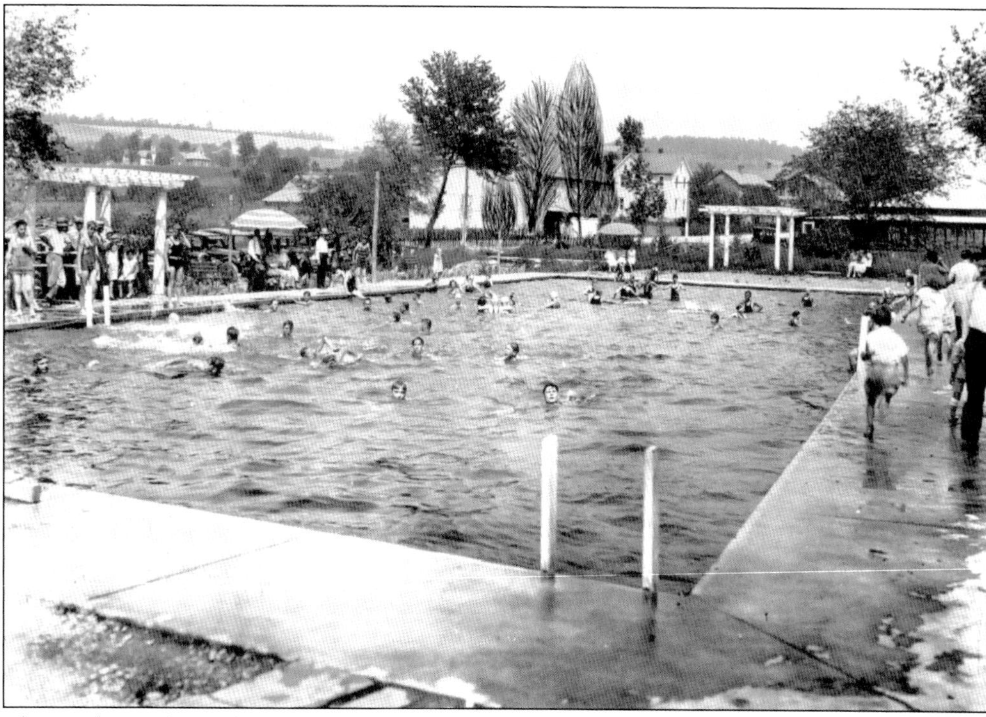

The pool was located in the field behind the Trading Post. In this view, the Pennsville Schoolhouse and the United Brethren Church can be seen in the distance at the upper left. The school is now a private residence, and the church has been gone for many years. (Courtesy Hilda Solliday Gaugler.)

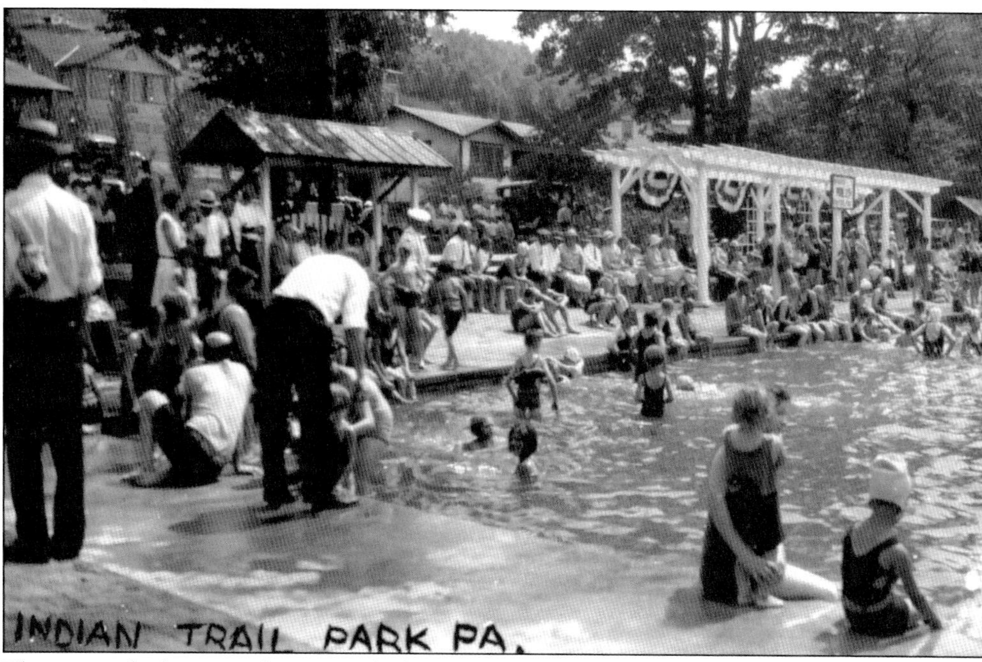

This view, looking southwest, includes some of the cottages that were built on the hill overlooking the park. (Courtesy Larry Hillborn.)

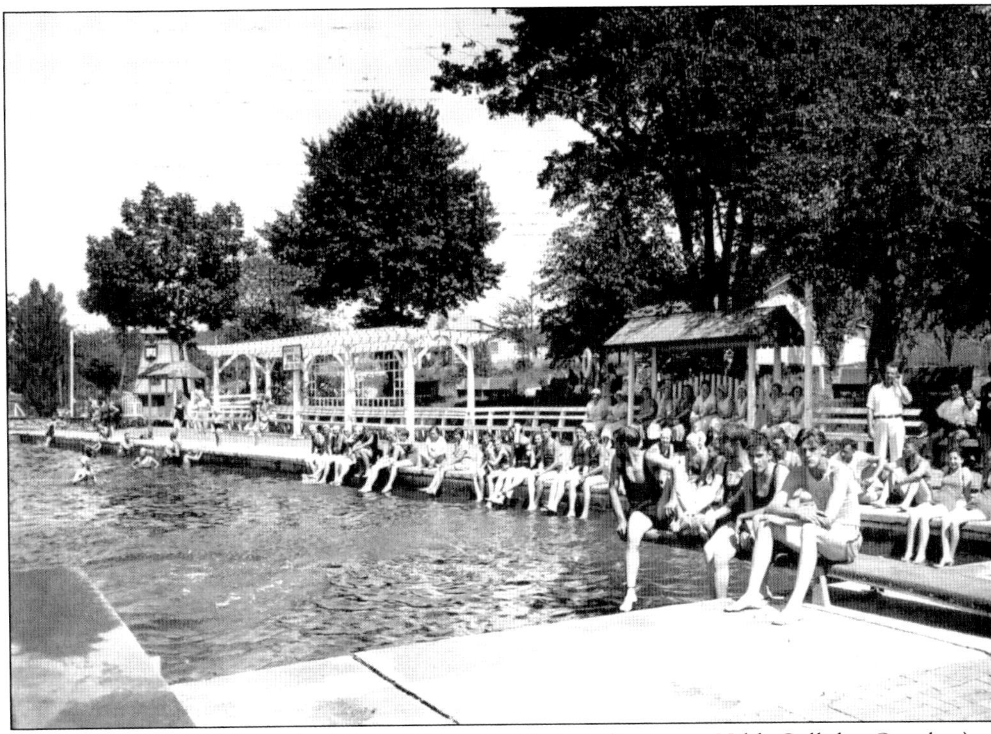

The windmill is visible on the left in this eastward view. (Courtesy Hilda Solliday Gaugler.)

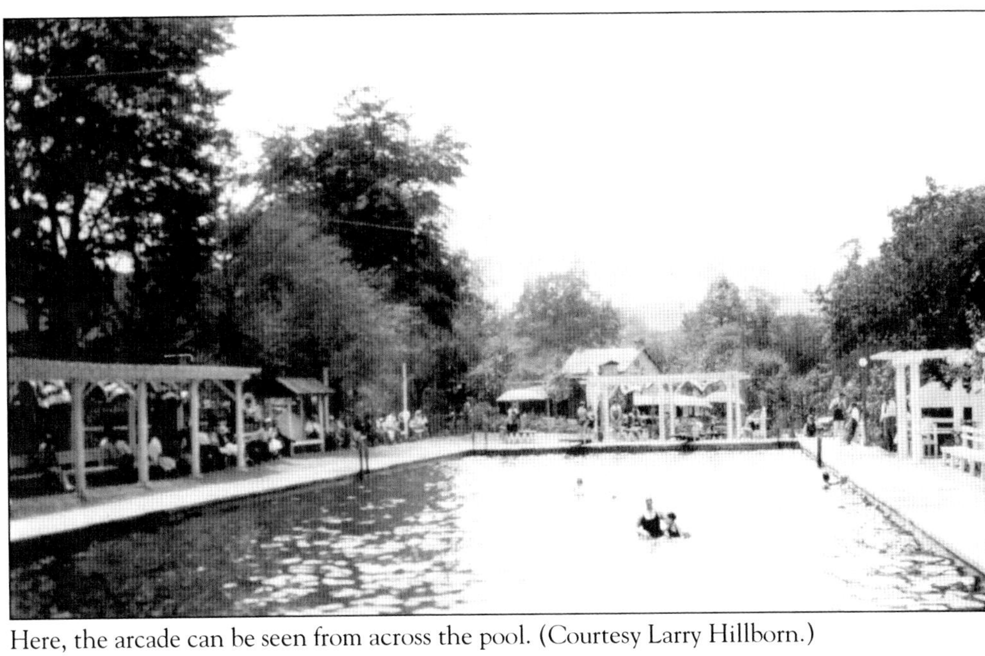

Here, the arcade can be seen from across the pool. (Courtesy Larry Hillborn.)

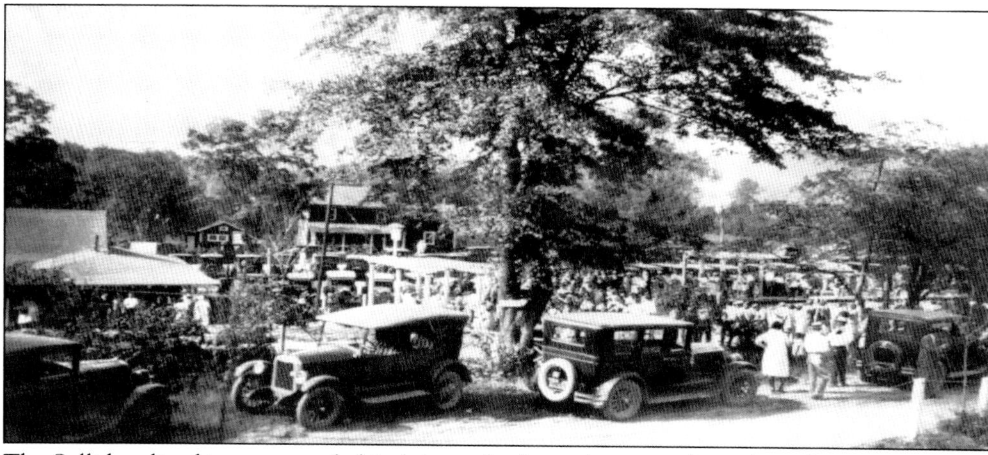

The Sollidays lived in a cottage behind the park, shown here on a busy day. The cars are parked on what is now Teak Drive. (Courtesy Hilda Solliday Gaugler.)

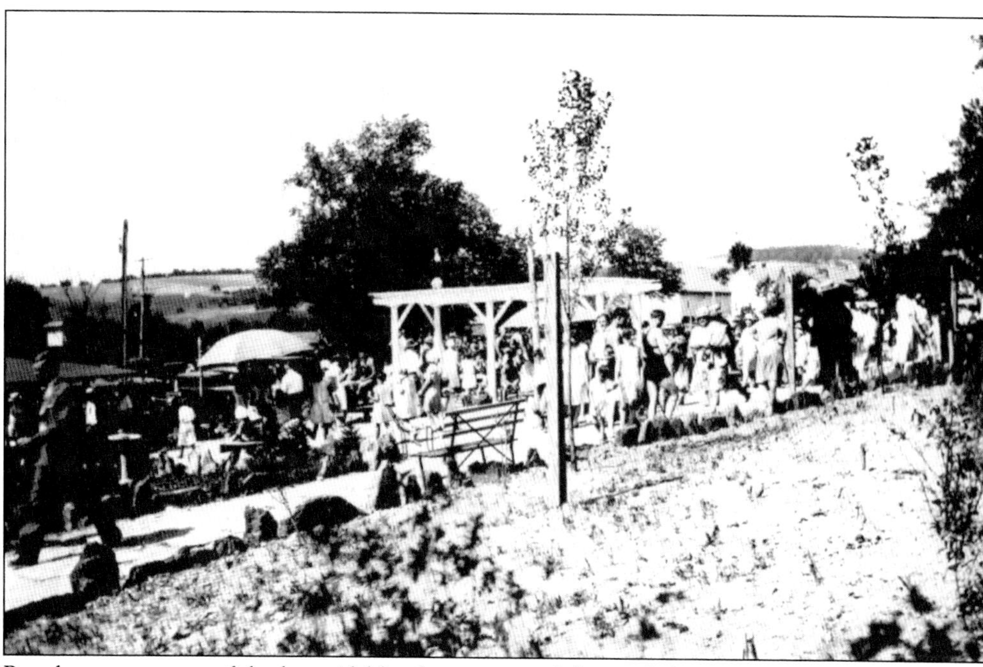

Benches were a part of the beautiful landscape around the pool. (Courtesy Larry Hillborn.)

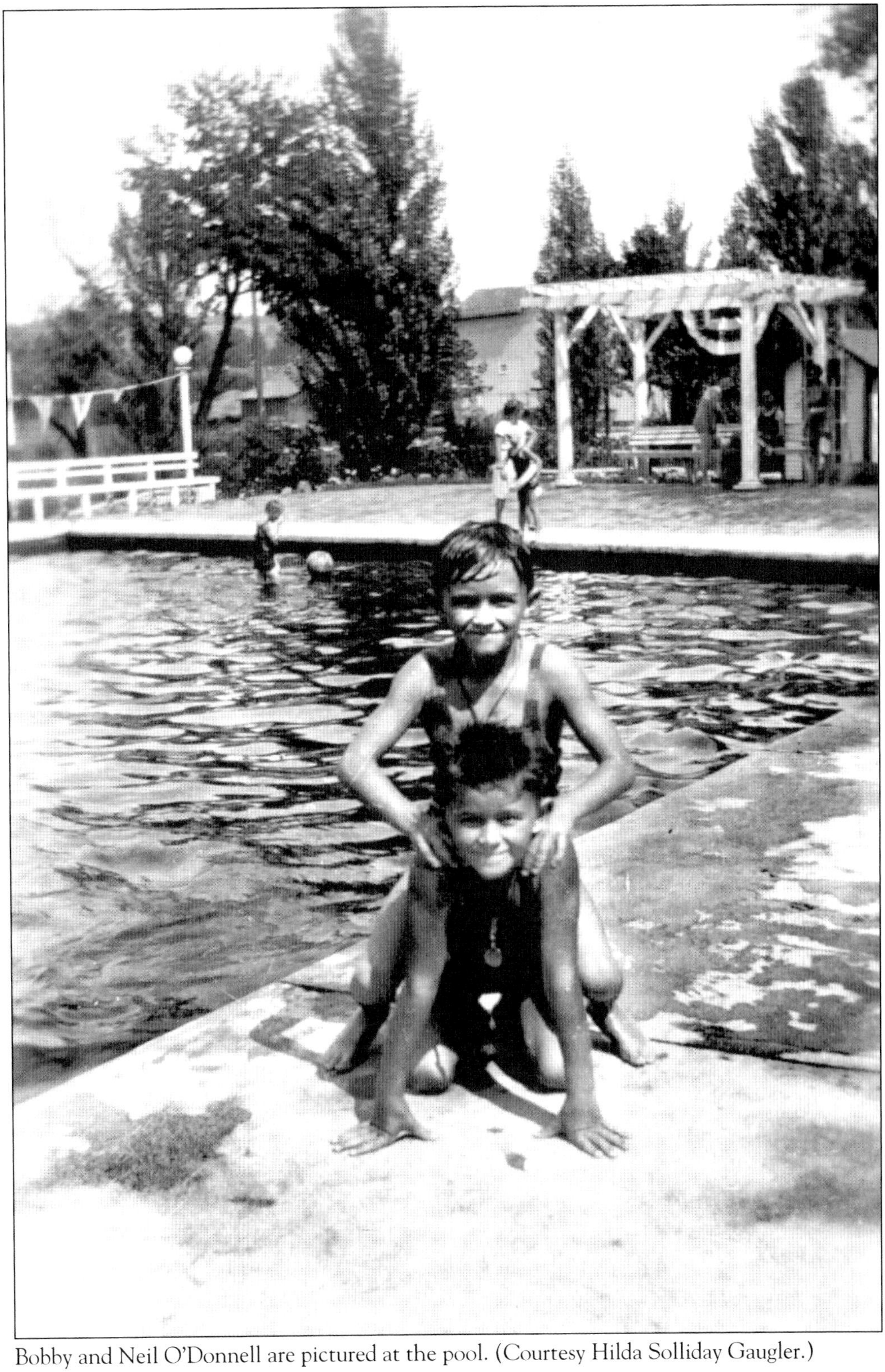

Bobby and Neil O'Donnell are pictured at the pool. (Courtesy Hilda Solliday Gaugler.)

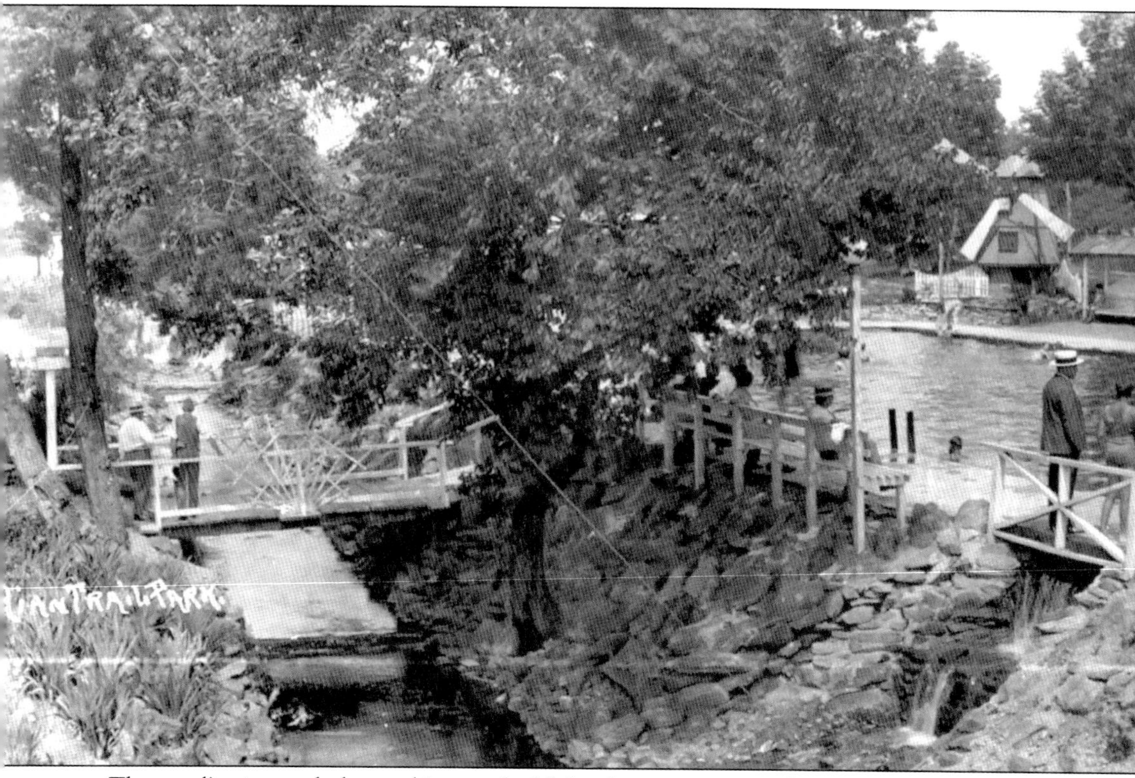

The pool's size and the park's wonderful landscaping are evident in this incredible view.

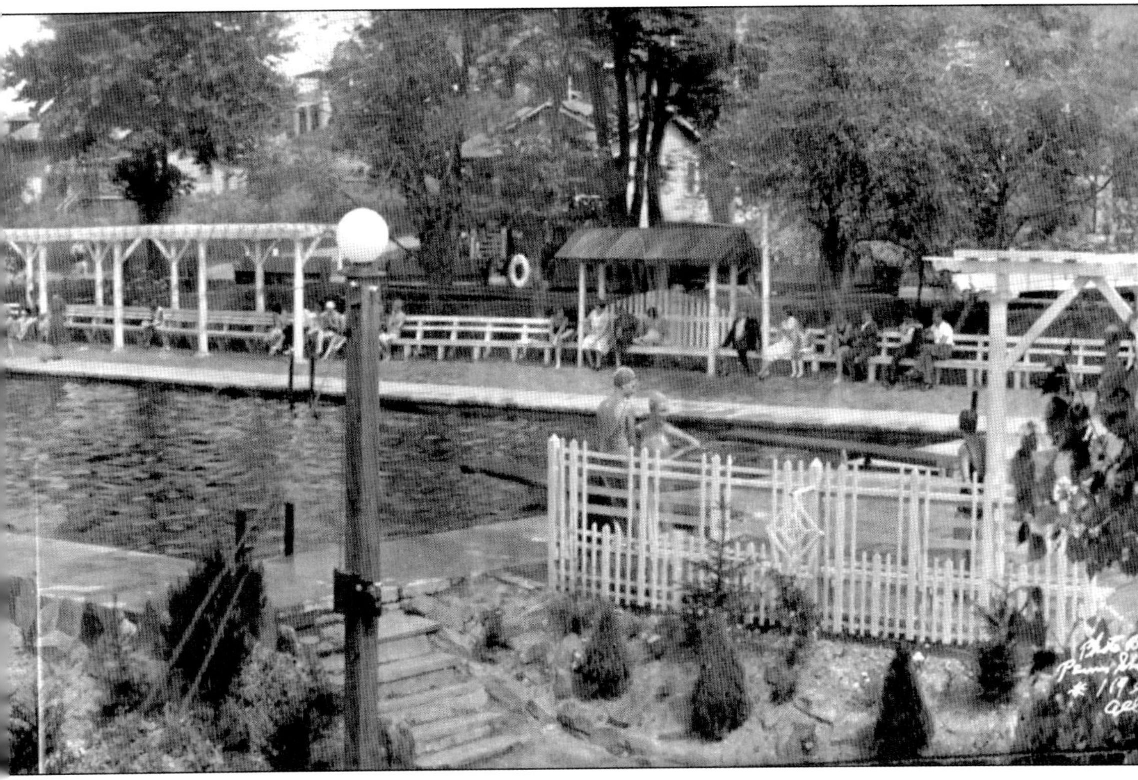

(Courtesy Hilda Solliday Gaugler.)

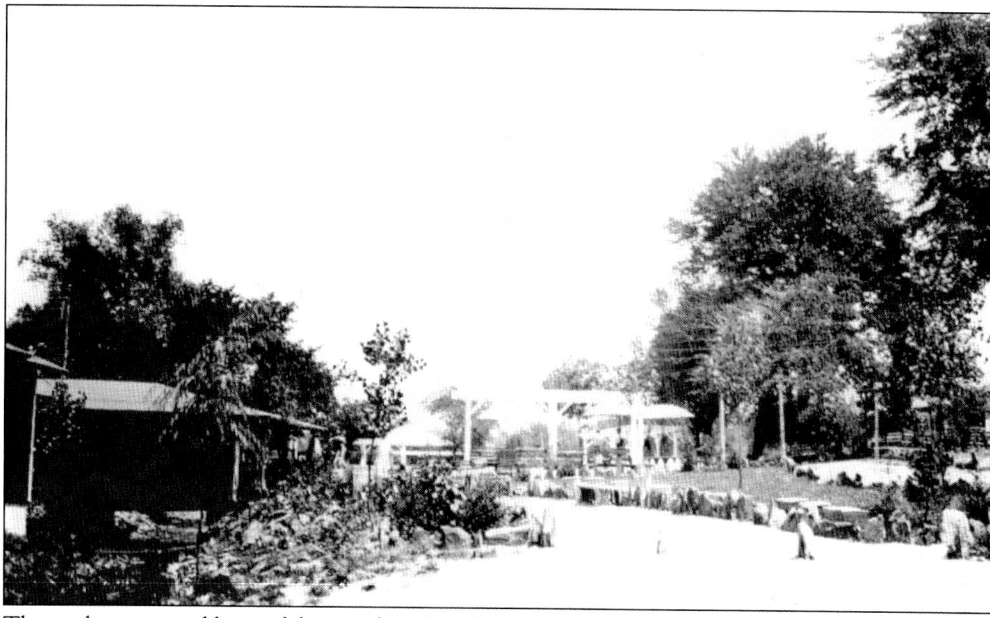

The park contained beautiful stone-lined walkways, as seen here. The back of the Trading Post is visible to the left. (Courtesy Larry Hillborn.)

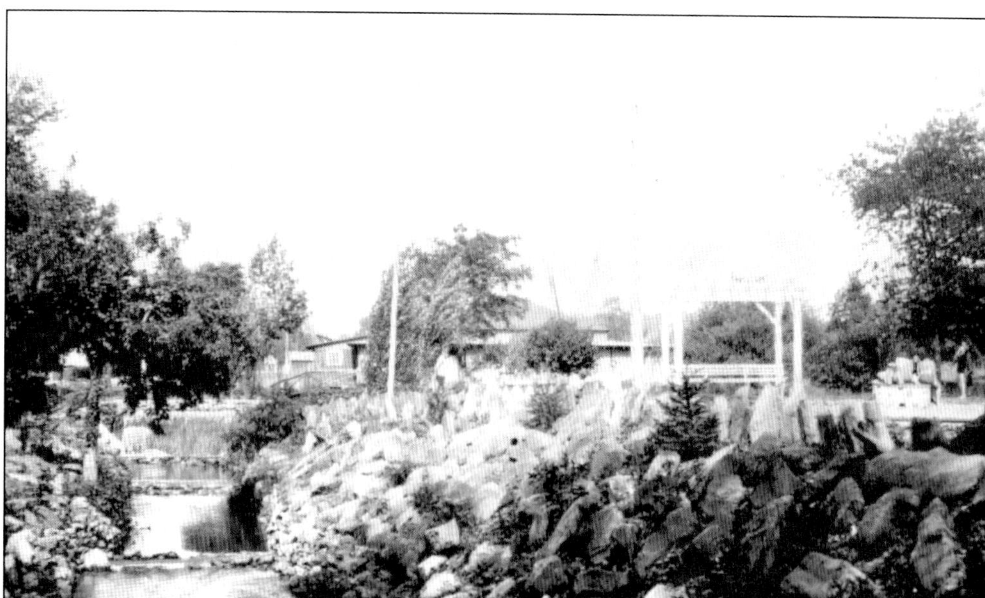

The pool is on the right in this view, looking up the creek behind the Trading Post. (Courtesy Hilda Solliday Gaugler.)

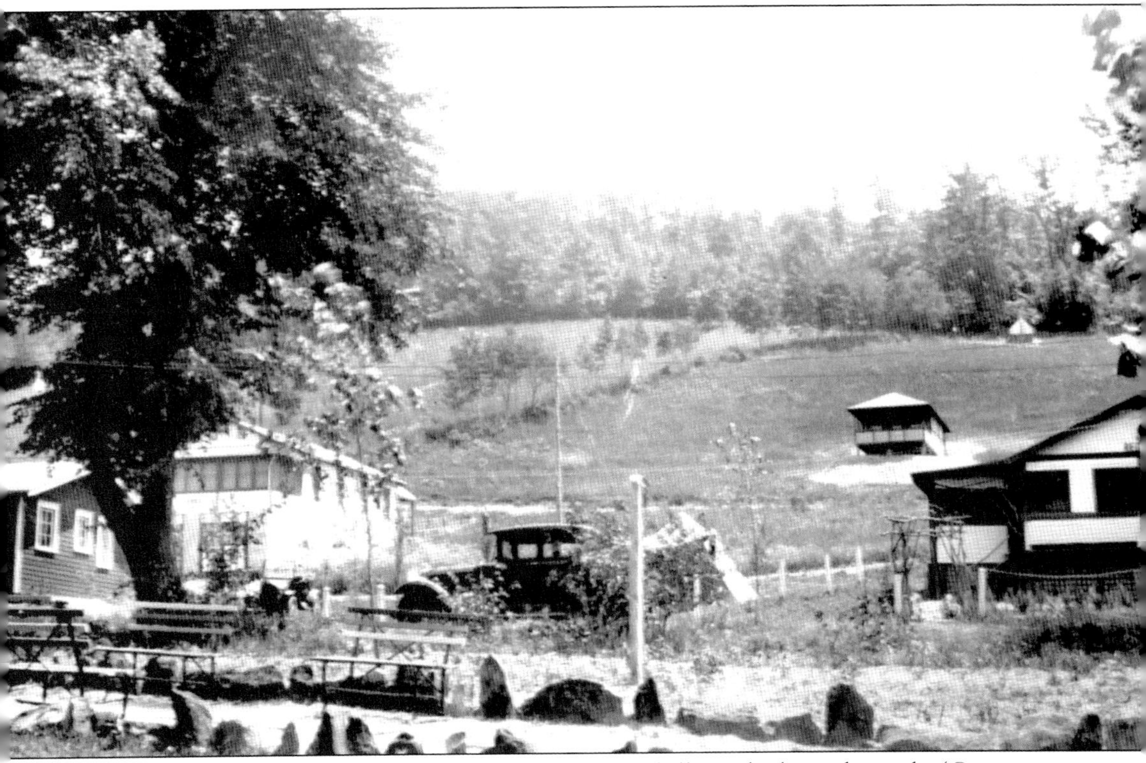

This photograph shows some of the cabins built on the hill overlooking the park. (Courtesy Larry Hillborn.)

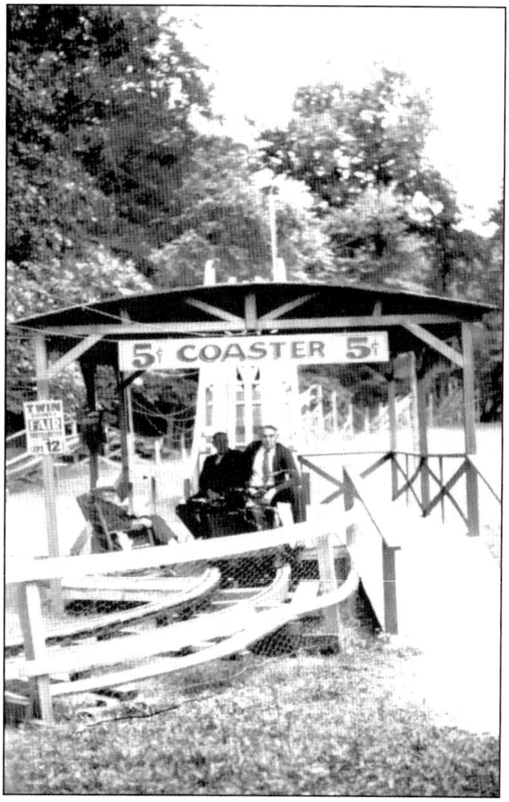

When this photograph was taken, a ride on the roller coaster cost 5¢. The poster to the left promotes the Twin County Fair, held outside of Northampton Borough for many years. (Courtesy Hilda Solliday Gaugler.)

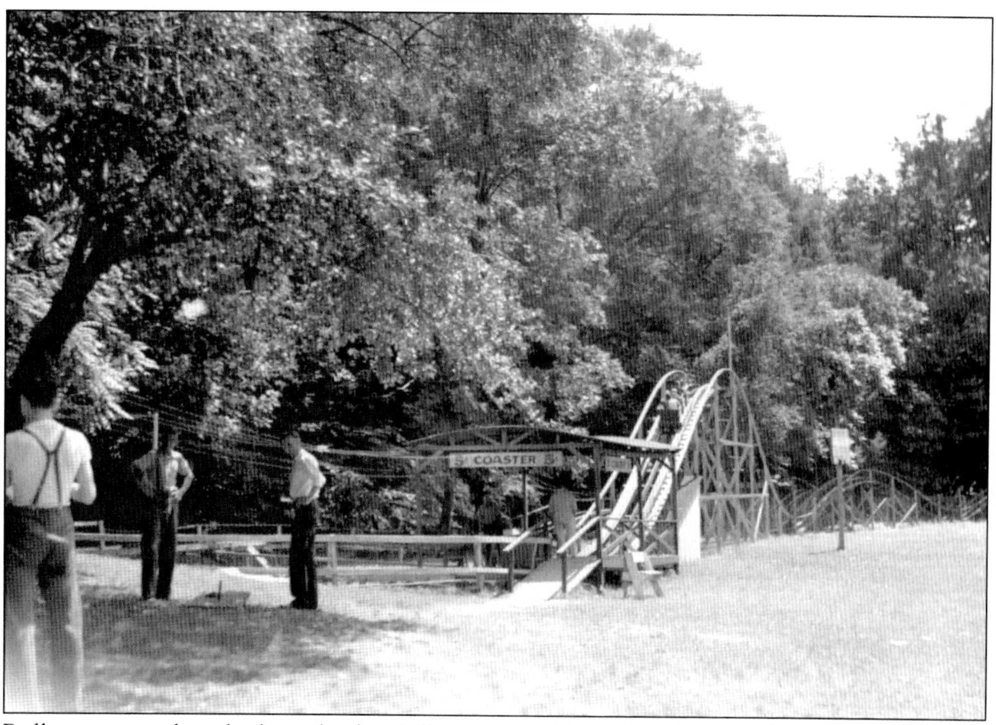

Roller coaster riders climb up the first hill. (Courtesy Hilda Solliday Gaugler.)

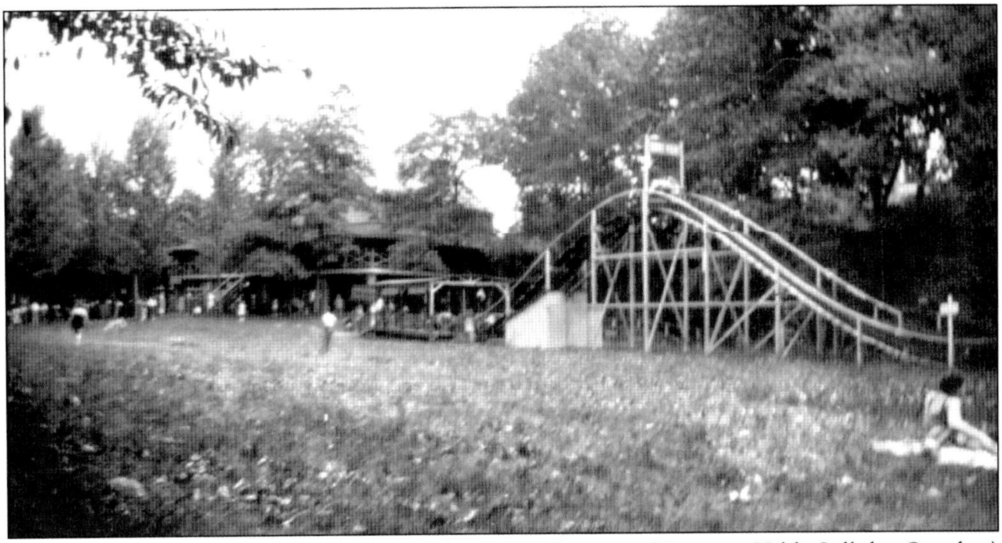

This picture of the roller coaster was taken from near the stage. (Courtesy Hilda Solliday Gaugler.)

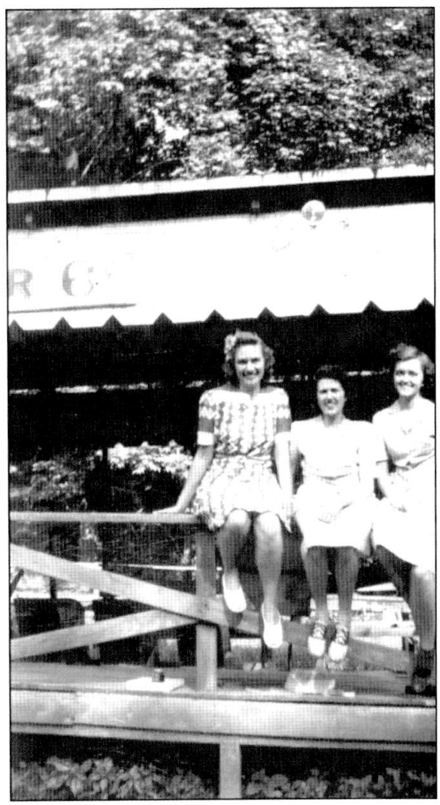

Hilda Solliday (left), Irene Solliday (center), and their cousin Pat Gable sit at the roller coaster station. By this time, the cost of a ride had risen to 6¢. (Courtesy Hilda Solliday Gaugler.)

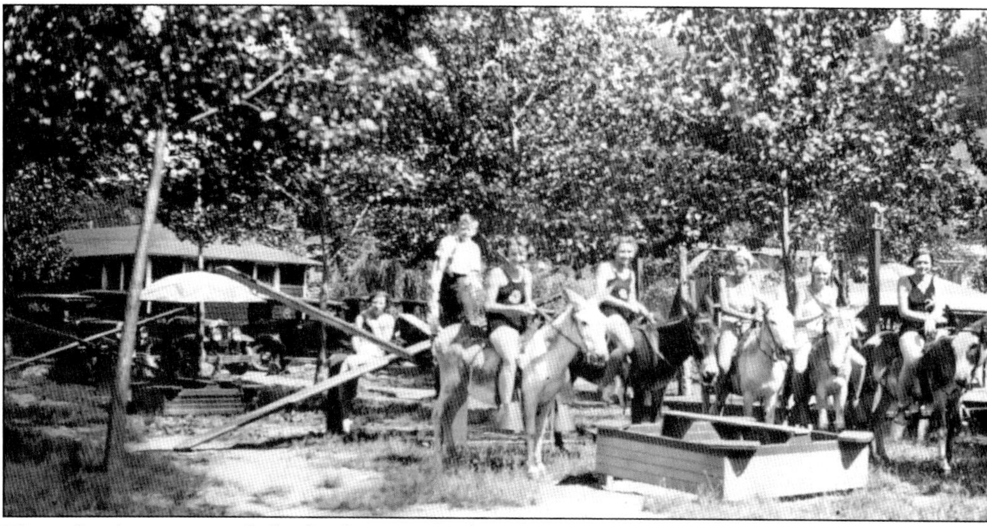

These five burros provided rides for patrons. (Courtesy Hilda Solliday Gaugler.)

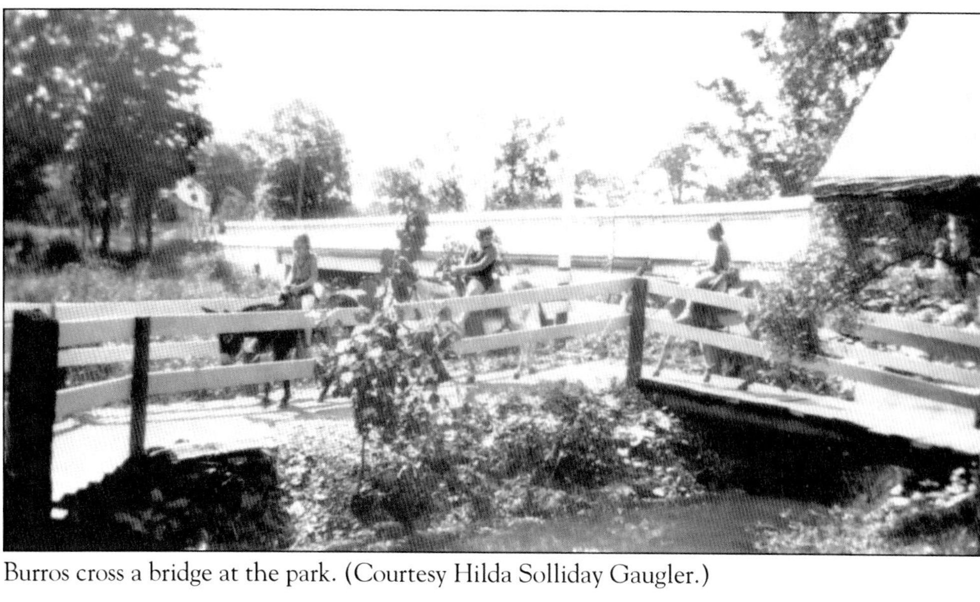

Burros cross a bridge at the park. (Courtesy Hilda Solliday Gaugler.)

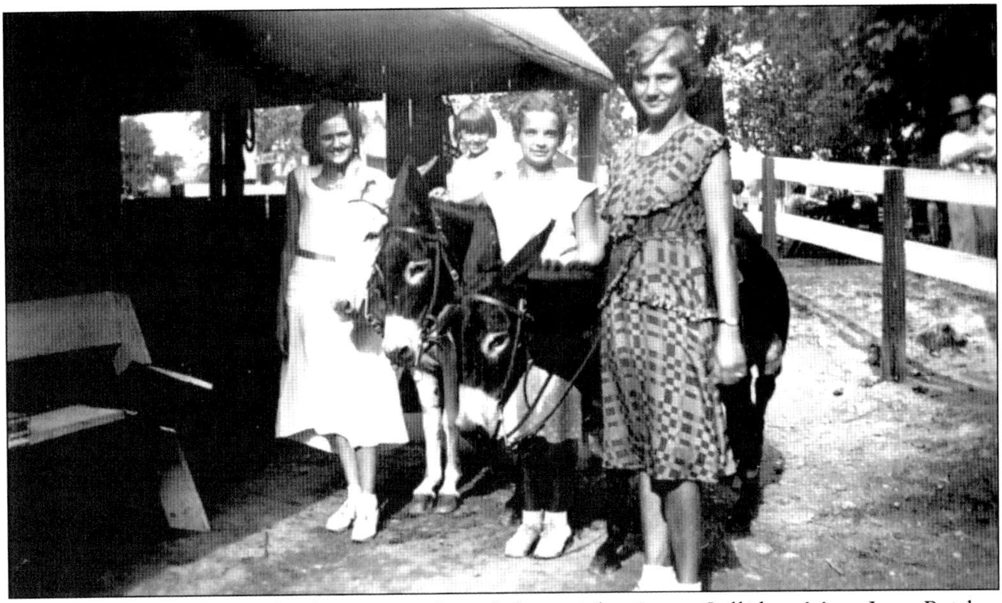

Appearing with two of the burros are, from left to right, Irene Solliday, Mary Jane Beitler, Verna Peters, and Hilda Solliday. (Courtesy Hilda Solliday Gaugler.)

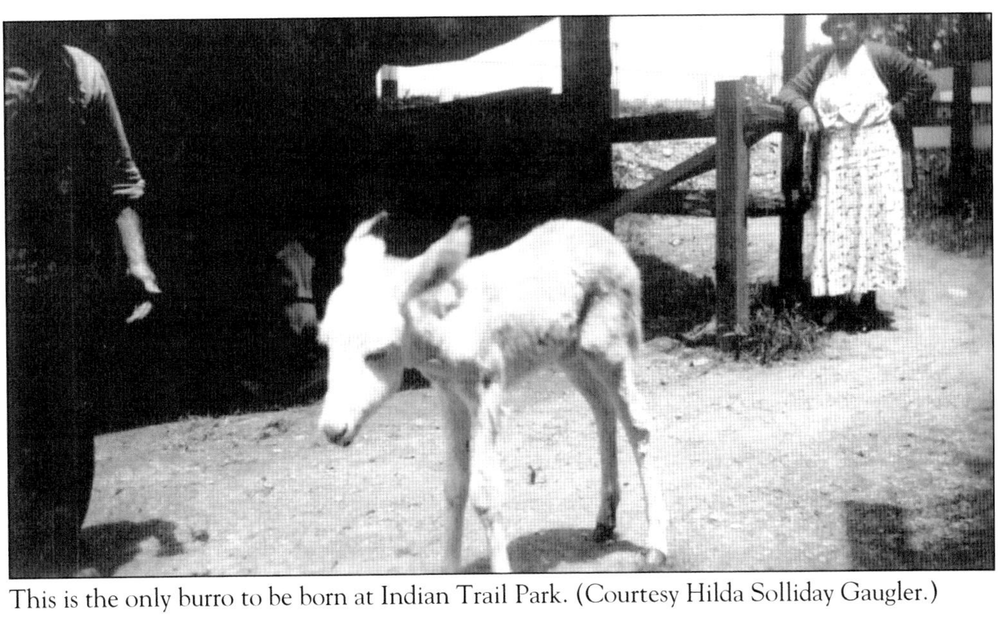

This is the only burro to be born at Indian Trail Park. (Courtesy Hilda Solliday Gaugler.)

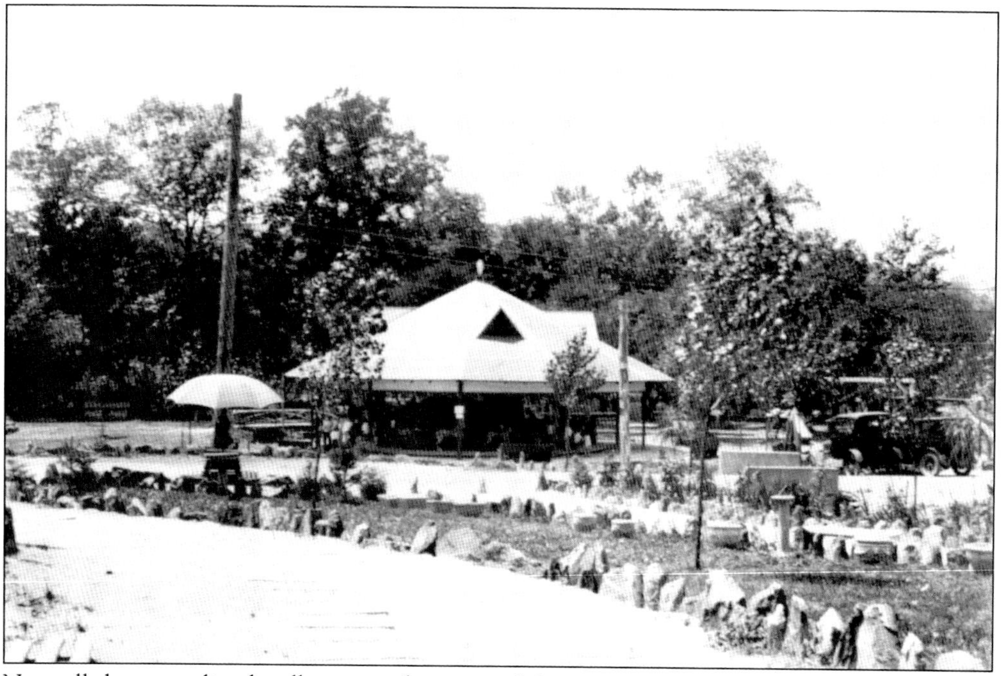

Note all the stone-lined walkways in this view of the merry-go-round, looking down from the pool. (Courtesy Larry Hillborn.)

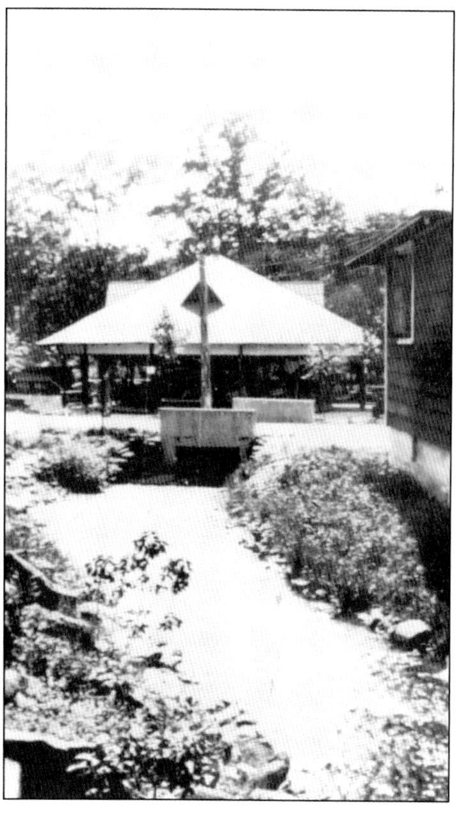

The merry-go-round can again be seen in this view, looking down from the bridge between the Trading Post and the pool. The back of the Trading Post is visible to the right. (Courtesy Hilda Solliday Gaugler.)

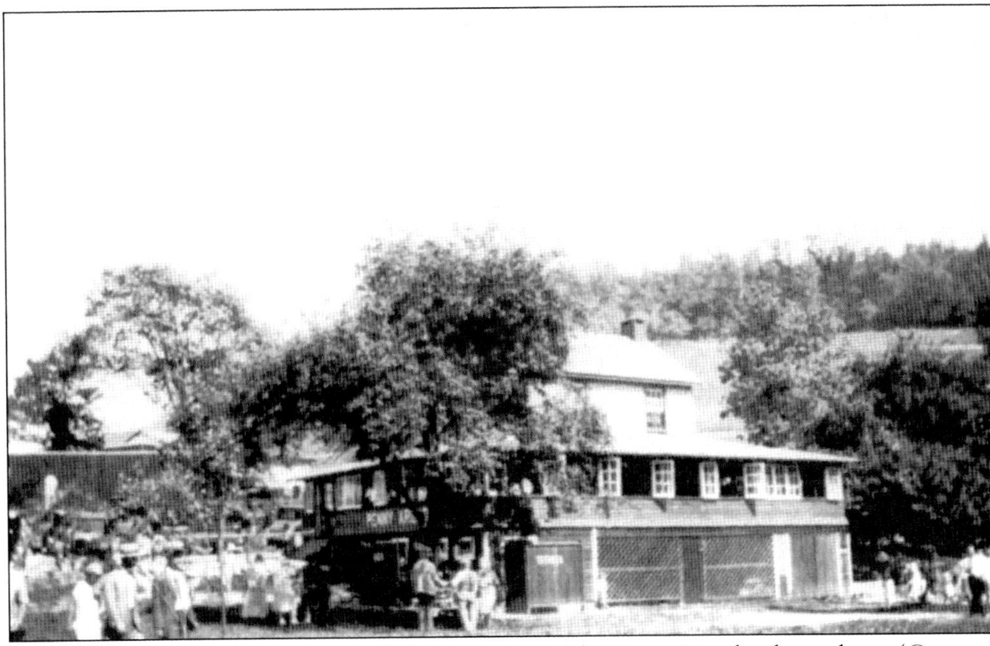

Harvey (page 13) sold his baskets in the lower part of the penny arcade, shown here. (Courtesy Hilda Solliday Gaugler.)

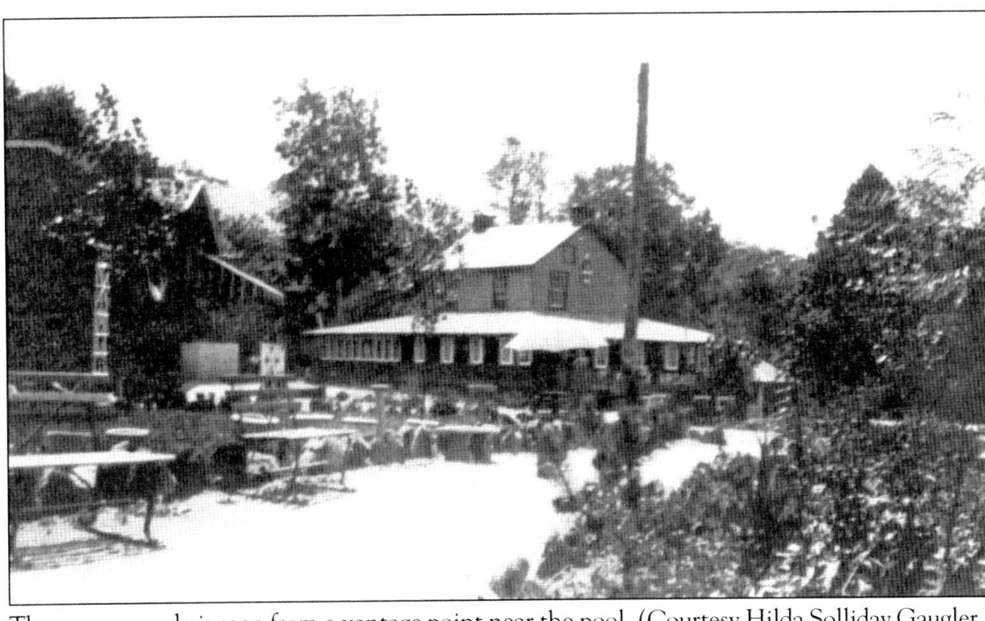

The penny arcade is seen from a vantage point near the pool. (Courtesy Hilda Solliday Gaugler.)

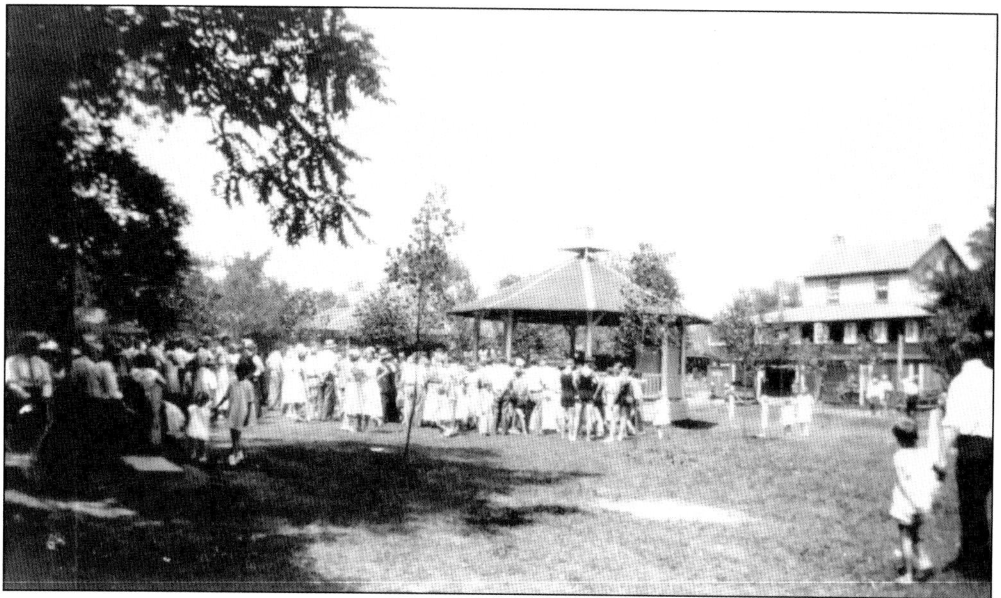

In this view, looking toward the front of the park, the penny arcade is visible to the right, and the merry-go-round is in the center behind the gazebo. (Courtesy Hilda Solliday Gaugler.)

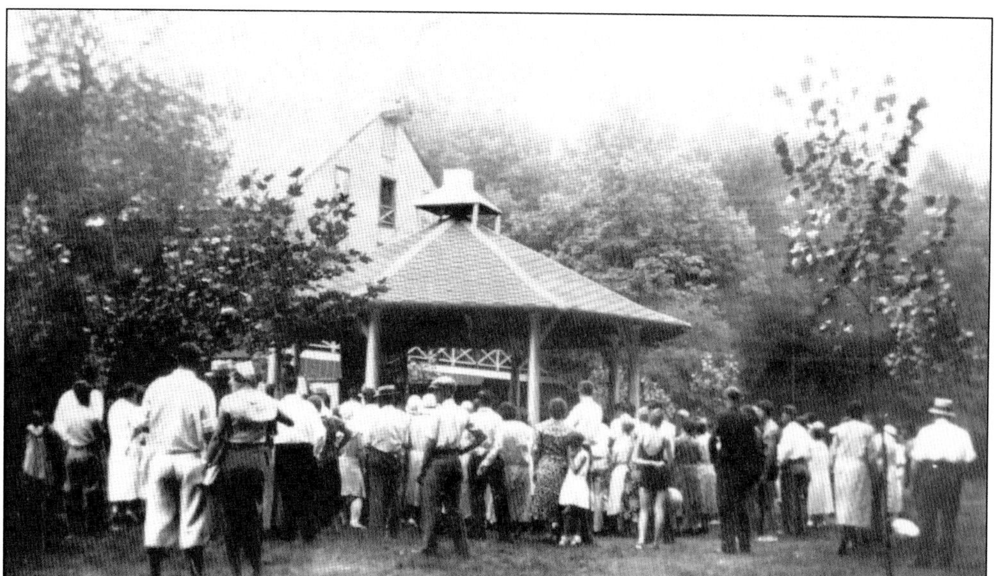

A crowd awaits the start of entertainment, while the gristmill occupies the background behind the gazebo. (Courtesy Hilda Solliday Gaugler.)

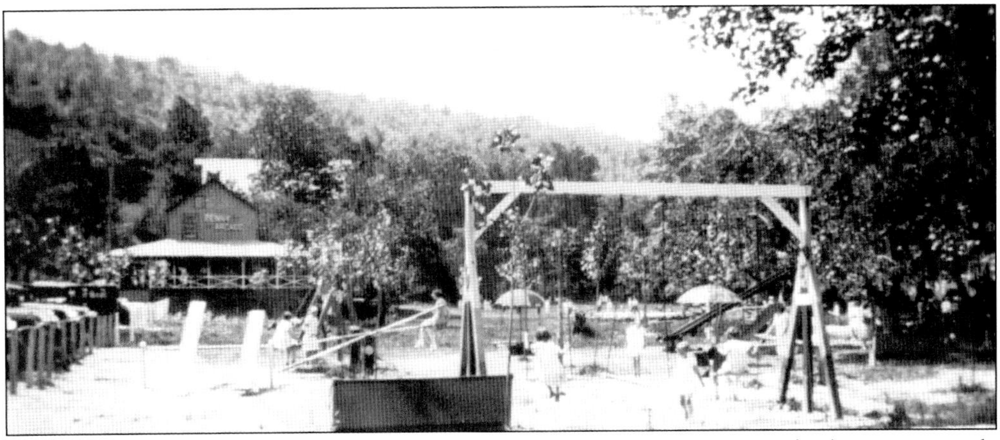

This view, looking south from what is now Route 248, shows the playground. The penny arcade is in the background to the left, and the roof of the gristmill can be seen above the arcade. (Courtesy Hilda Solliday Gaugler.)

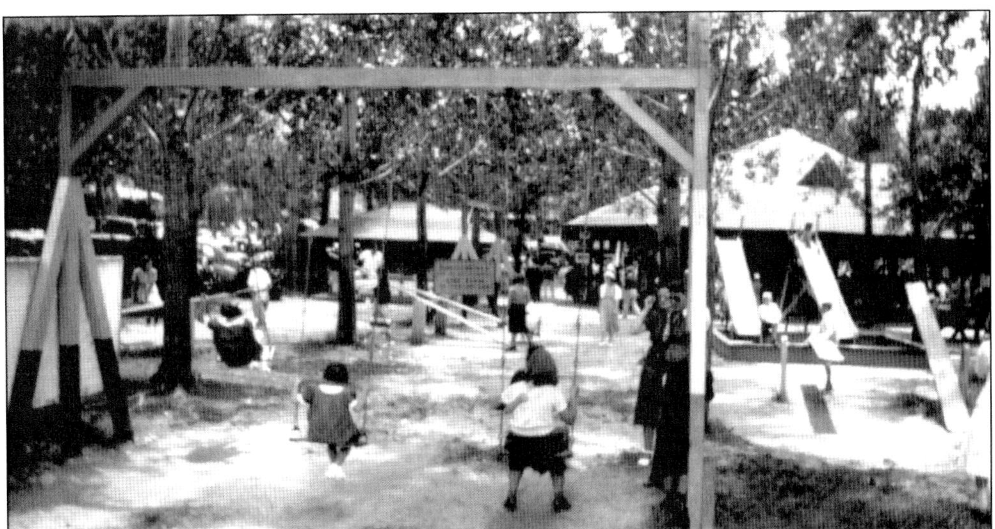

In this later image of the playground, the trees seen in the previous view are now grown. (Courtesy Hilda Solliday Gaugler.)

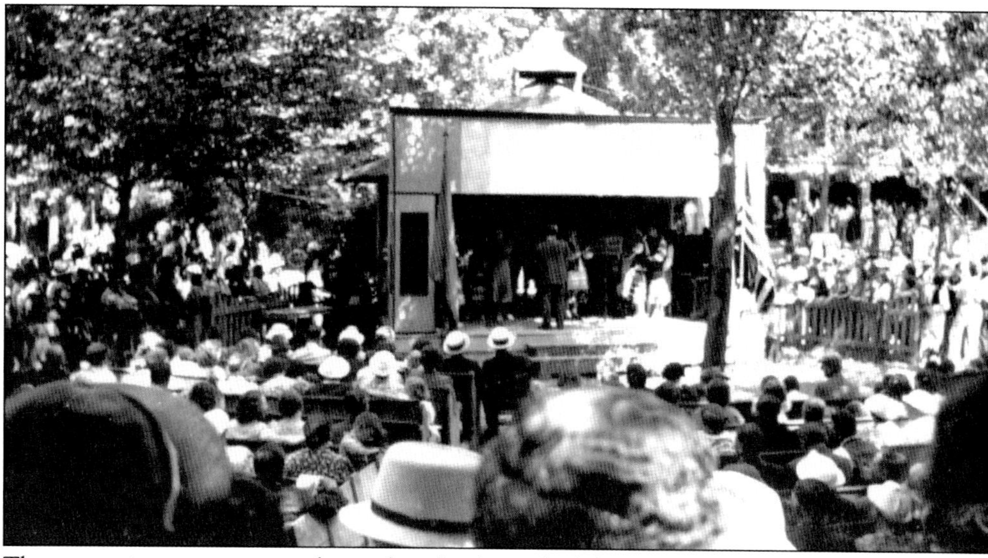

The entertainment stage was located at the far end of the park. Here, a large crowd enjoys a show. (Courtesy Hilda Solliday Gaugler.)

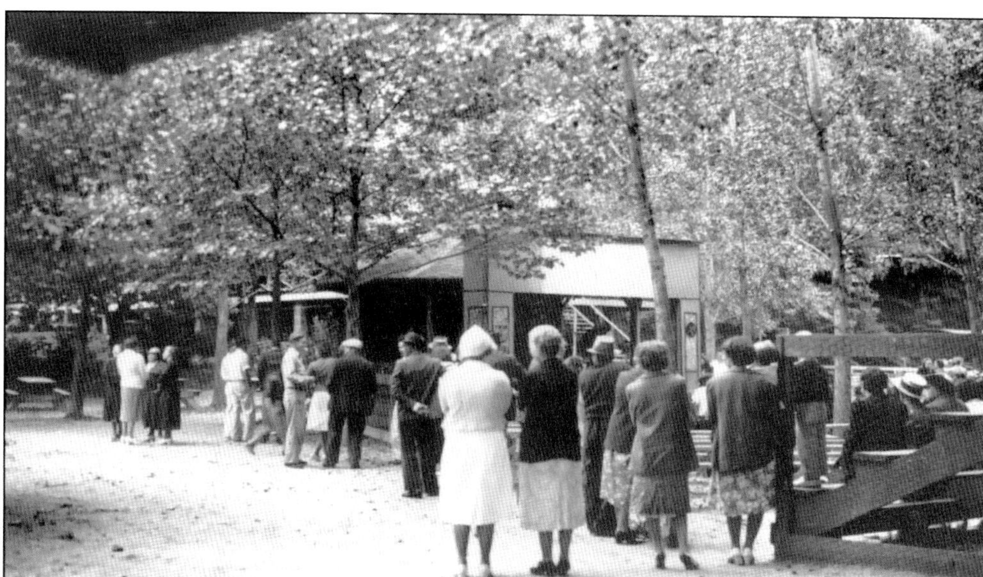

A crowd waits for a show to begin. (Courtesy Hilda Solliday Gaugler.)

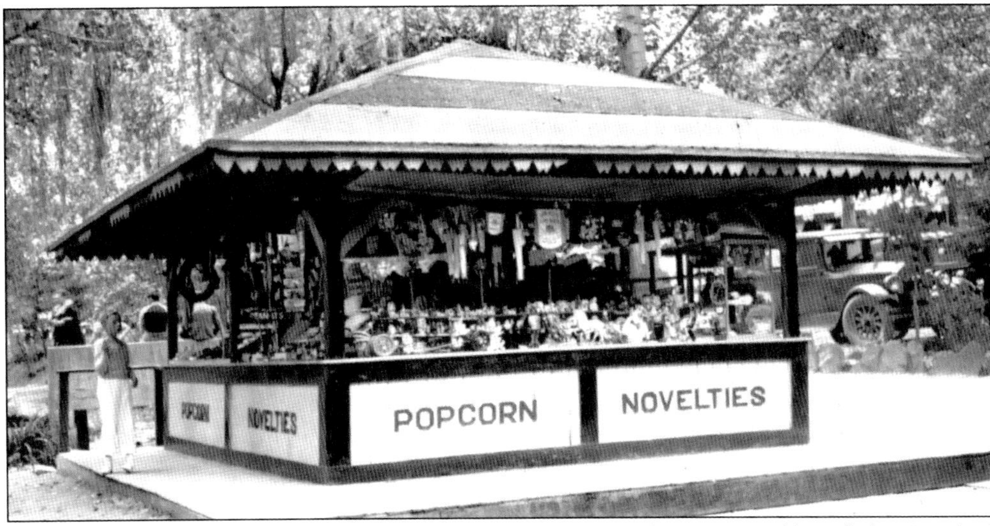

The popcorn and novelties stand offered a variety of souvenirs. (Courtesy Hilda Solliday Gaugler.)

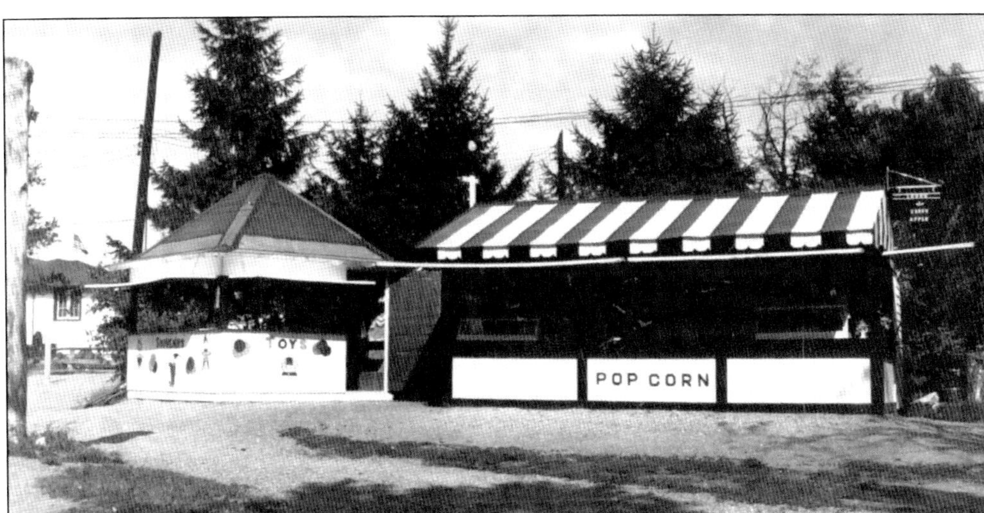

The popcorn stand was later expanded, as shown here. (Courtesy Hilda Solliday Gaugler.)

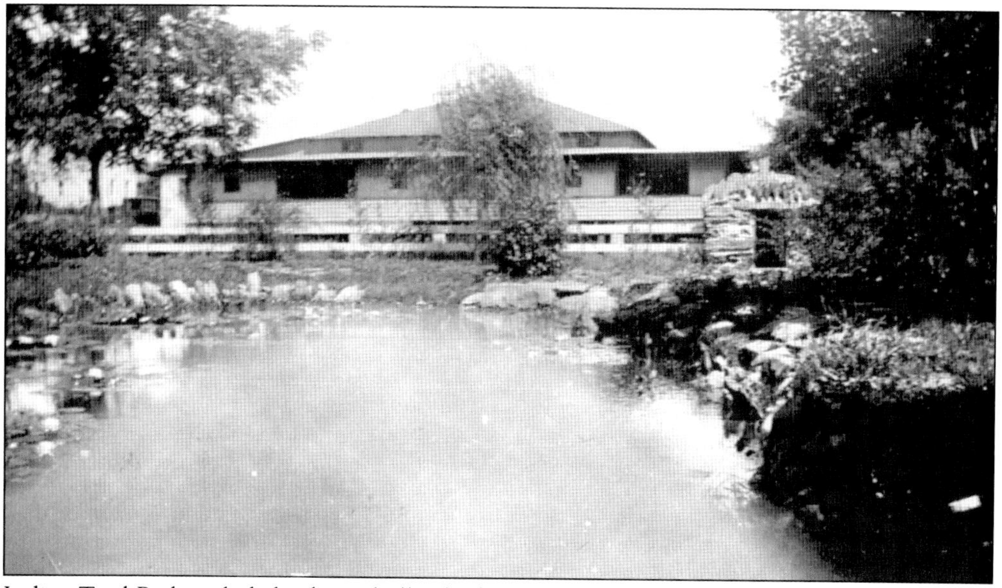

Indian Trail Park included a dance hall, which was located east of the Trading Post on what is now Route 248. (Courtesy Hilda Solliday Gaugler.)

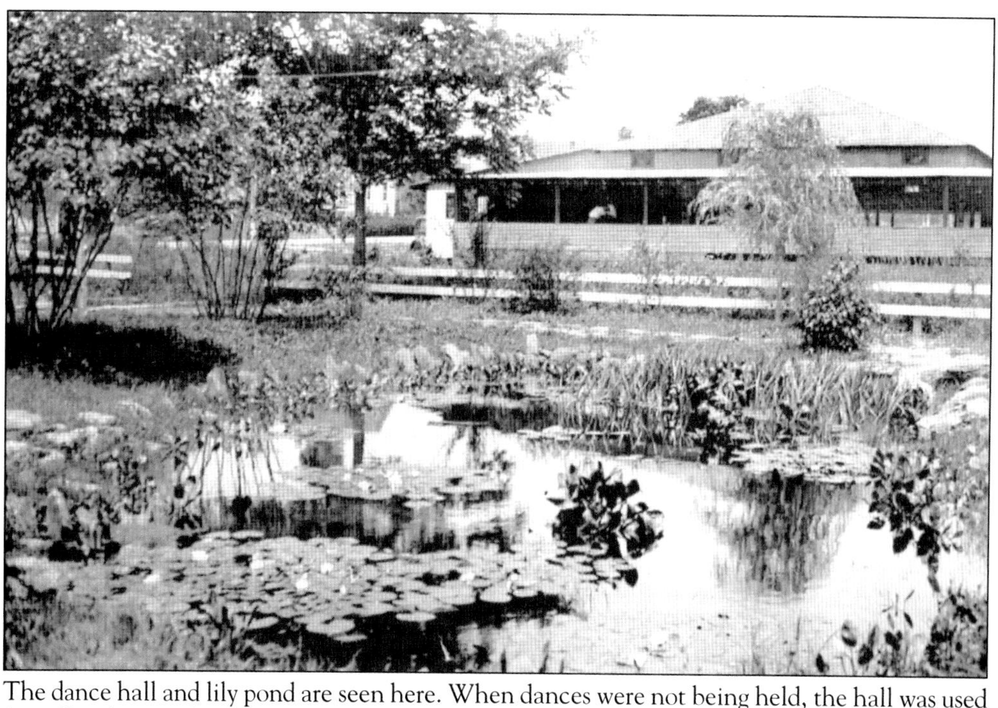

The dance hall and lily pond are seen here. When dances were not being held, the hall was used for roller-skating. (Courtesy Hilda Solliday Gaugler.)

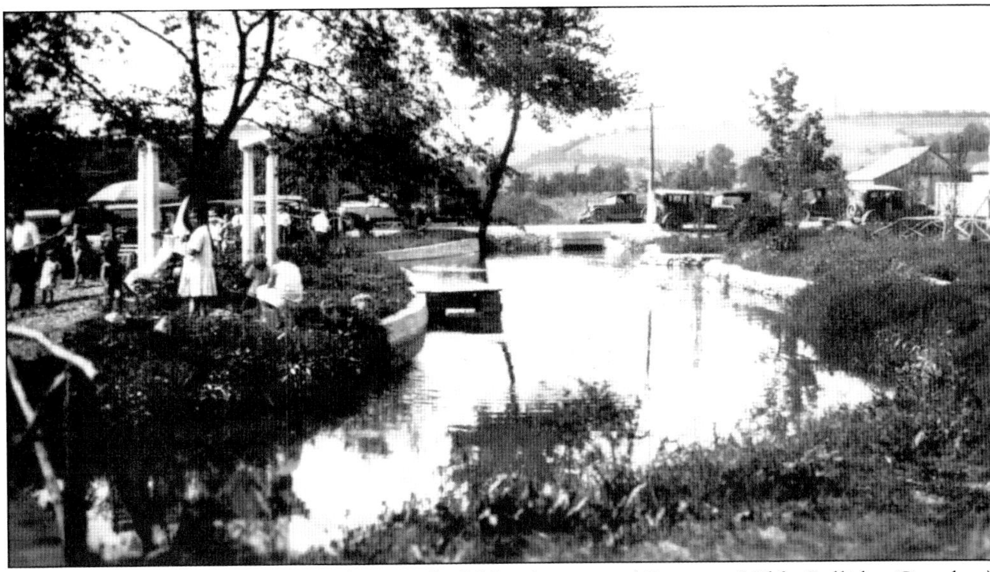

This view shows more of the park's wonderful landscaping. (Courtesy Hilda Solliday Gaugler.)

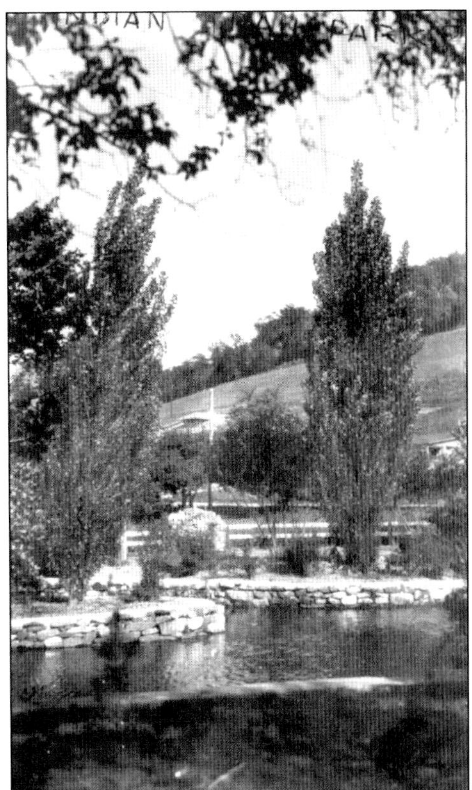

The ponds featured beautiful stonework. (Courtesy Hilda Solliday Gaugler.)

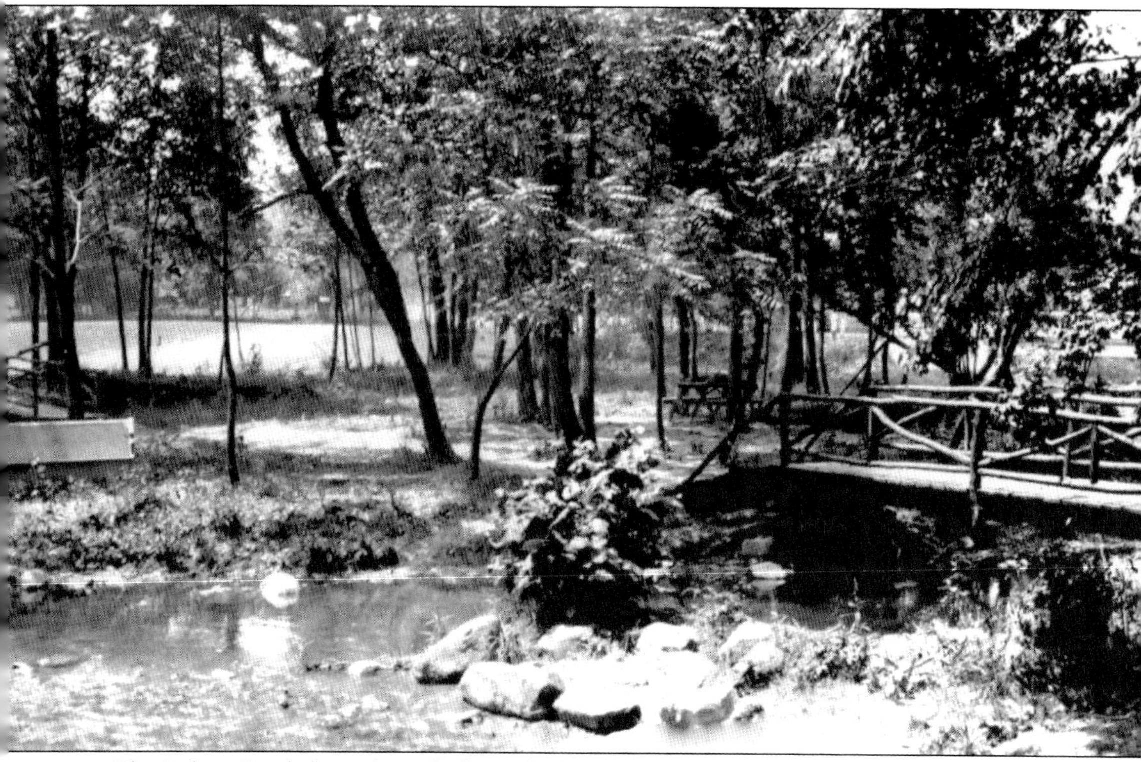

The Indian Creek flows through the park. (Courtesy Hilda Solliday Gaugler.)

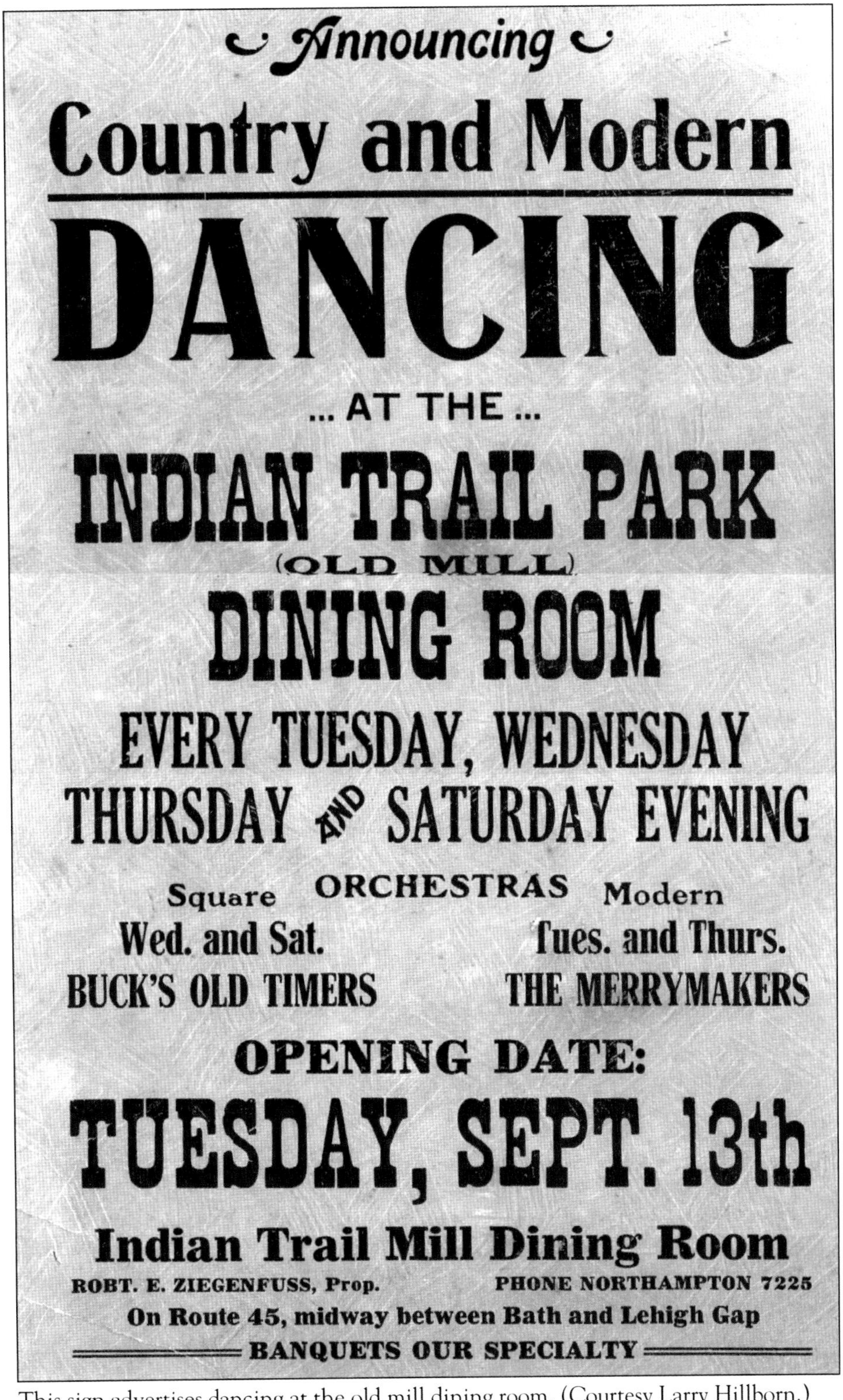

This sign advertises dancing at the old mill dining room. (Courtesy Larry Hillborn.)

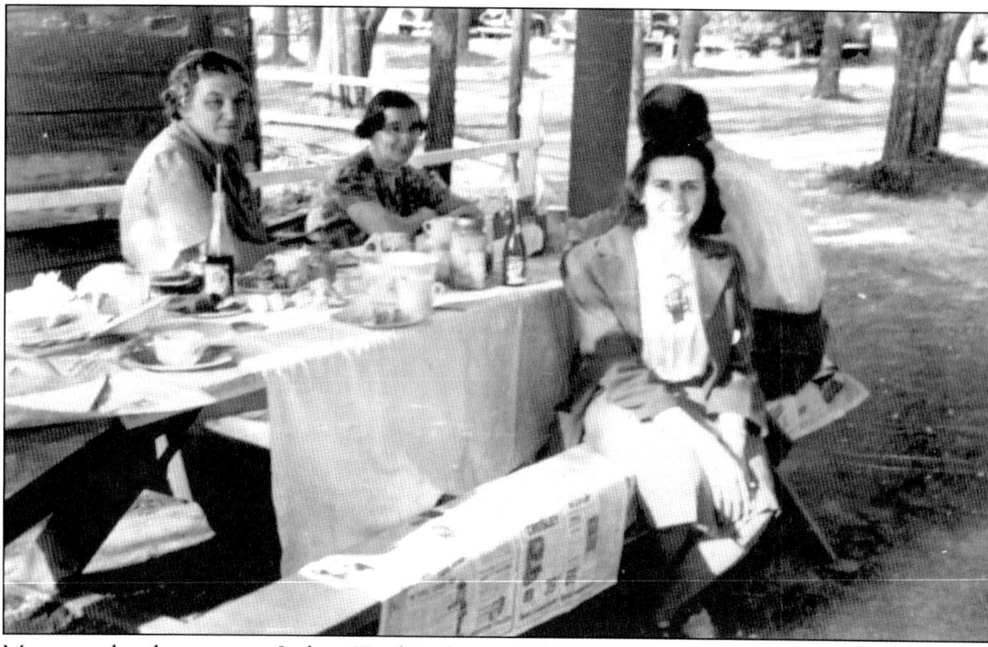

Most people who came to Indian Trail Park enjoyed a picnic along the creek, as shown in this 1942 scene. (Courtesy Hilda Solliday Gaugler.)

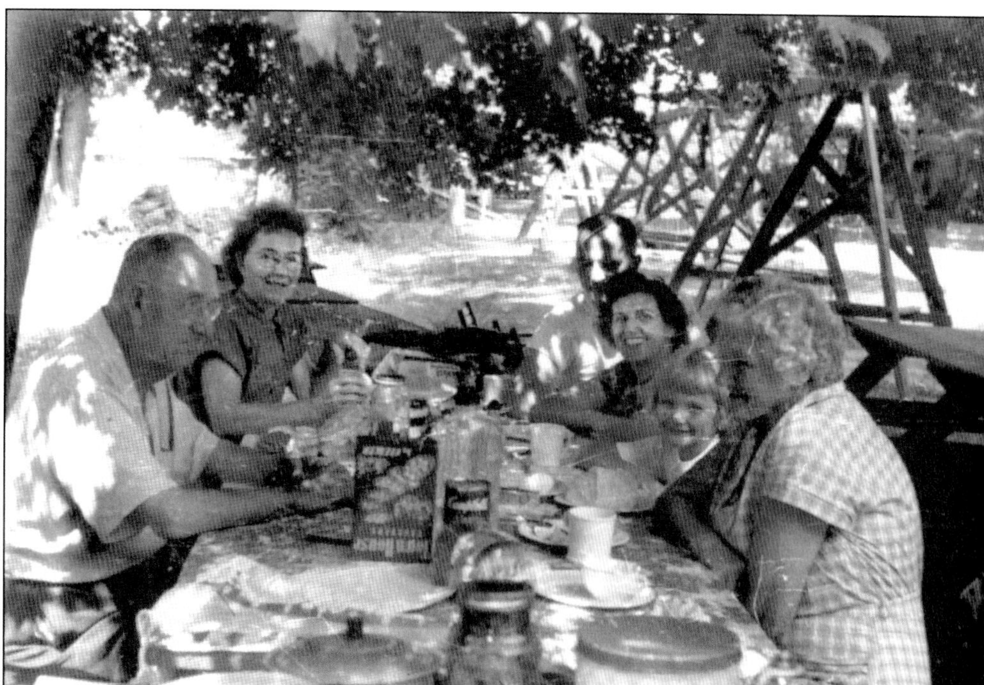

In this photograph of a picnic, the playground can be seen in the background. (Courtesy Hilda Solliday Gaugler.)

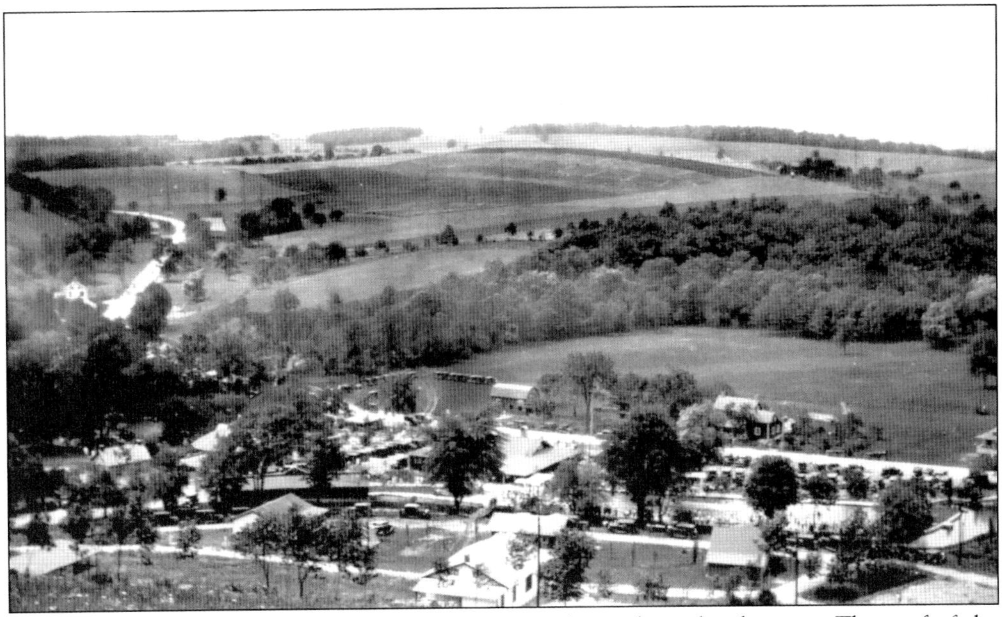

Looking down from the hilltop, this view captures the park in the distance. The roof of the Trading Post is visible in the center. (Courtesy Hilda Solliday Gaugler.)

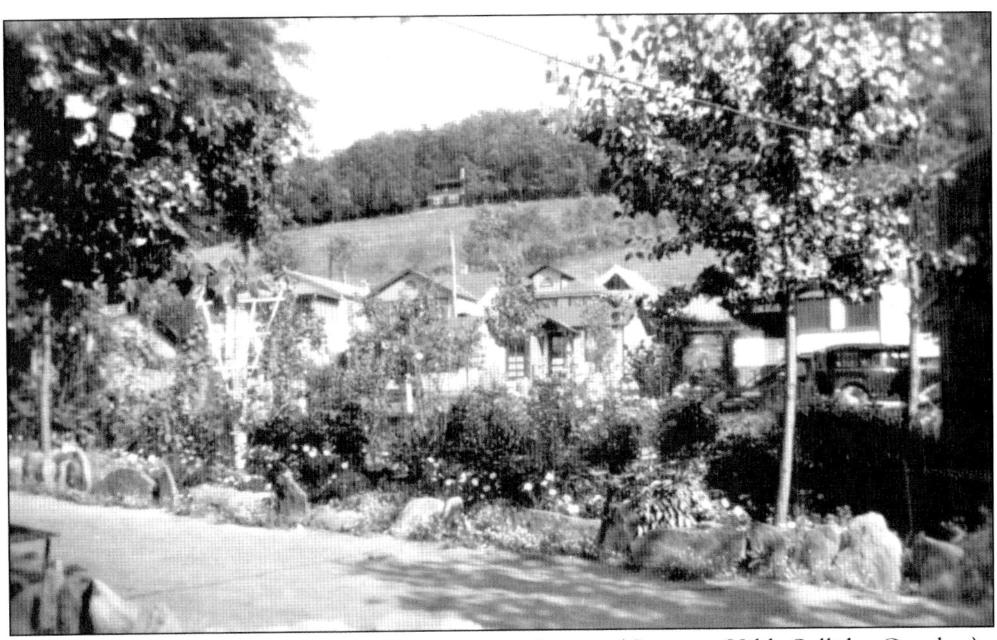

Cottages like these have since become permanent homes. (Courtesy Hilda Solliday Gaugler.)

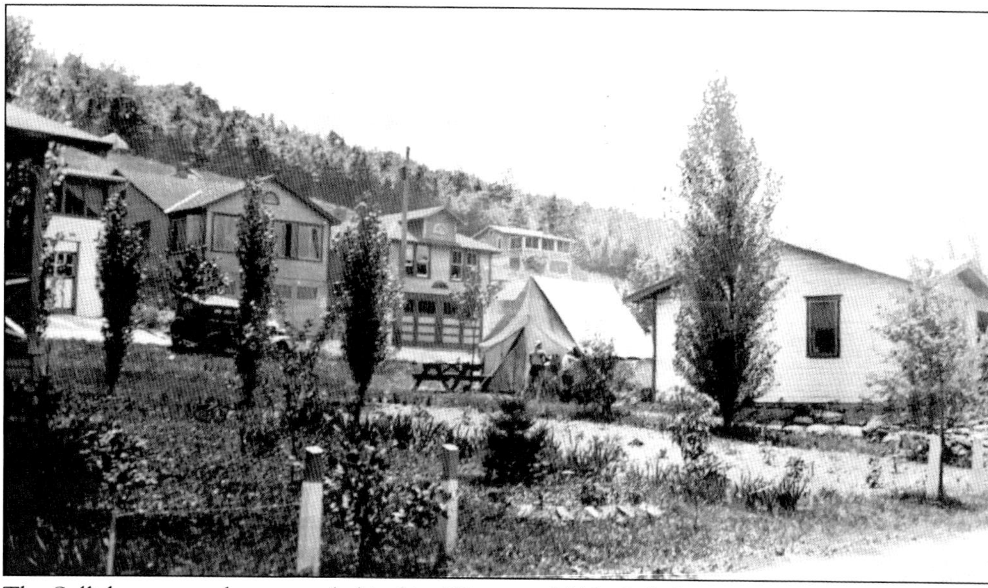

The Solliday cottage has a tent behind it. (Courtesy Hilda Solliday Gaugler.)

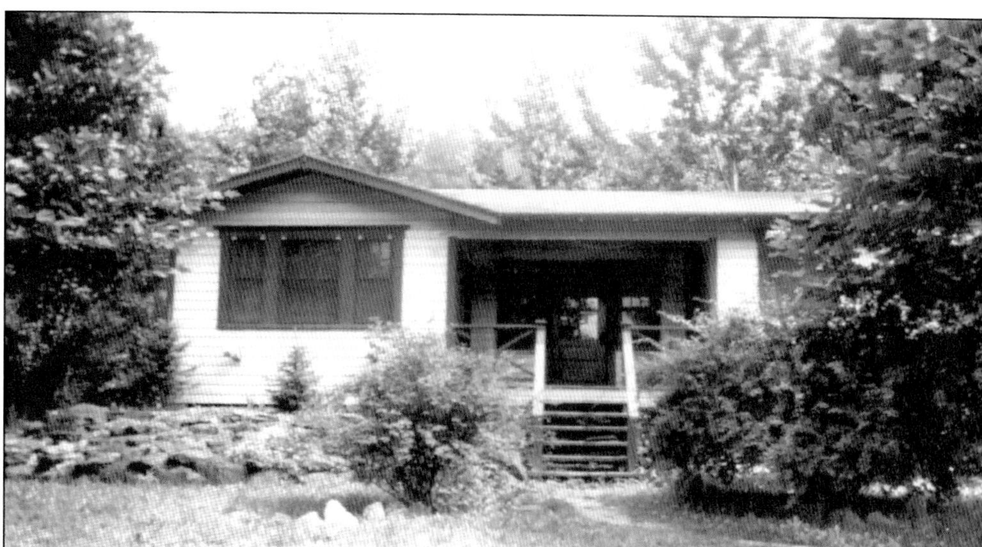

The front of the Solliday cottage is shown here. (Courtesy Hilda Solliday Gaugler.)

Two

Indian Trail Park

Changing Owners

In 1939, Rollin E. and Anna C. Minnich bought the property east of Cinchona Road, which contained the pool and the Trading Post, from the Sollidays. Rollin Minnich Jr. was responsible for the pool and the bathhouse. He met his future wife, Belle Fogelman, when she worked as a waitress in his parents' restaurant. The Minniches ran the restaurant and pool until 1945, when they sold them. The restaurant was then operated by Miles Weaver and then by Dick and Jean Lott. The property containing the restaurant and pool was later purchased by C. P. Fenstermaker. When the Lehigh Township Historical Society rebuilt the Trading Post, a sign reading, "C. P. Fenstermaker Justice of the Peace," was found in the bathroom floor.

Leroy Kahle and Thomas Long purchased the property to the west of Cinchona Road on November 30, 1949, from the Sollidays' Indian Trail Park Company. Leroy Kahle ran the park with his wife, Suzanne, and their family. Thomas Long was never very active at Indian Trail Park because he was busy running Bushkill Park, near Easton. On April 8, 1957, Kahle bought out Long, becoming sole owner.

Leroy and Suzanne Kahle had a daughter, Joan, who married Ronald Bergen. Joan and Ronald had four children—Leslie, Kerry, Ron, and Scott. Both families lived on the second floor of the park's gristmill. Leroy and Suzanne lived on one side; Ronald, Joan, and their children occupied the other. Each side contained a kitchen, living room, and two bedrooms.

On March 20, 1959, Leroy Kahle purchased the land south of the creek, where the pool was located, from C. P. Fenstermaker. At the same time, the Bergen family needed more space, so Ronald purchased the land north of the creek, were the Trading Post was, from Fenstermaker. The Trading Post had been used as a restaurant until 1959, when the Bergens moved in. After they moved out, the building stood vacant.

When Kahle bought the pool, he eliminated the admission fee. Although swimming was free, lifeguards were no longer provided and the snack bar was removed.

The pool was fed by water diverted from the creek. In the deep end, a pipe emptied back to the stream and a large cork in the pipe held in the water. Because the water was not chlorinated, it needed to be changed several times during the summer. It took about three days to refill. The pool was not drained for the winter but was left to freeze, and local children were allowed to skate on the ice.

Every Sunday, the Kahles provided entertainment. Suzanne sold ride tickets from a booth on the bridge crossing the creek that comes down behind the Trading Post. While the Kahles owned the park, a couple named Leon and Margaret ran the popcorn stand. Although they were from Mahanoy City, they lived in a small trailer on the park property during the summer. Joan Bergen operated the refreshment stand, and eight-year-old Leslie Bergen operated the dart and novelty stands. The dart booth was located on the lower level of the penny arcade. On the upper level was a huge room with pinball machines. Shooting games included one with an air gun to hit moving targets.

Most of the rides were operated by local children. Leroy Kahle would pick them up in the morning, and Suzanne would drive them home at night. Leroy worked on the rides himself and rebuilt many of them, including the roller coaster.

Suzanne died in 1969, and Leroy sold the park in 1972 to Leslie and Judith Tuttle. Leroy remarried and moved to Florida shortly before his death in 1974. Before he sold the park, he removed two merry-go-round horses for the family to keep. They were taken to Florida.

Rollin Minnich Sr. and Anna C. Minnich stand on the steps of the house where they lived while running the Indian Trail Park pool and restaurant. (Courtesy Rollin Minnich Jr.)

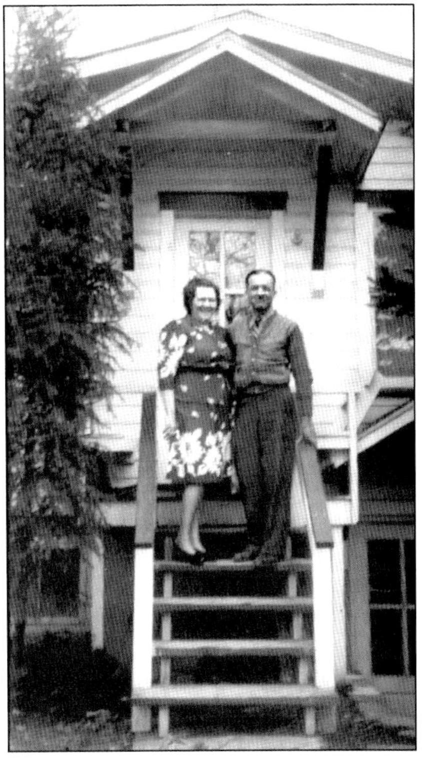

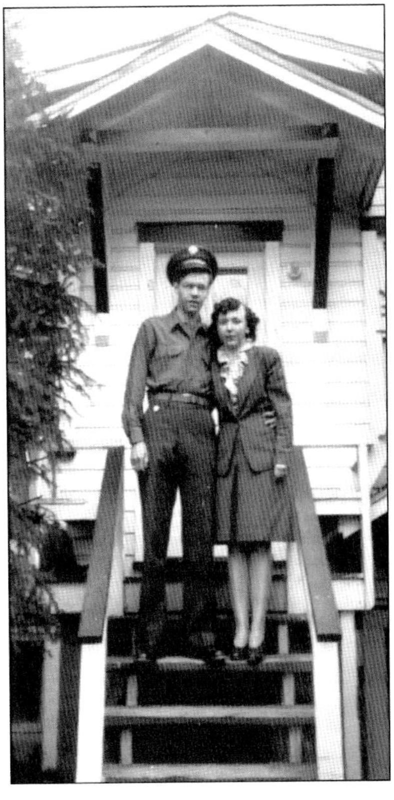

Rollin Minnich Jr. and Belle Minnich appear in front of his parents' home. The younger Rollin was drafted into World War II. When he left for the war, his parents operated the restaurant and pool at Indian Trail Park, but by the time he returned, they had already bought Edgemont Park. (Courtesy Rollin Minnich Jr.)

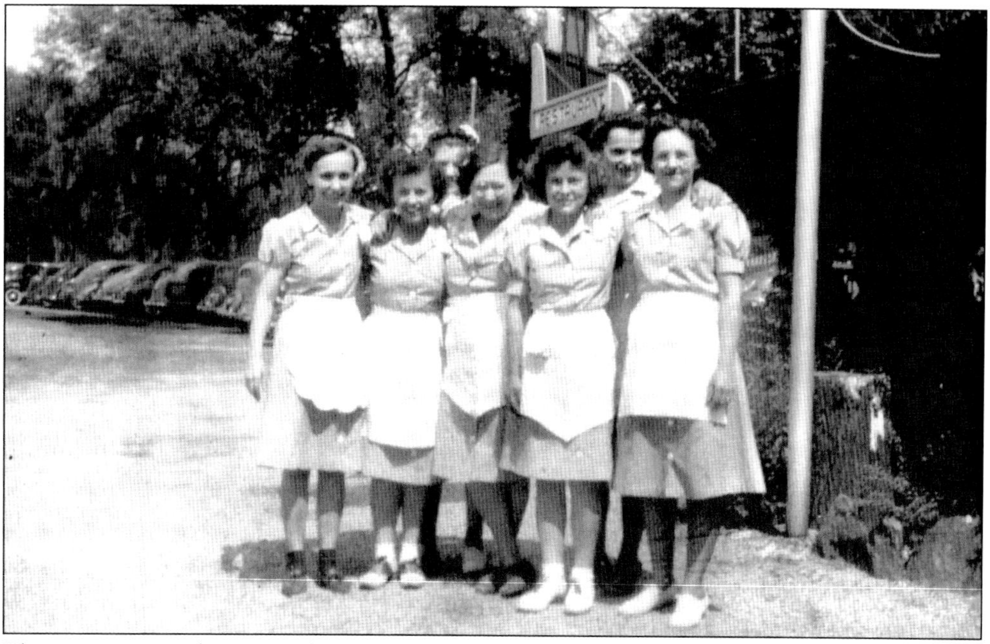

The waitresses at the Minnich-operated restaurant in the Trading Post are, from left to right, Belle Fogelman (Minnich), Olive Kleppinger (Heiney Diehl), Hilda Silfies's daughter, Anna Minnich, Dixie Kleppinger, Althea Fogelman (Rinker), and Hilda Silfies. Sarah Jacoby also worked in the kitchen, and her daughter Elda worked there after the Minniches sold the restaurant. Olive Diehl, the largest private contributor to the rebuilding of the Trading Post, passed away in 2004. (Courtesy Rollin Minnich Jr.)

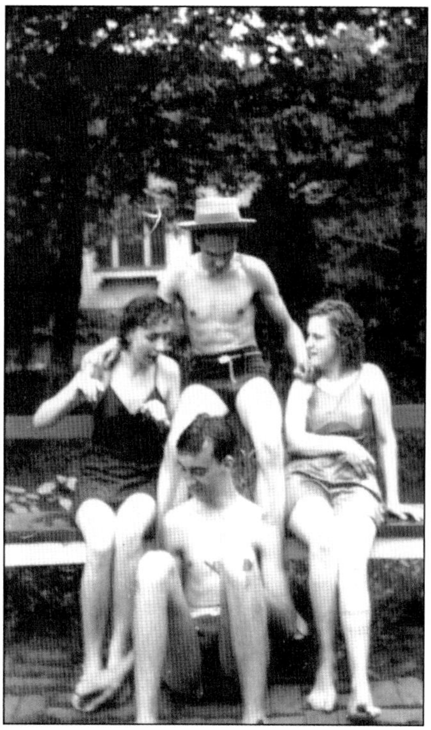

At the pool are, from left to right, Belle Fogelman, Rollin Minnich Jr., Harvey Wetherhold, and Ruth Frey. (Courtesy Rollin Minnich Jr.)

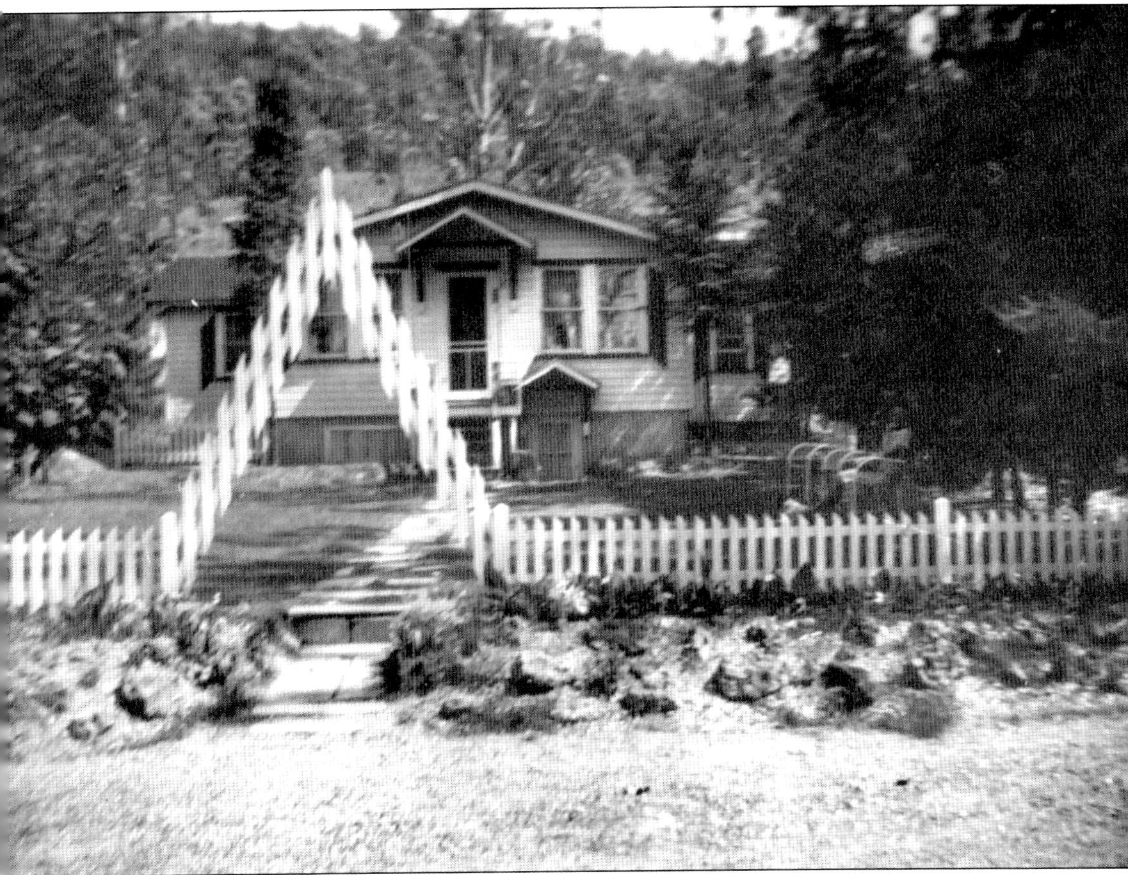

The Minniches lived in this house when they operated the pool and the restaurant at Indian Trail Park. (Courtesy Rollin Minnich Jr.)

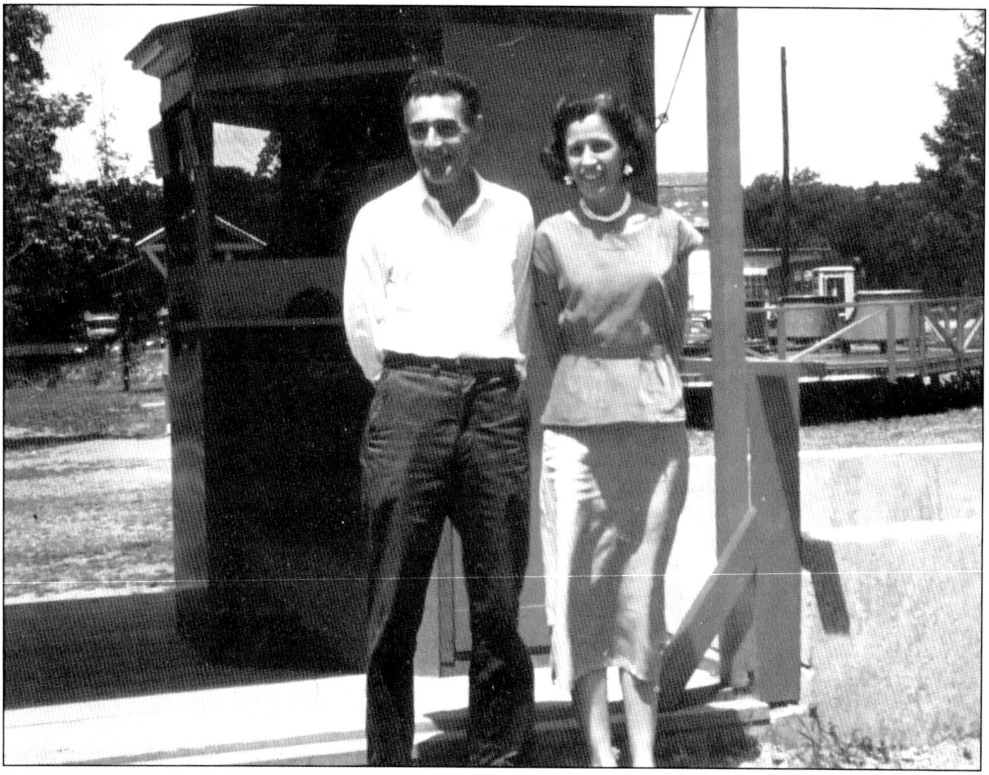

In this c. 1950 view, Leroy and Suzanne Kahle appear by the ticket booth, which was located on the bridge that crossed the creek near the merry-go-round. The whip can be seen in the background. (Courtesy Leslie Greffe.)

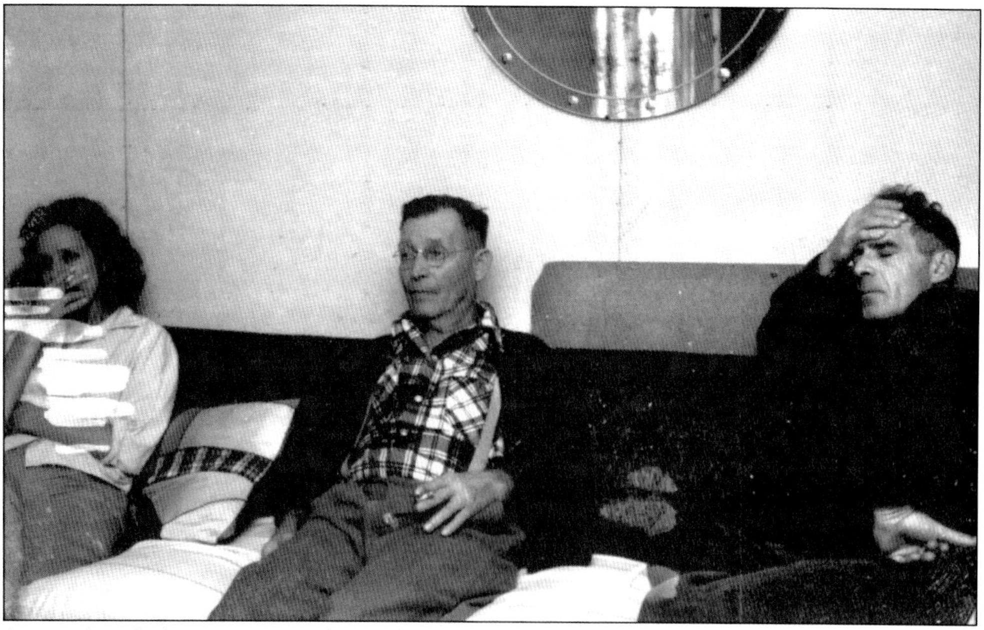

An unidentified woman, Leon (center), and Leroy Kahle sit on a couch in the old mill, which served as a home for the Kahle and Bergen families. (Courtesy Leslie Greffe.)

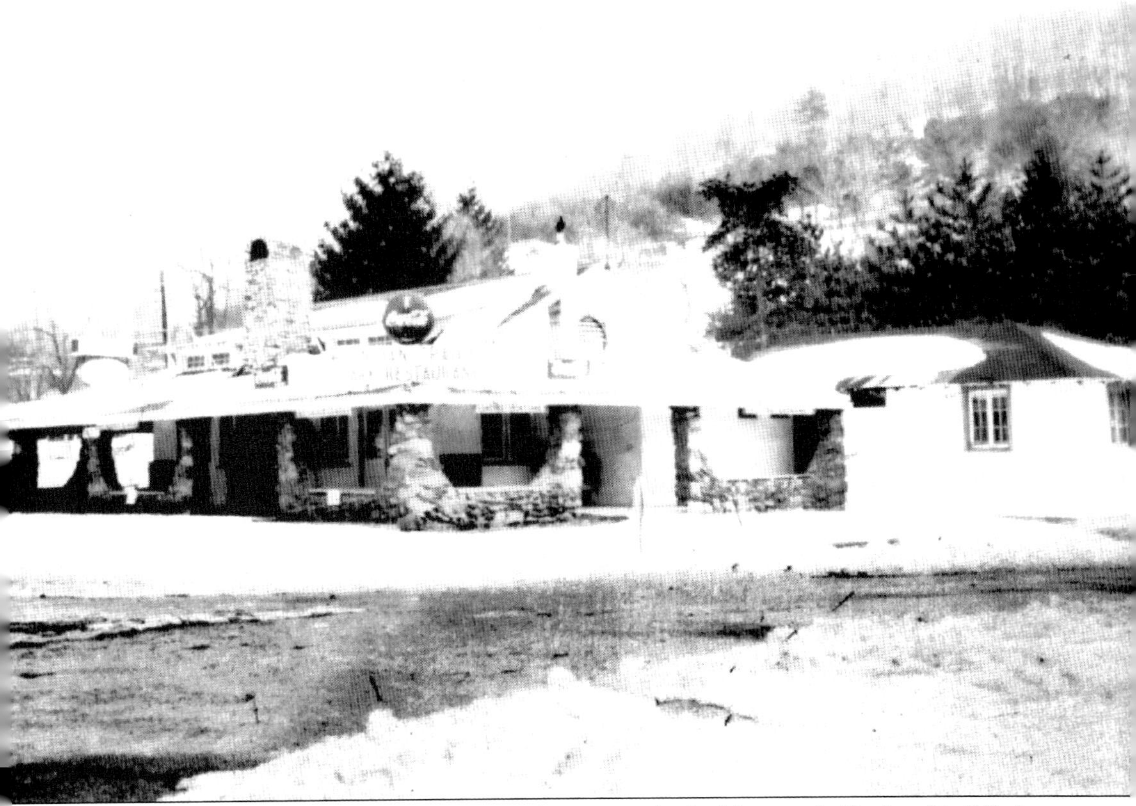

In this 1950s winter view of the Trading Post, the sign on the building reads, "Indian Trail Park Restaurant." (Courtesy Leslie Greffe.)

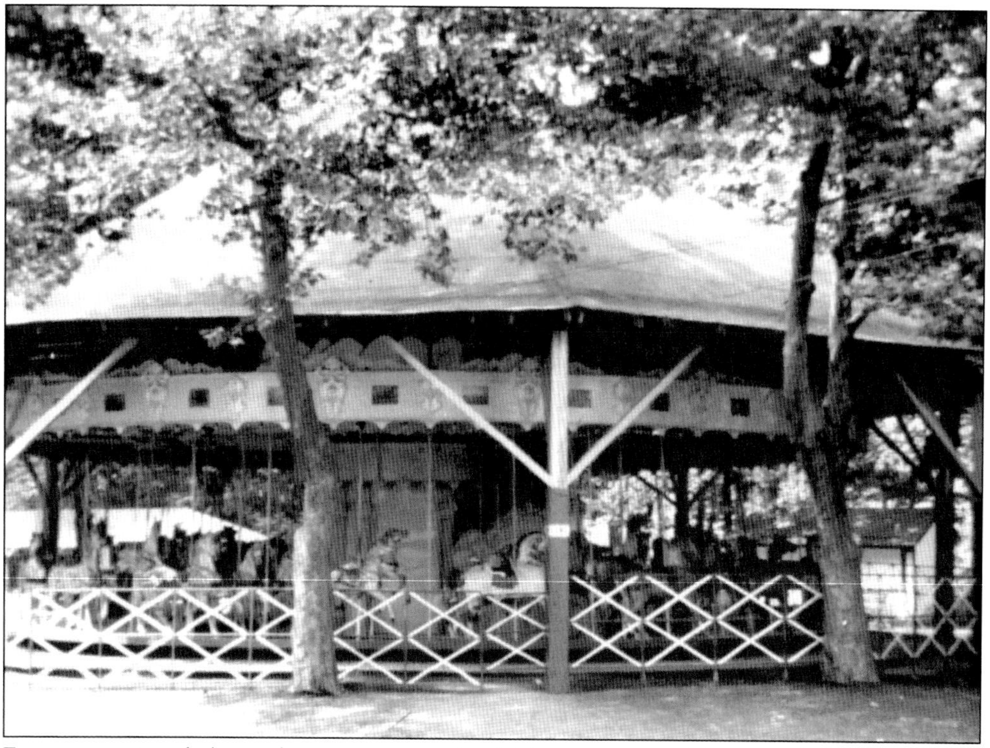

Everyone enjoyed the park merry-go-round, which was operated by Darrel Schaffer around 1960. (Courtesy Leslie Greffe.)

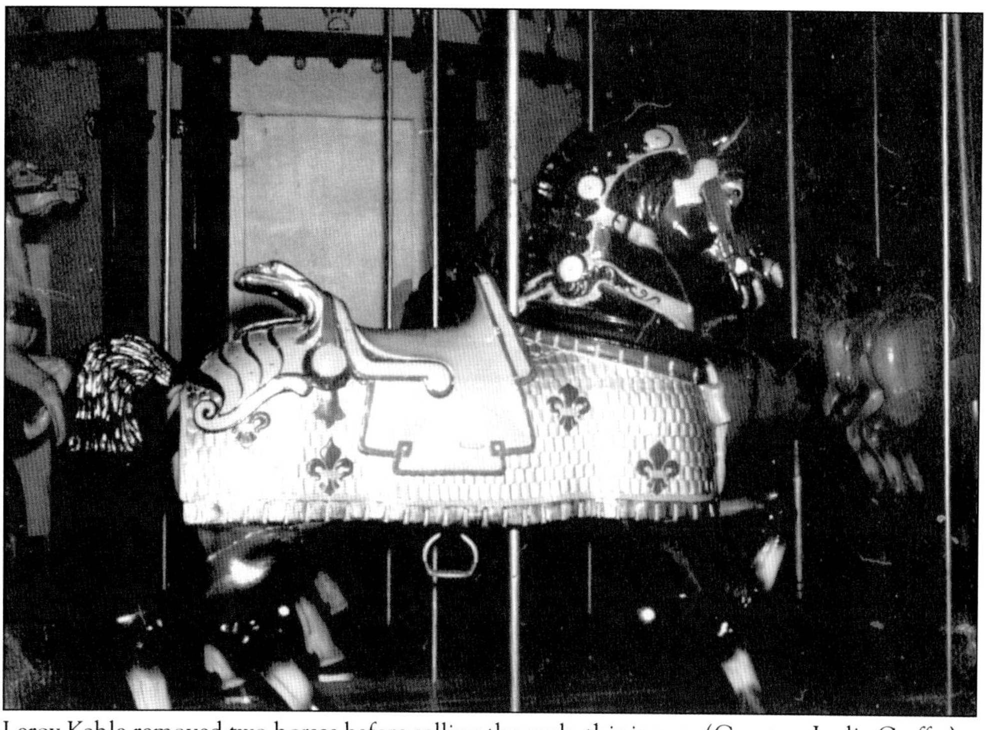

Leroy Kahle removed two horses before selling the park; this is one. (Courtesy Leslie Greffe.)

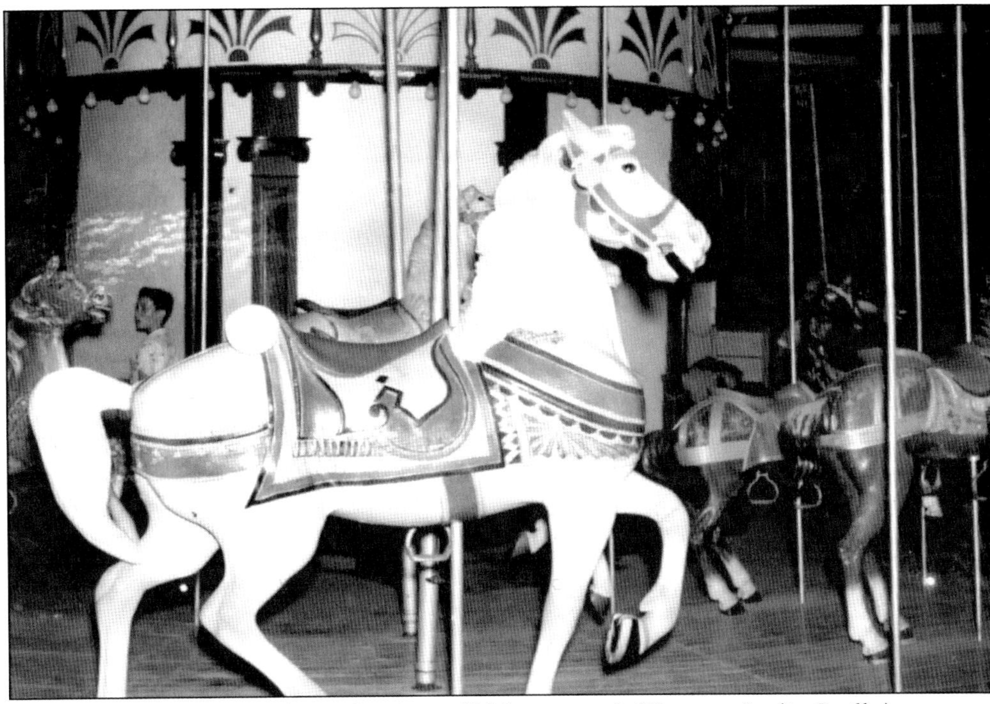

Shown here is the second horse that Leroy Kahle removed. (Courtesy Leslie Greffe.)

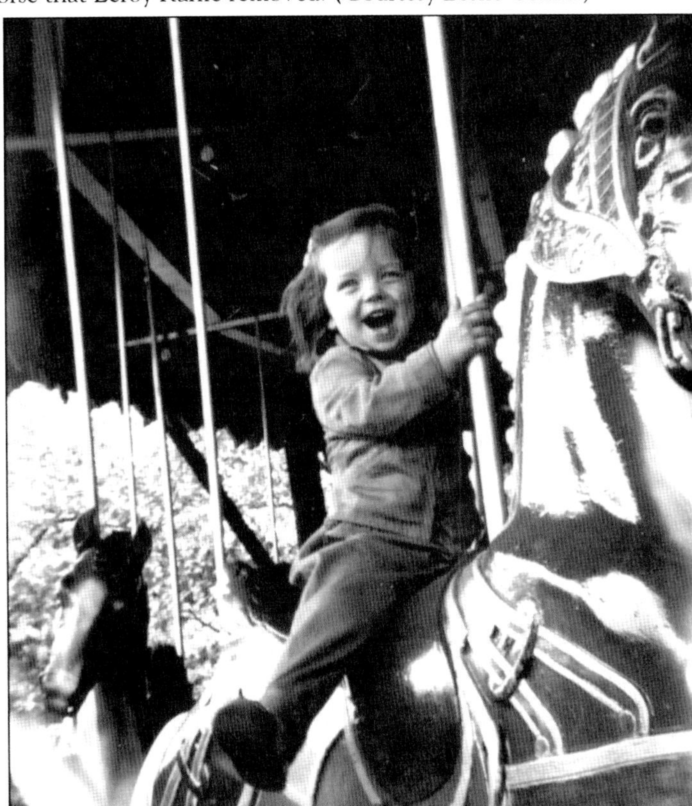

Leslie Bergen rides the merry-go-round in 1951. (Courtesy Leslie Greffe.)

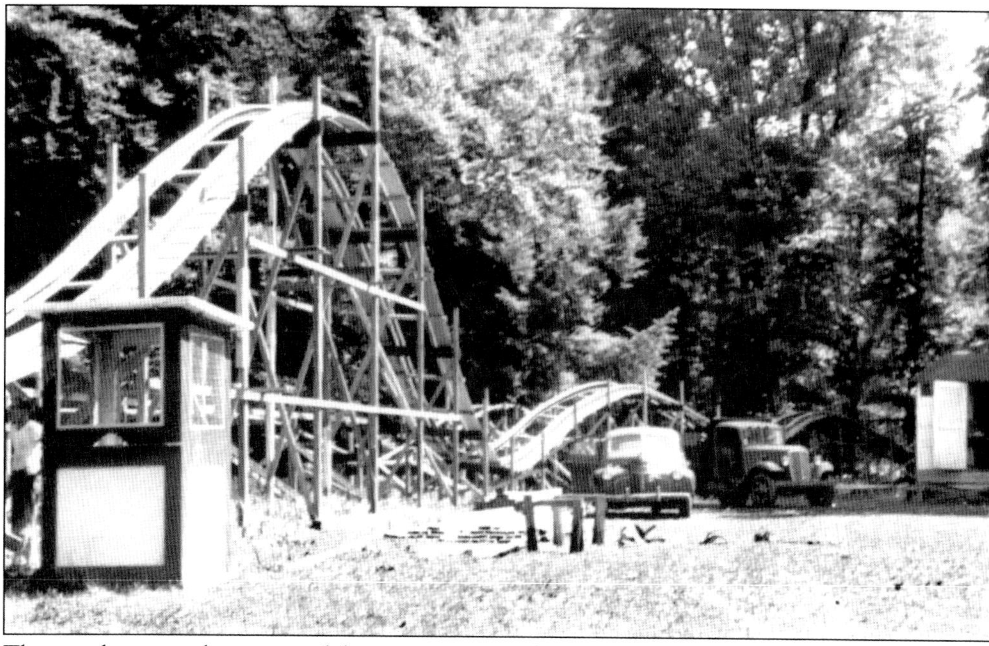

The wood seen in the center of this image was used to repair the roller coaster. Note the ticket booth next to the coaster. The old dump truck to the right was used to pick up the garbage throughout the park. (Courtesy Leslie Greffe.)

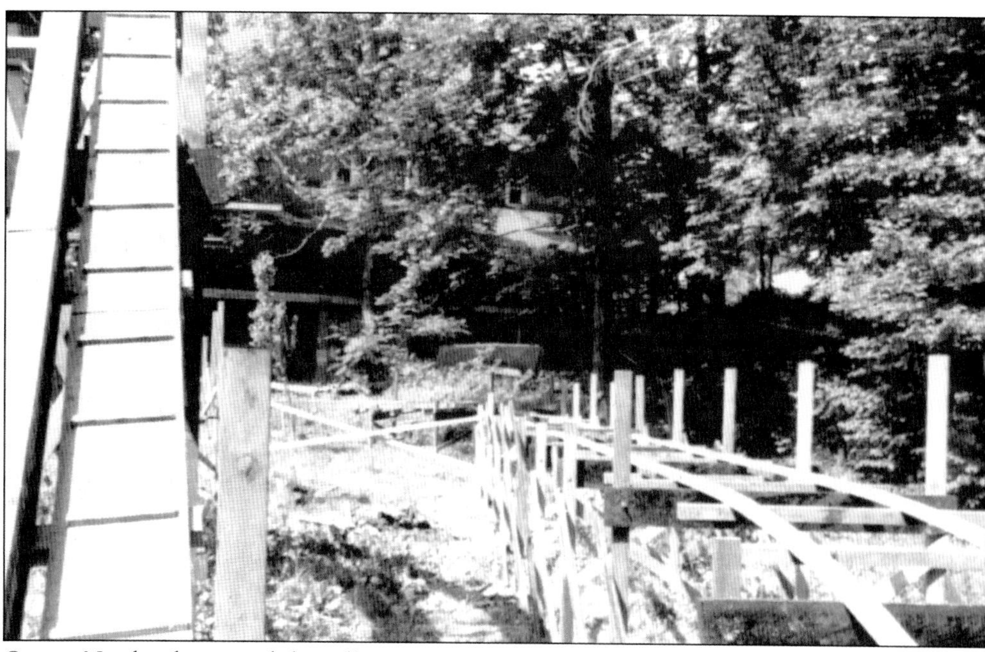

George Newhard operated the roller coaster for a number of years and may have been working in that capacity when this photograph was taken. (Courtesy Leslie Greffe.)

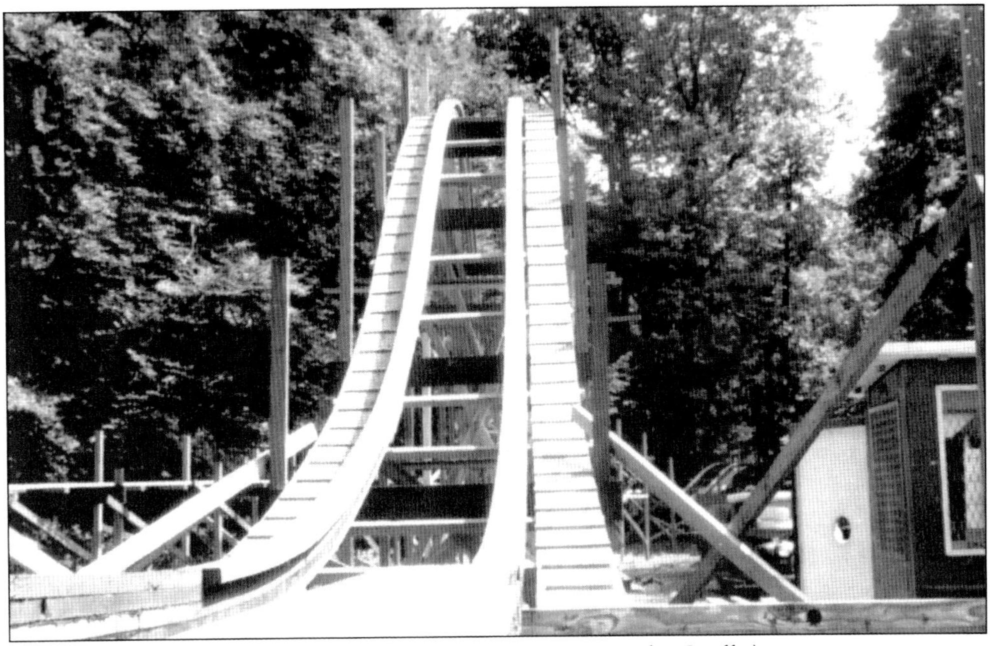

The first hill on the roller coaster awaits traffic. (Courtesy Leslie Greffe.)

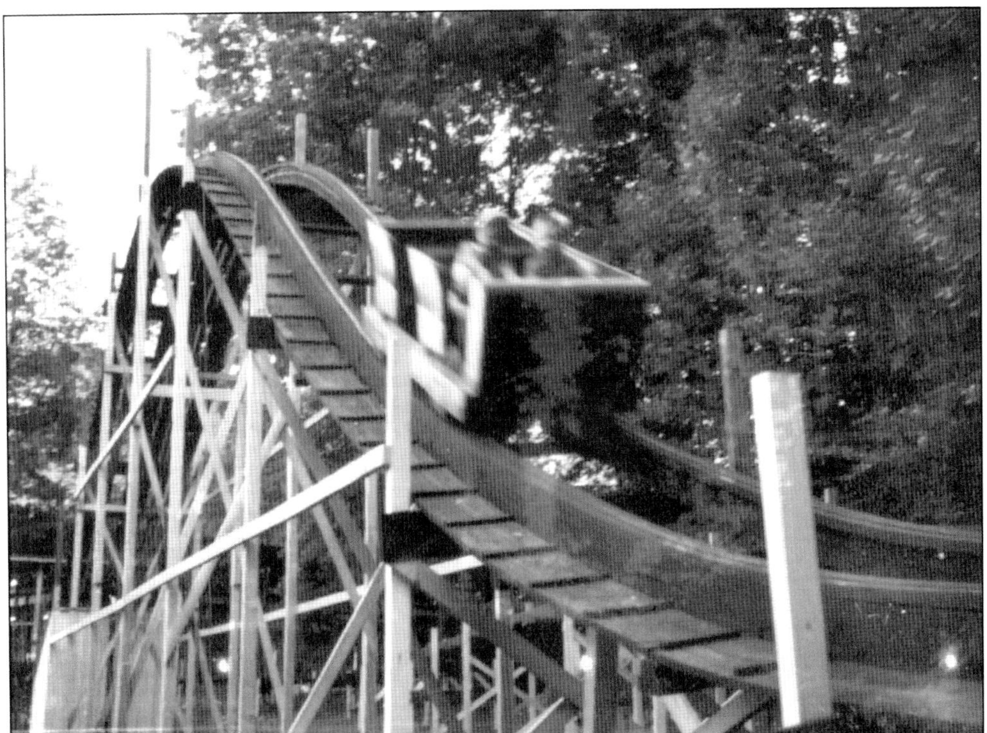

A coaster car rolls down the first hill. (Courtesy Leslie Greffe.)

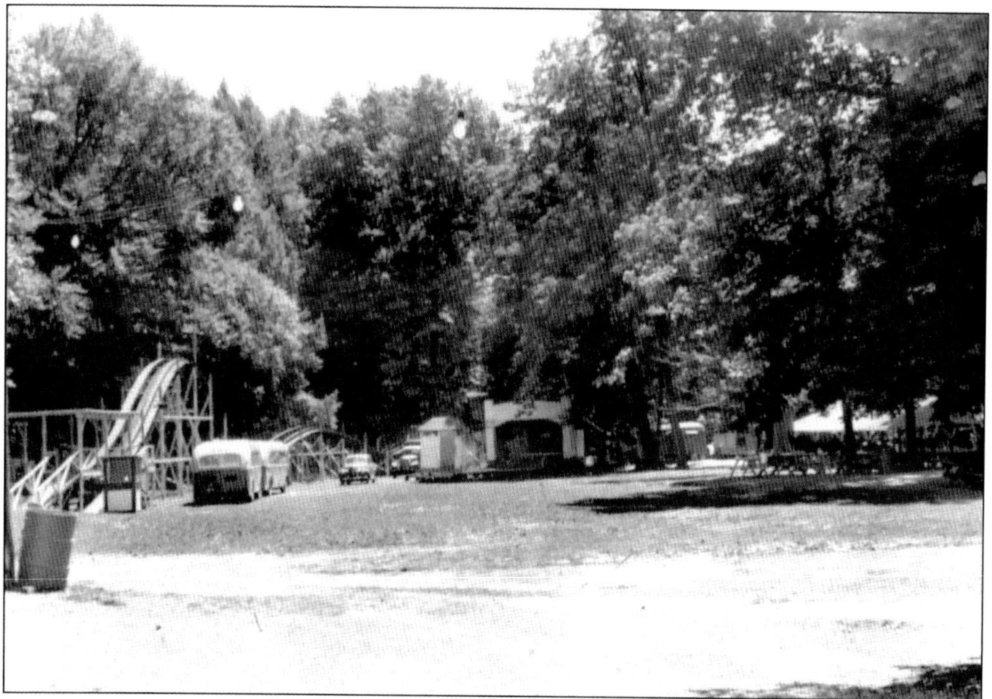

In this photograph, taken from near the merry-go-round, the roller coaster can be seen to the left, the stage to the center, and the picnic area to the right. The buses parked near the coaster were purchased by Leroy Kahle to bring groups of picnickers to the park. At the end of the season, Kahle used the buses to treat his workers to a trip, one of which was to Crystal Cave. (Courtesy Leslie Greffe.)

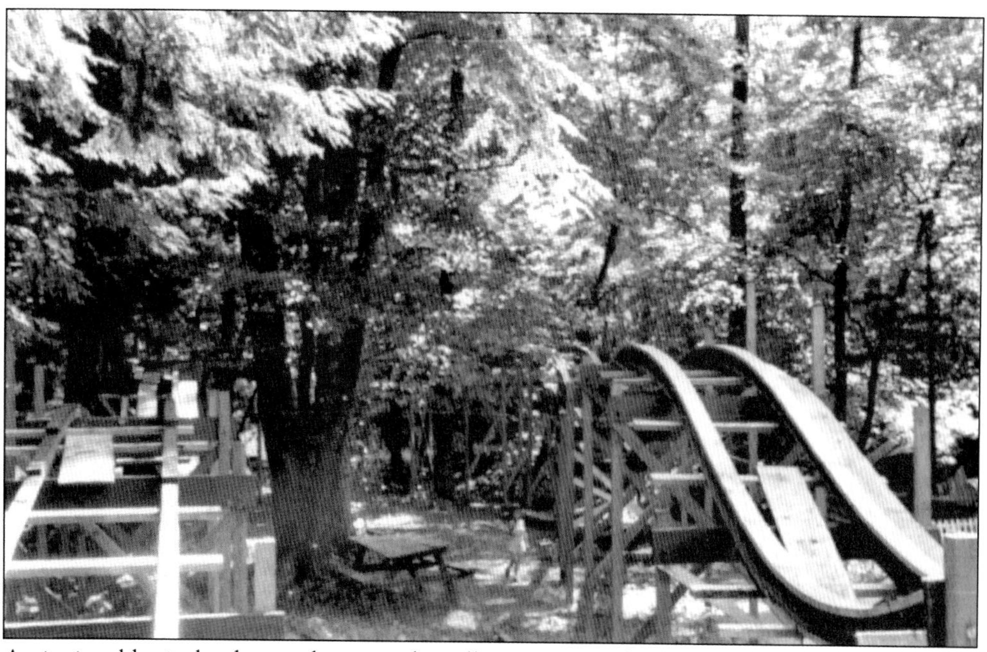

A picnic table sits by the tree between the roller coaster tracks. (Courtesy Leslie Greffe.)

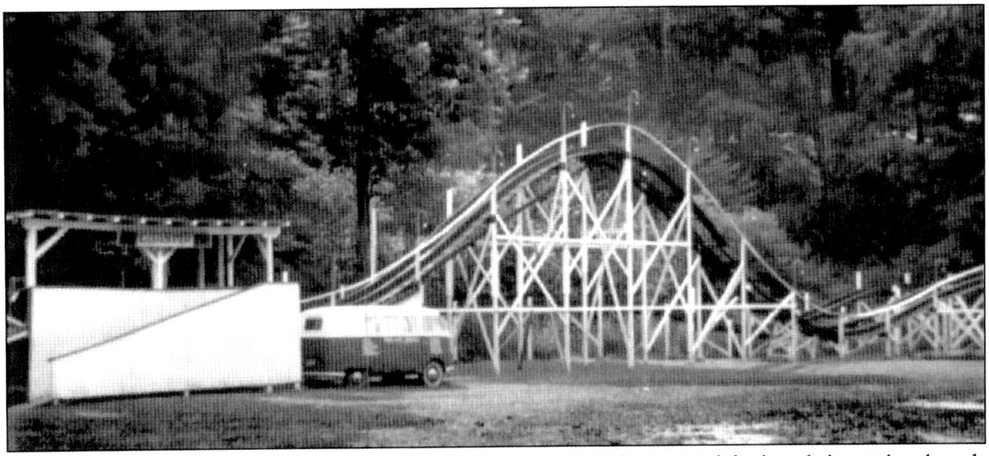

In this later view of the roller coaster, the loading area has been modified and the ticket booth is no longer adjacent. (Courtesy Leslie Greffe.)

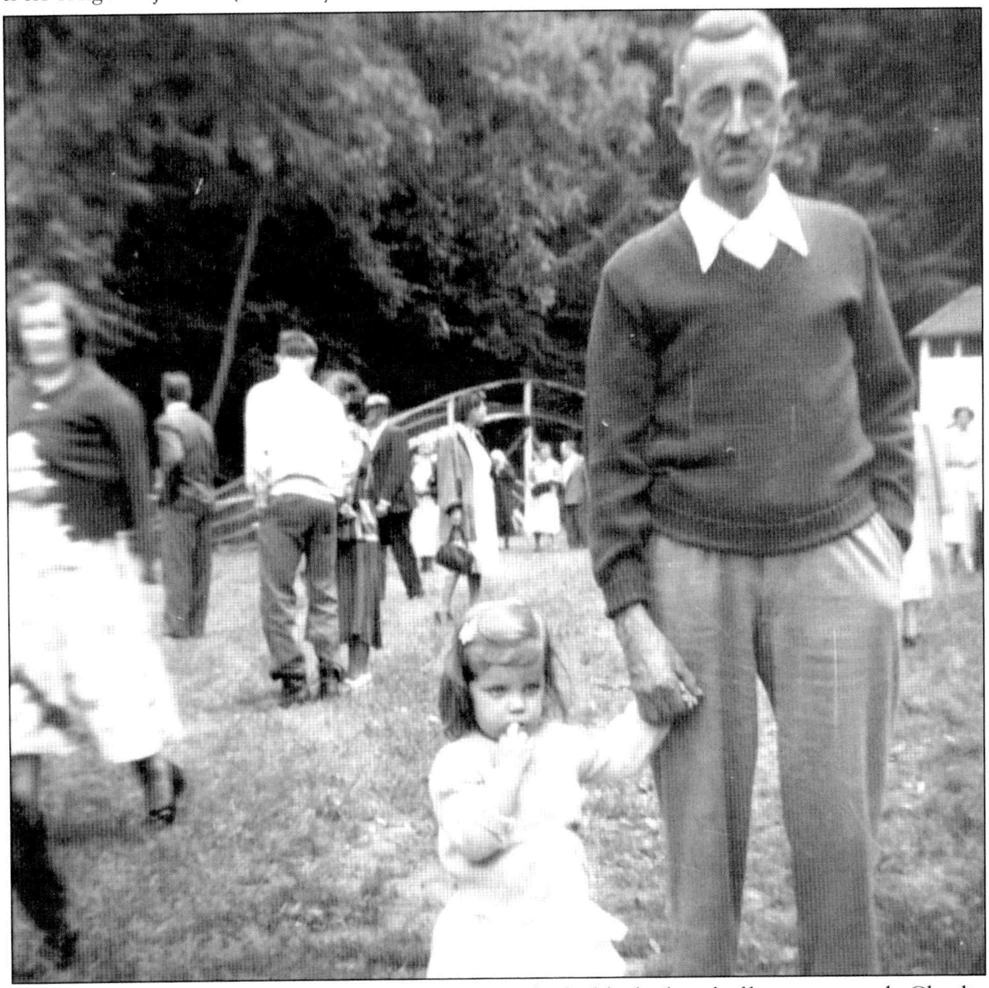

The roller coaster is visible behind Leslie Bergen, who holds the hand of her great-uncle Charlie Bergen. (Courtesy Leslie Greffe.)

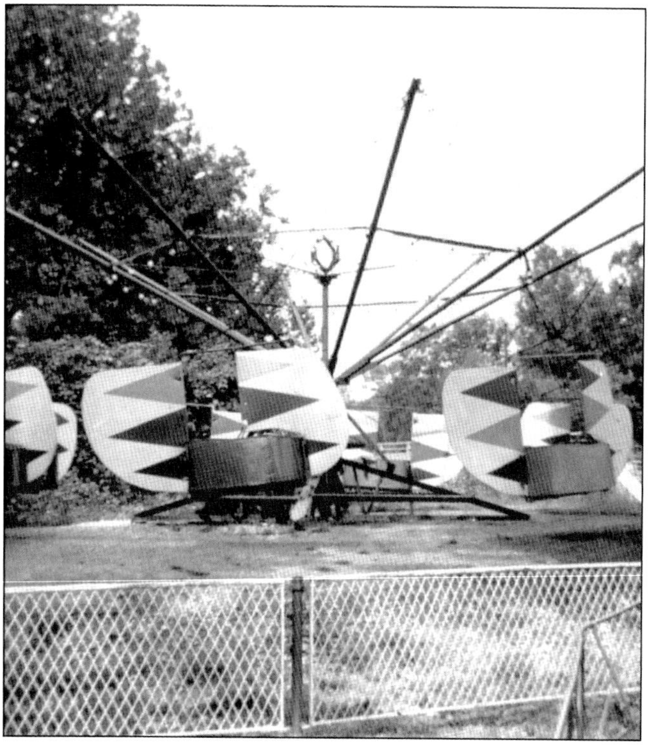

Riders of the Flying Scooter could steer the front rudder to make the scooter go higher or lower. (Courtesy Leslie Greffe.)

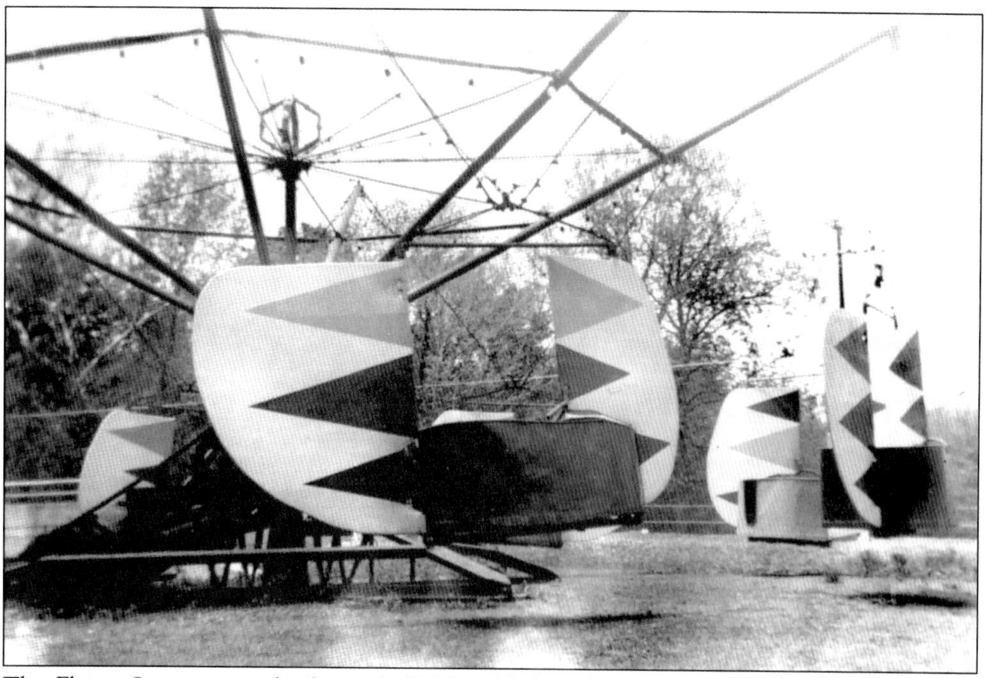

The Flying Scooter was the last ride Kahle added to the park (likely around 1964). Allen Newhard operated the ride. (Courtesy Leslie Greffe.)

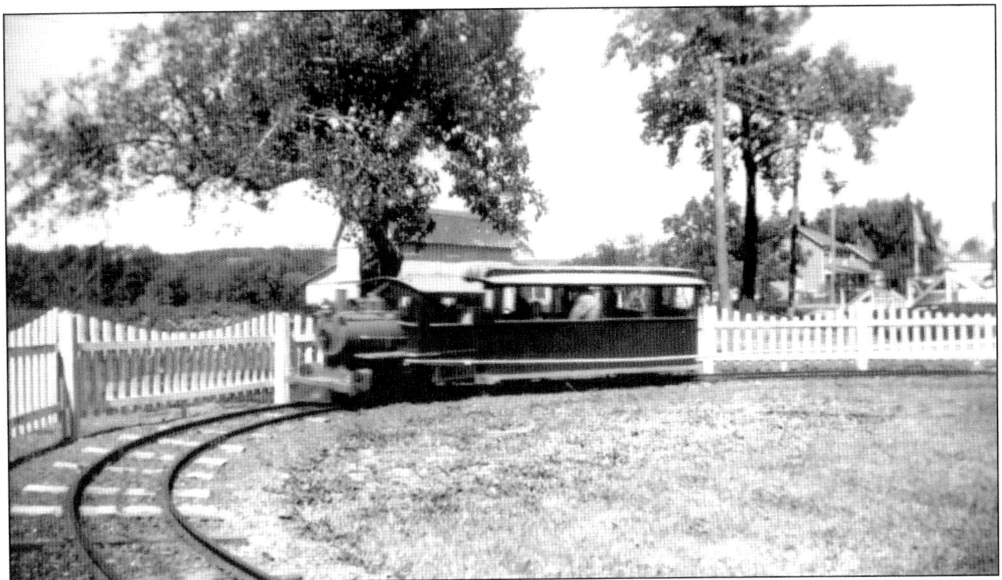

Dale Miller ran the train about 1960. Adam Newhard also operated the ride. (Courtesy Blaine Kahle.)

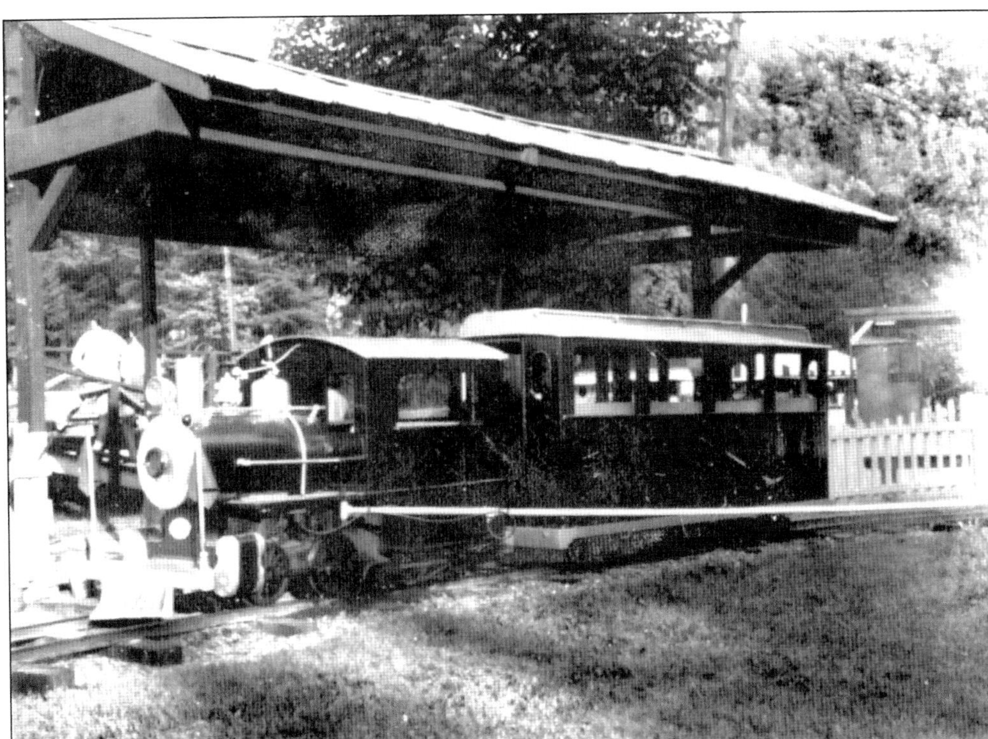

Electricity, supplied through the white pole connected to the engine, powered the train. (Courtesy Leslie Greffe.)

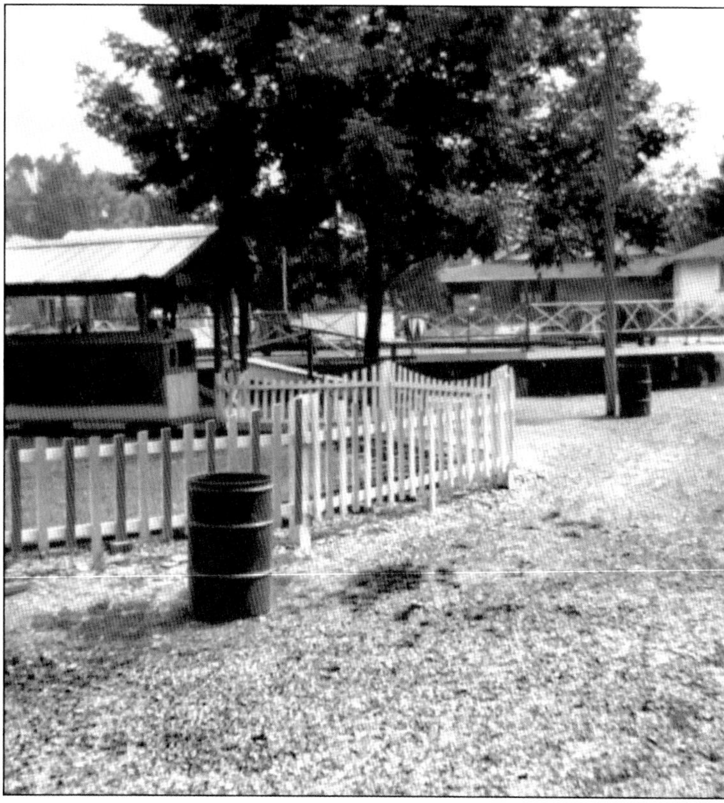

In this view, looking across the park, the back of the train can be seen to the left behind the fence. The whip is visible in the center, and the Trading Post is behind it to the right. (Courtesy Leslie Greffe.)

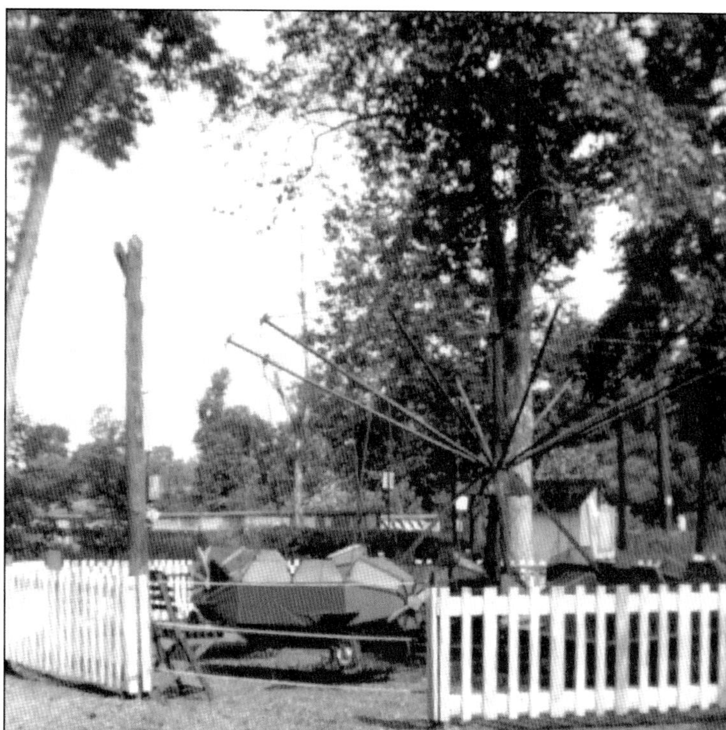

The park featured a kids' airplane ride, operated by Gary Reph. (Courtesy Leslie Greffe.)

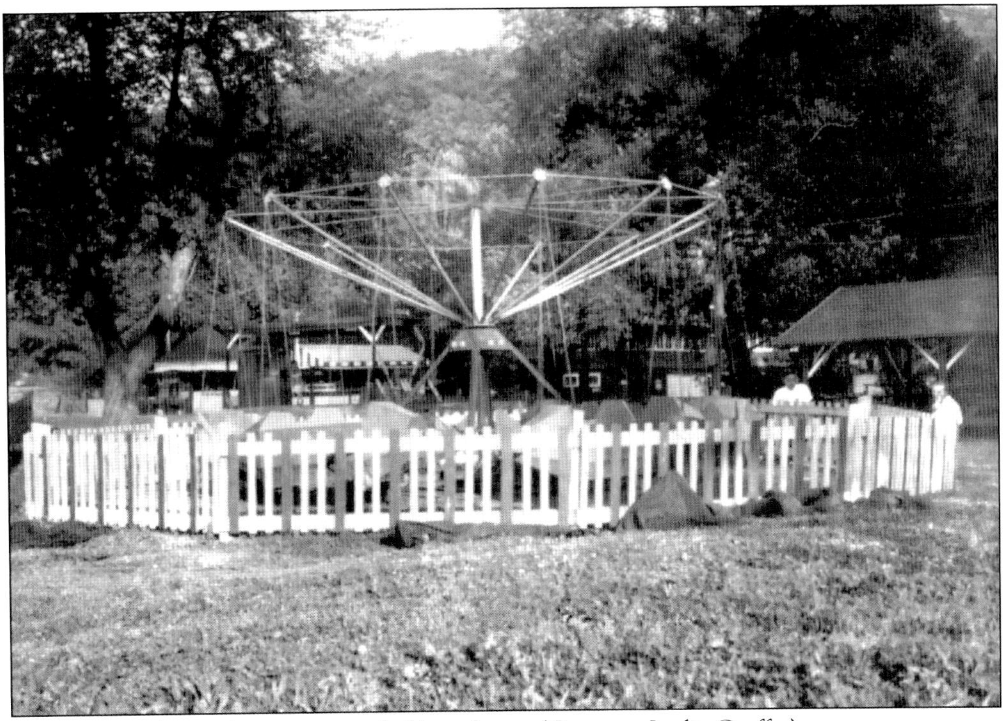

The kids' airplane ride was surrounded by a fence. (Courtesy Leslie Greffe.)

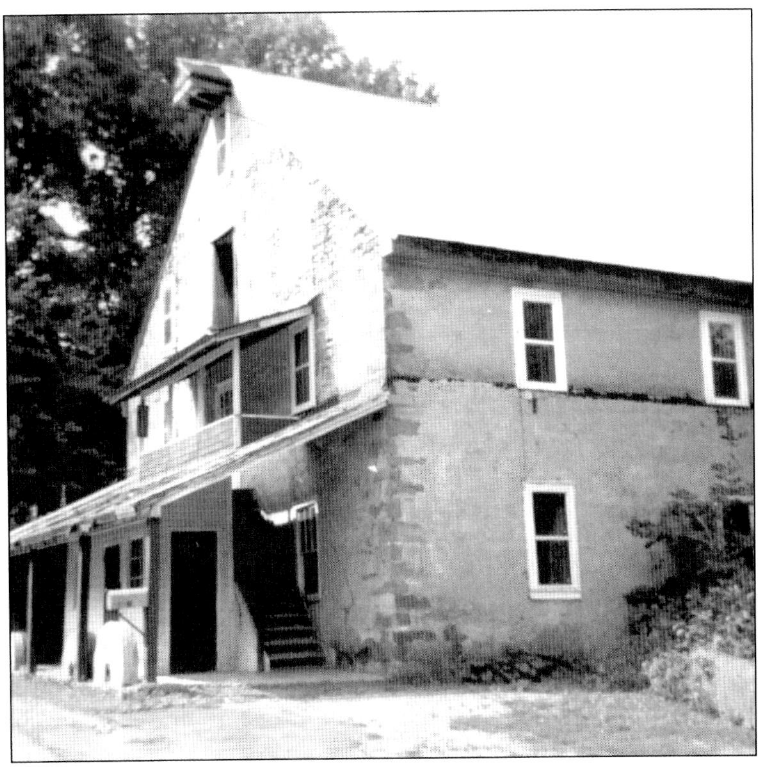

In this c. 1950s view, two grinding stones sit in front of the old gristmill. The Kahles and Bergens lived on the second floor of the mill. (Courtesy Leslie Greffe.)

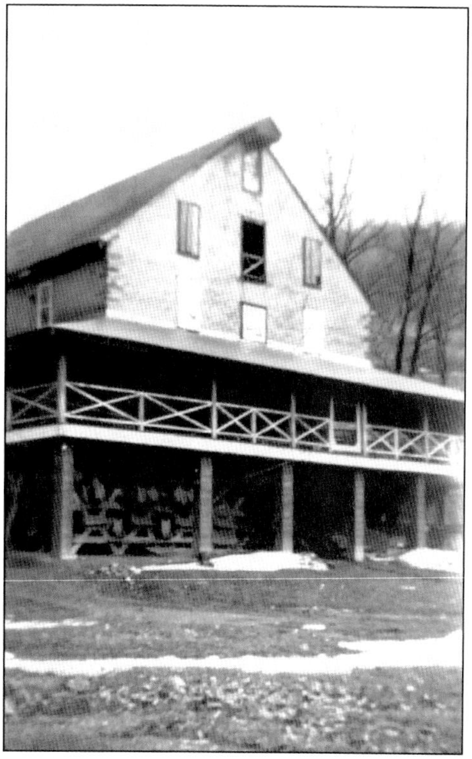

Patrons looking at the gristmill from the park were provided this view. (Courtesy Leslie Greffe.)

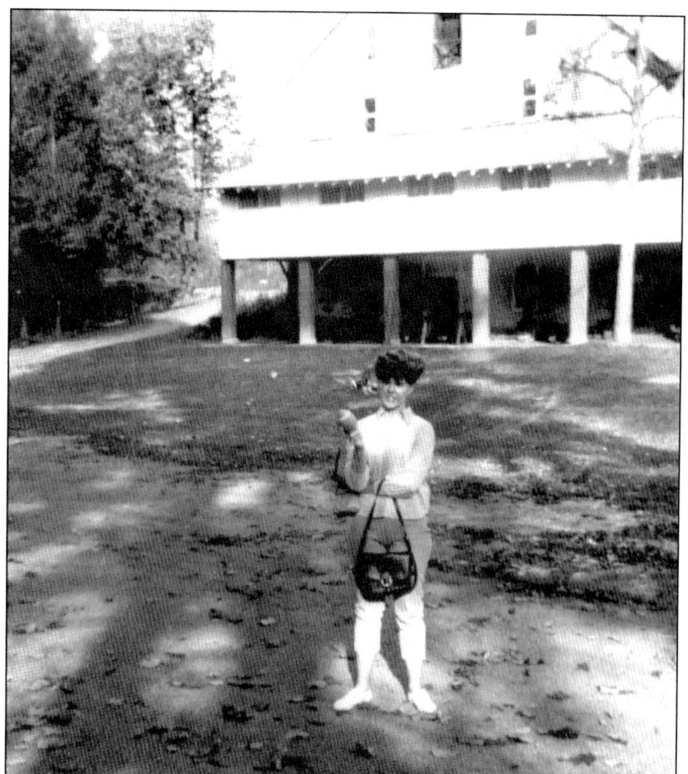

Kerry Bergen stands in front of the mill. (Courtesy Leslie Greffe.)

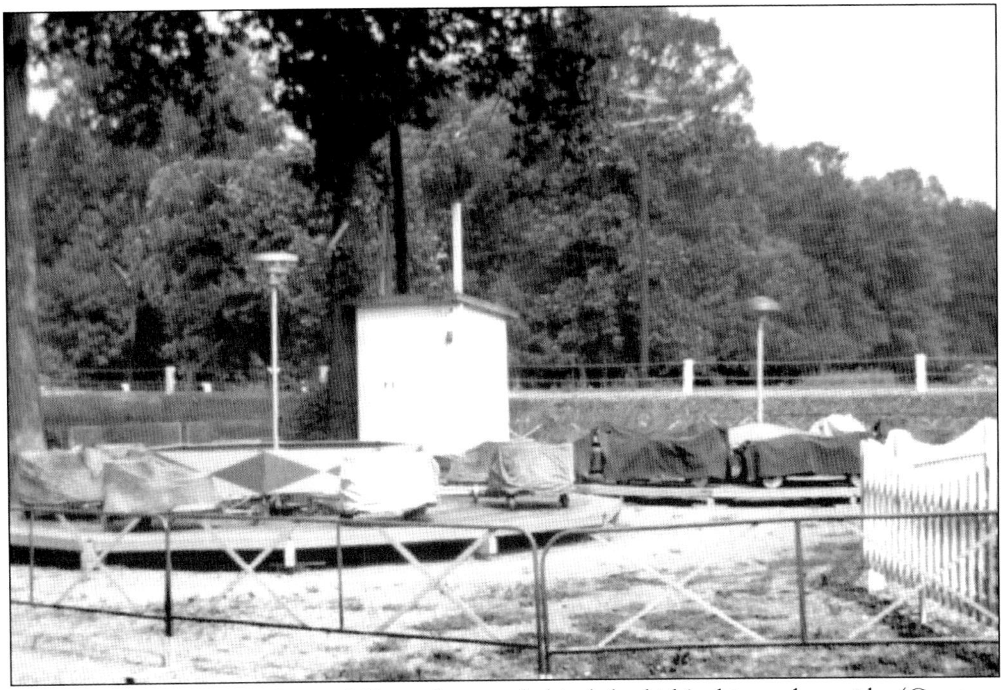

The road now known as Route 248 can be seen behind the kids' whip and car ride. (Courtesy Leslie Greffe.)

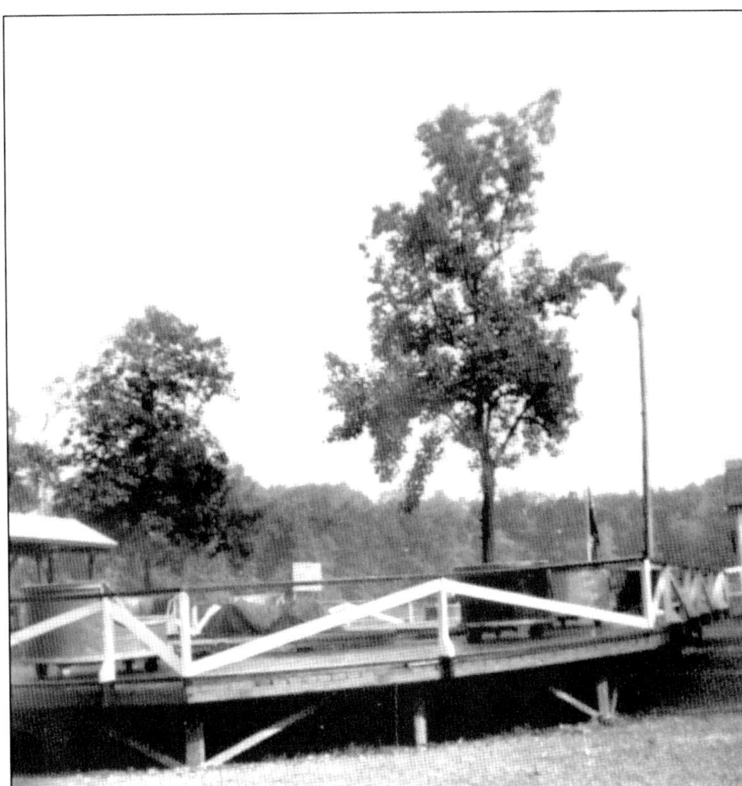

The train station is visible to the left in this photograph of the whip. (Courtesy Leslie Greffe.)

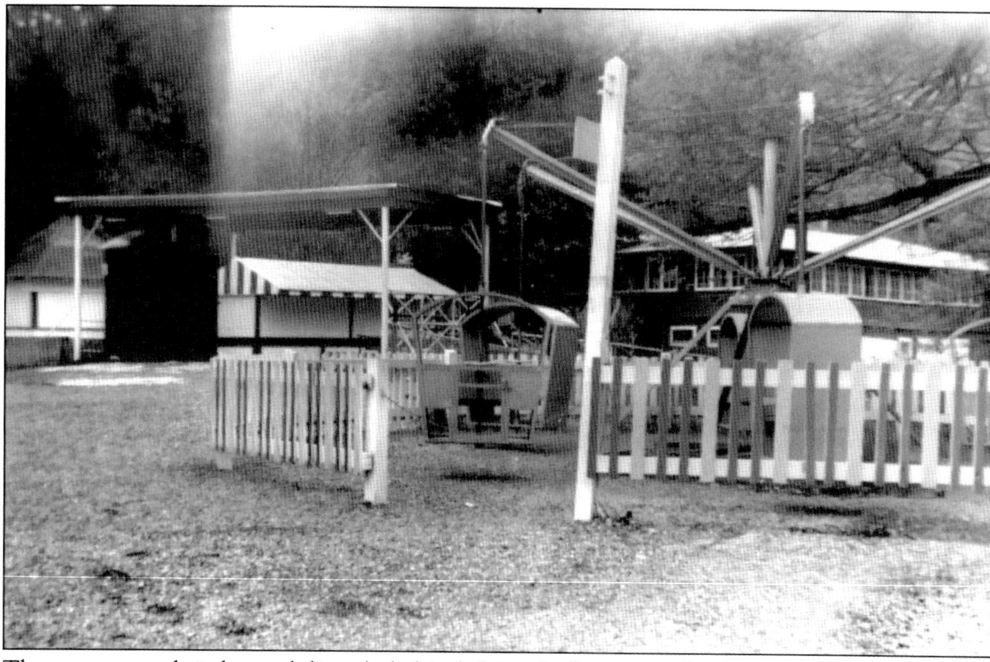

The penny arcade is located directly behind this ride, known as the Spinner, and the popcorn stand is behind it to the left. (Courtesy Leslie Greffe.)

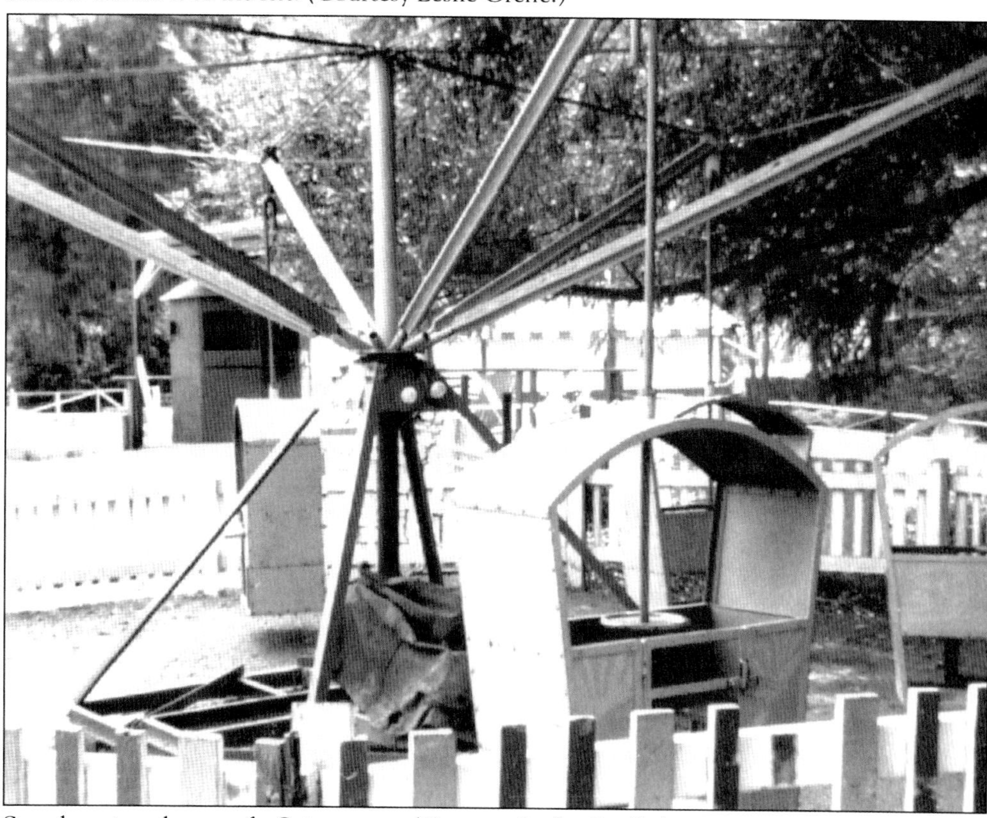

Seen here is a closeup of a Spinner car. (Courtesy Leslie Greffe.)

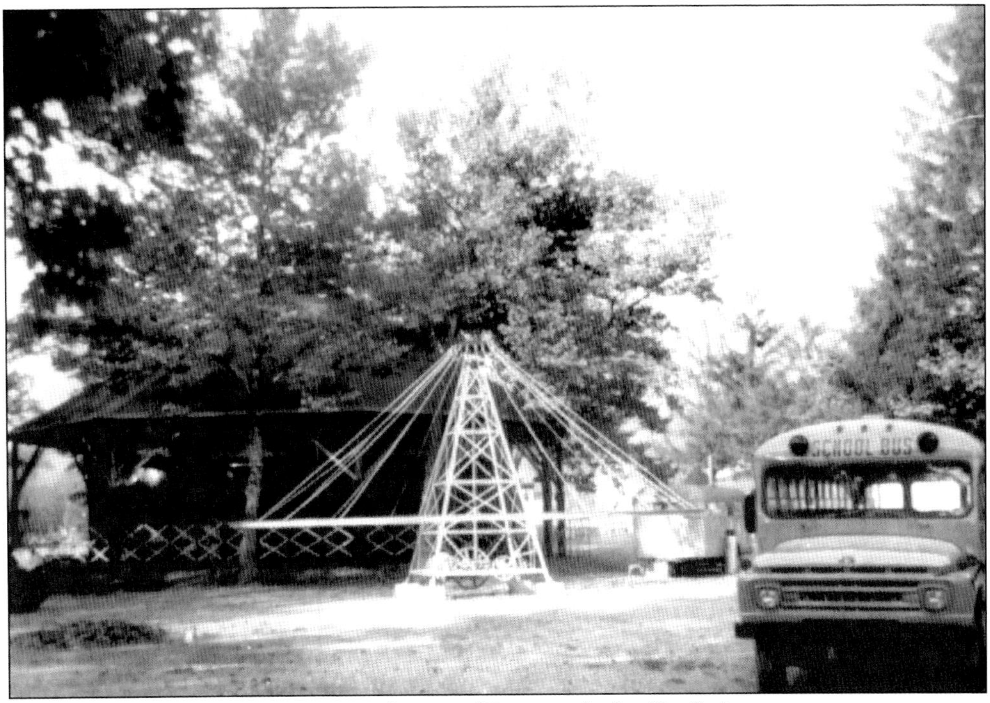

This ride's name and function are unknown. (Courtesy Leslie Greffe.)

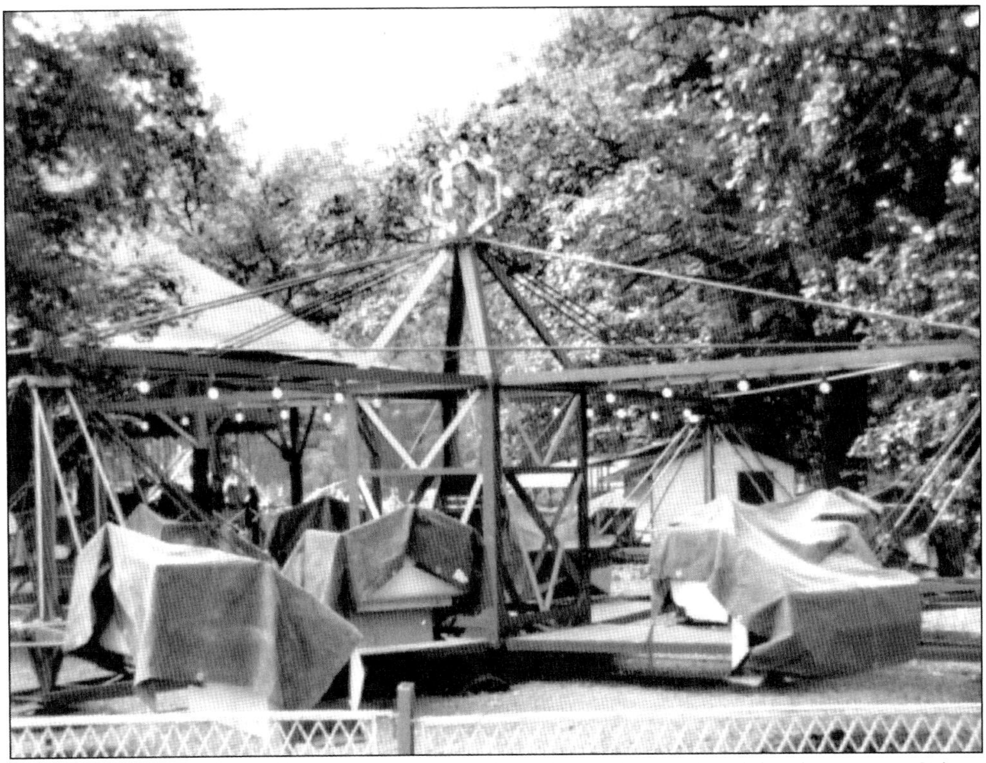

Rides such as the Merry Mixer were covered when the park was closed for the winter. Others were taken apart and stored in the bottom of the mill. (Courtesy Leslie Greffe.)

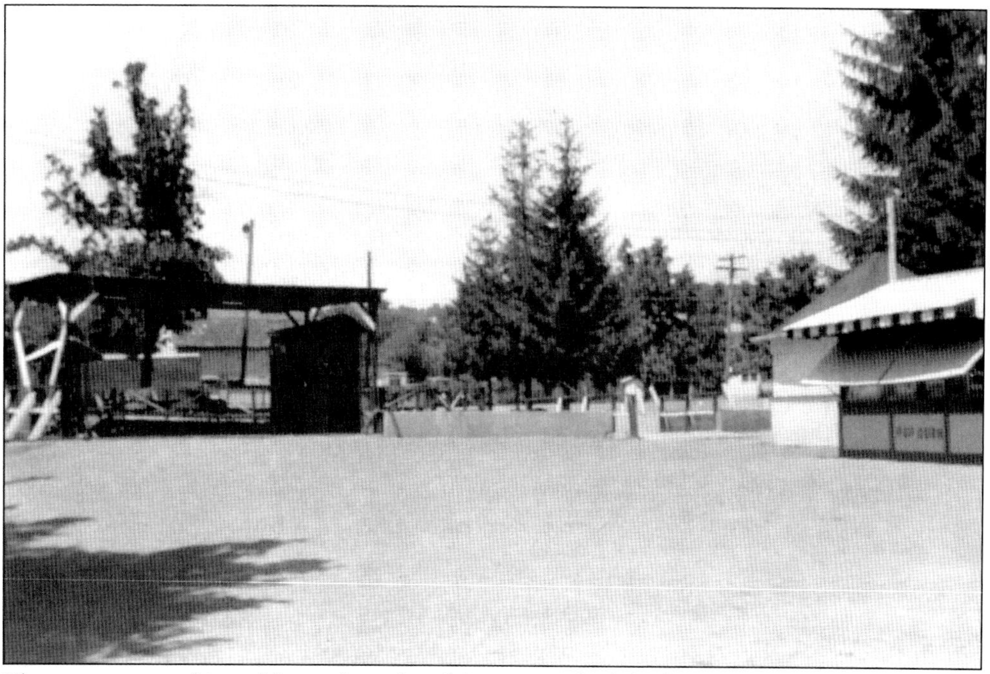

The popcorn stand is visible on the right of this view, which looks toward the road now known as Route 248. The bridge with the park ticket booth is on the left. (Courtesy Leslie Greffe.)

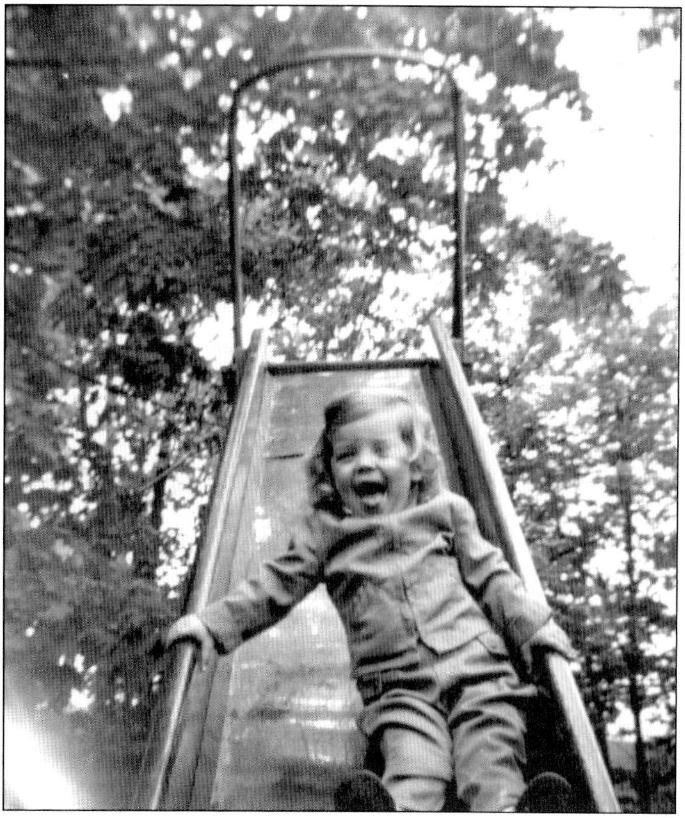

Leslie Bergen zips down the park slide in 1951. (Courtesy Leslie Greffe.)

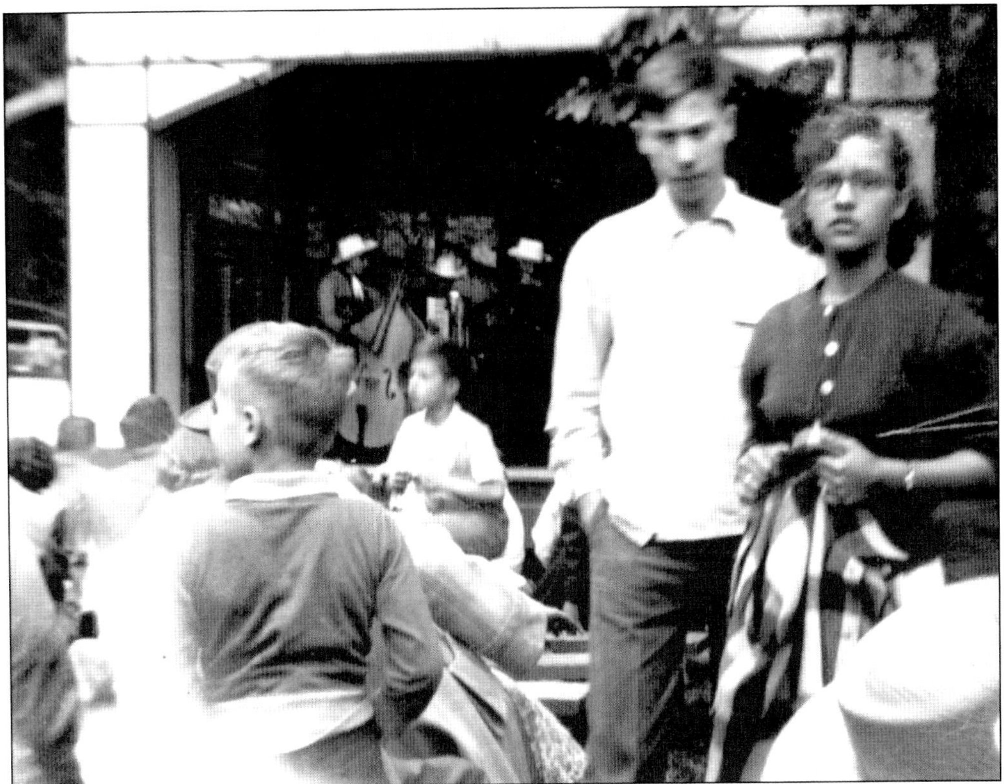

Entertainment at the park was still popular in the 1950s. Here, a band performs on the stage in front of a crowd. (Courtesy Leslie Greffe.)

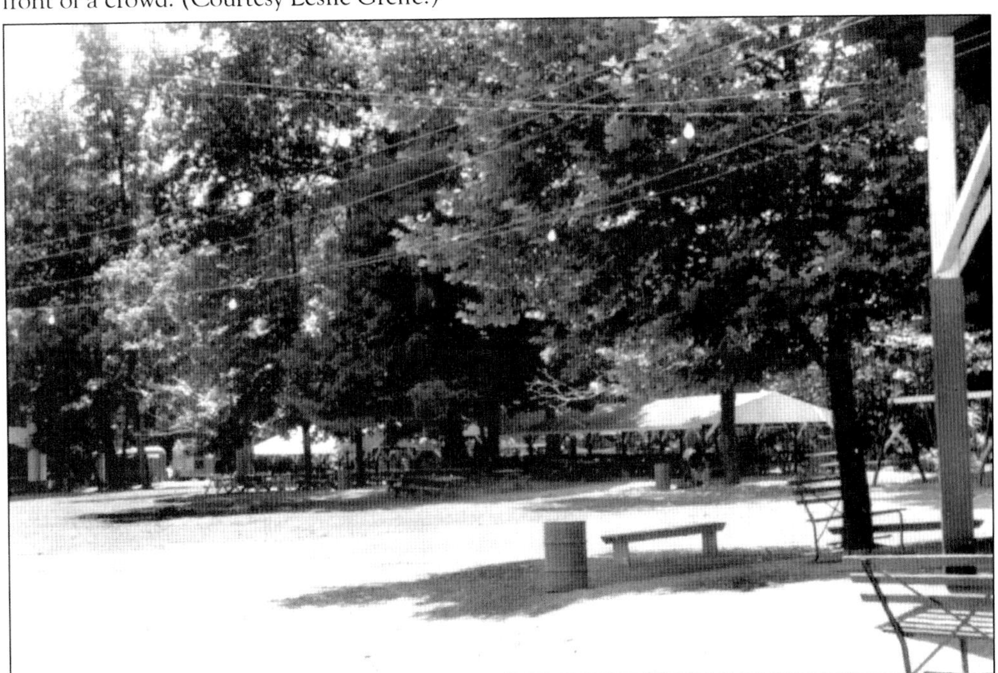

This is the picnic area as it appeared from the merry-go-round. (Courtesy Leslie Greffe.)

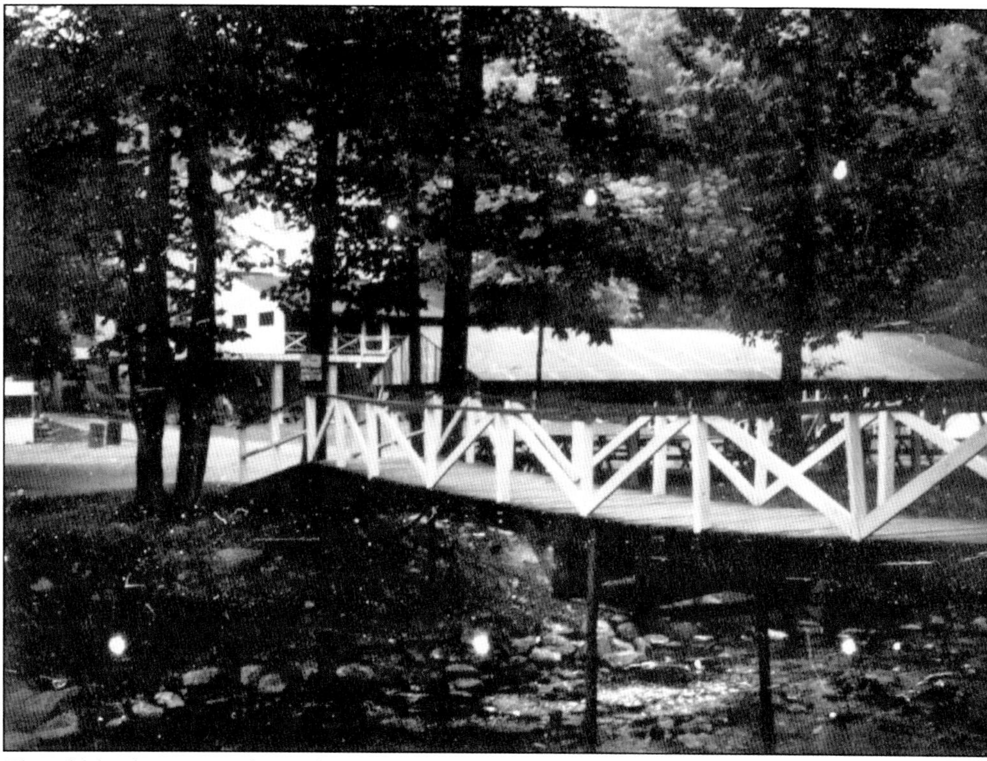

The old bridge across the Indian Creek was located in the same spot as the current bridge. (Courtesy Leslie Greffe.)

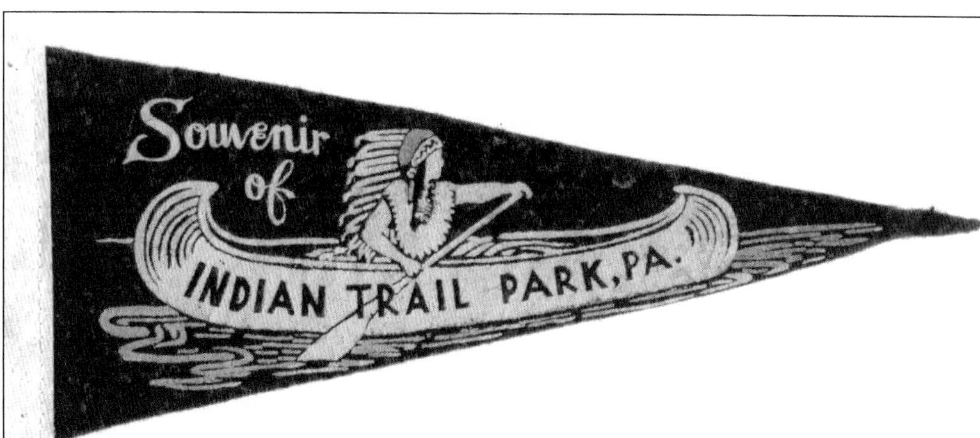

Pennants such as this one were among the souvenirs available at Indian Trail Park. (Courtesy Larry Hillborn.)

Three

Indian Trail Park

Hard Times

Leslie and Judith Tuttle purchased the park from Leroy Kahle in 1972 and ran it until the summer of 1977, when, according to newspaper reports, antiques they had stored in one of the park buildings were stolen. On September 9, 1977, the park was sold at sheriff's sale to the First National Bank of Allentown, which then sold the park to Lehigh Township on April 21, 1978, for $72,000.

Lehigh Township leased the park to Saullo Amusements in 1981. The company added the Looper, the Octopus, a little train, the Cuddle-Up, a Ferris wheel, a little merry-go-round, and children's bumper cars. Many of these rides were from the defunct Lakewood Park in Barnesville.

The swimming pool was closed and filled to allow for a miniature golf course. The Trading Post was converted into an arcade with pinball machines and was used as a park office. In June 1984, Saullo Amusements ended its lease with the township, and Indian Trail Park began to transform from an amusement park to a township recreation park. In September 1984, the Ferris wheel, Flying Scooter, Octopus, and Looper rides were sold at auction to Jerry Farrow of Funtime Amusements in Maryland.

In 1986, the township decided to demolish the old gristmill, which had ceased operation around 1920, served as a park restaurant after 1929, and eventually became a residence. Citizens calling themselves the Indian Trail Grist Mill Inc. stepped forward to save it. The group, incorporated as a nonprofit in 1987, tried unsuccessfully to obtain a 99-year lease to the building and one acre of land surrounding it. In October 1988, the township attempted to find someone to lease and run Indian Trail as an amusement park but received no bids. Finally, in 1990, the township advertised for bids to demolish the mill, and it was removed shortly thereafter.

In 1985, the Trading Post was leased out to First Chapter of Bath and converted into a garment factory. The five-year lease stipulated rent of $100 per month for the first three years and $150 per month for the last two. First Chapter also agreed to complete $8,762 worth of repairs to the building.

R&S Poultry then leased the Trading Post and used it as a store. After R&S closed, sometime in the 1990s, the building stood vacant. It was beginning to look like the Trading Post was doomed to suffer the same fate as the old mill. However, the Lehigh Township Historical

Society, founded in 2001, signed a lease with the township in November 2002 for the building and one acre surrounding it. The roof had been leaking for years, and by the time the society began restoration work in December 2002, the front walls had rotted to the point where they were no longer sound. In November 2003, as the roof was being removed for replacement, workers discovered that the back wall was also rotted and infested with termites. A few days later, this wall was removed. A windstorm then swiftly knocked down the remaining wall.

Not defeated, the society decided to reconstruct the Trading Post to look as much like the original as possible. Atas International of Fogelsville donated the metal roofing materials. Alcoa donated the vinyl siding and aluminum trim, and Quality Roofing Supply of Allentown provided the shingles for the main roof. Costa Construction of Allentown then successfully rebuilt.

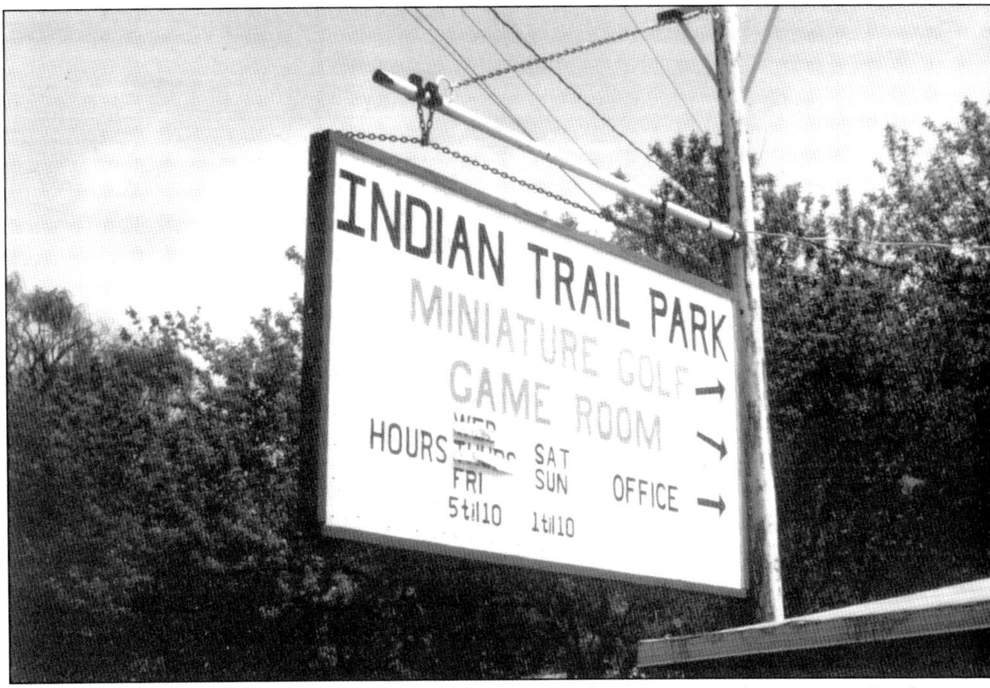

This sign hung next to the Trading Post during the park's last years of operation. By this time, the pool had been filled and a miniature golf coarse set up in its place. The Trading Post was used as a game room during these years. (Courtesy Larry Hillborn.)

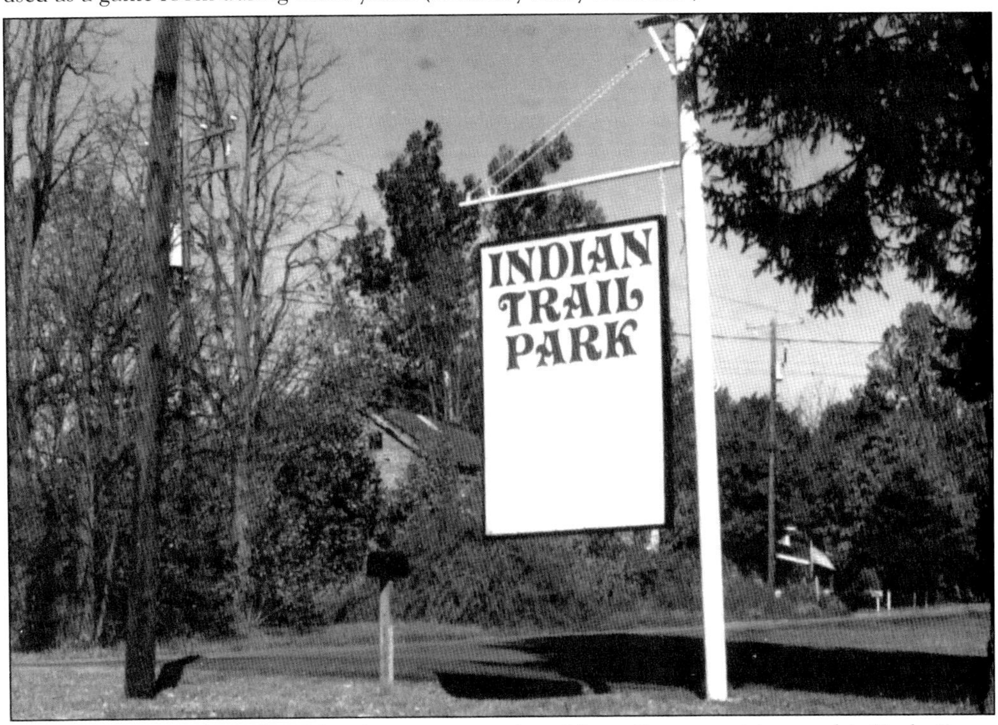

The sign remained until 2003, when it was replaced by a Scout working on his Eagle Scout project. (Courtesy Larry Hillborn.)

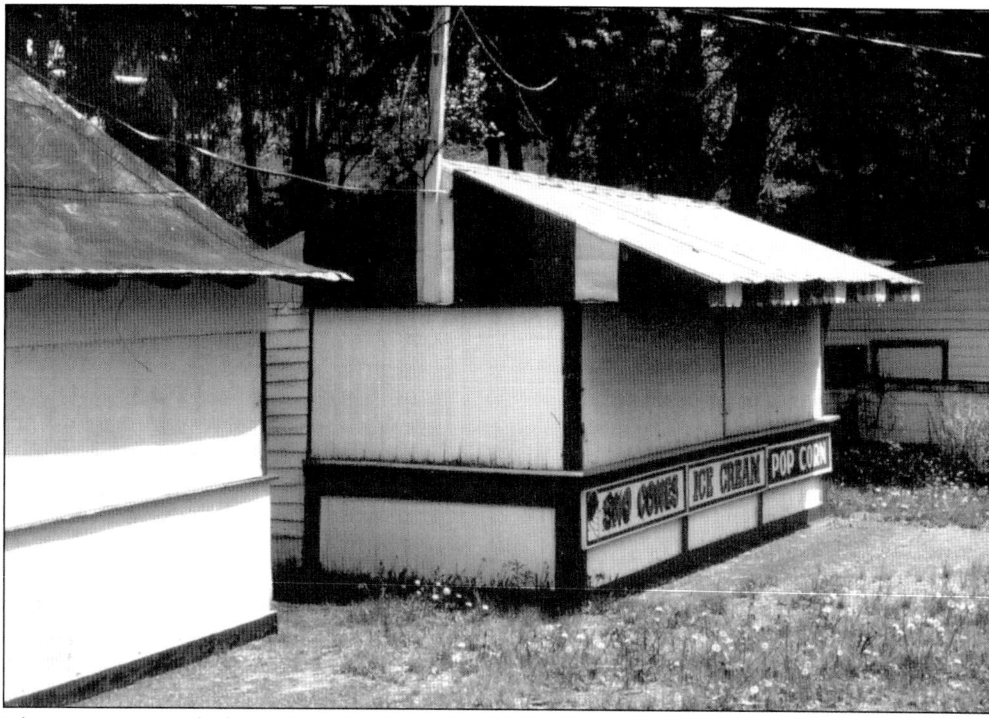

The popcorn stand, shown here in the early 1980s, also sold ice-cream and Sno cones at one time. (Courtesy Larry Hillborn.)

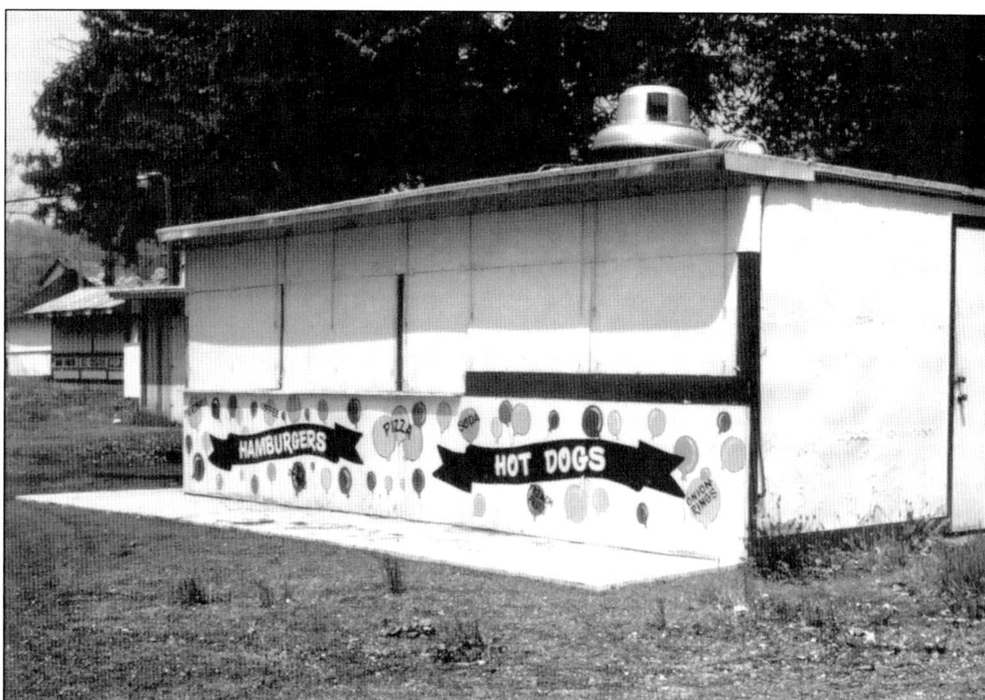

The hot dog and hamburger stand, seen in the 1980s, provided onion rings, pierogies, pizza, and soda in addition to the mainstays. (Courtesy Larry Hillborn.)

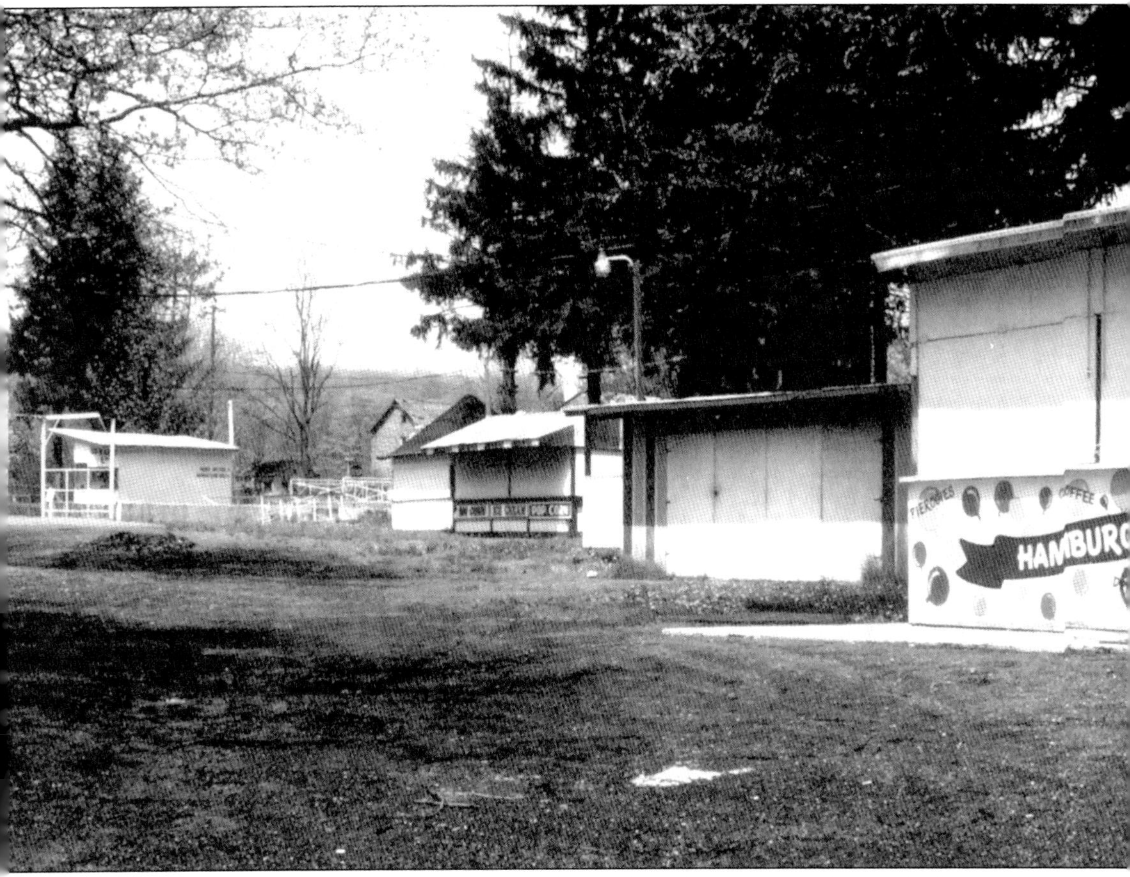

Go-carts were added during the final years at the park and were located past the hot dog, hamburger, and popcorn stands. (Courtesy Larry Hillborn.)

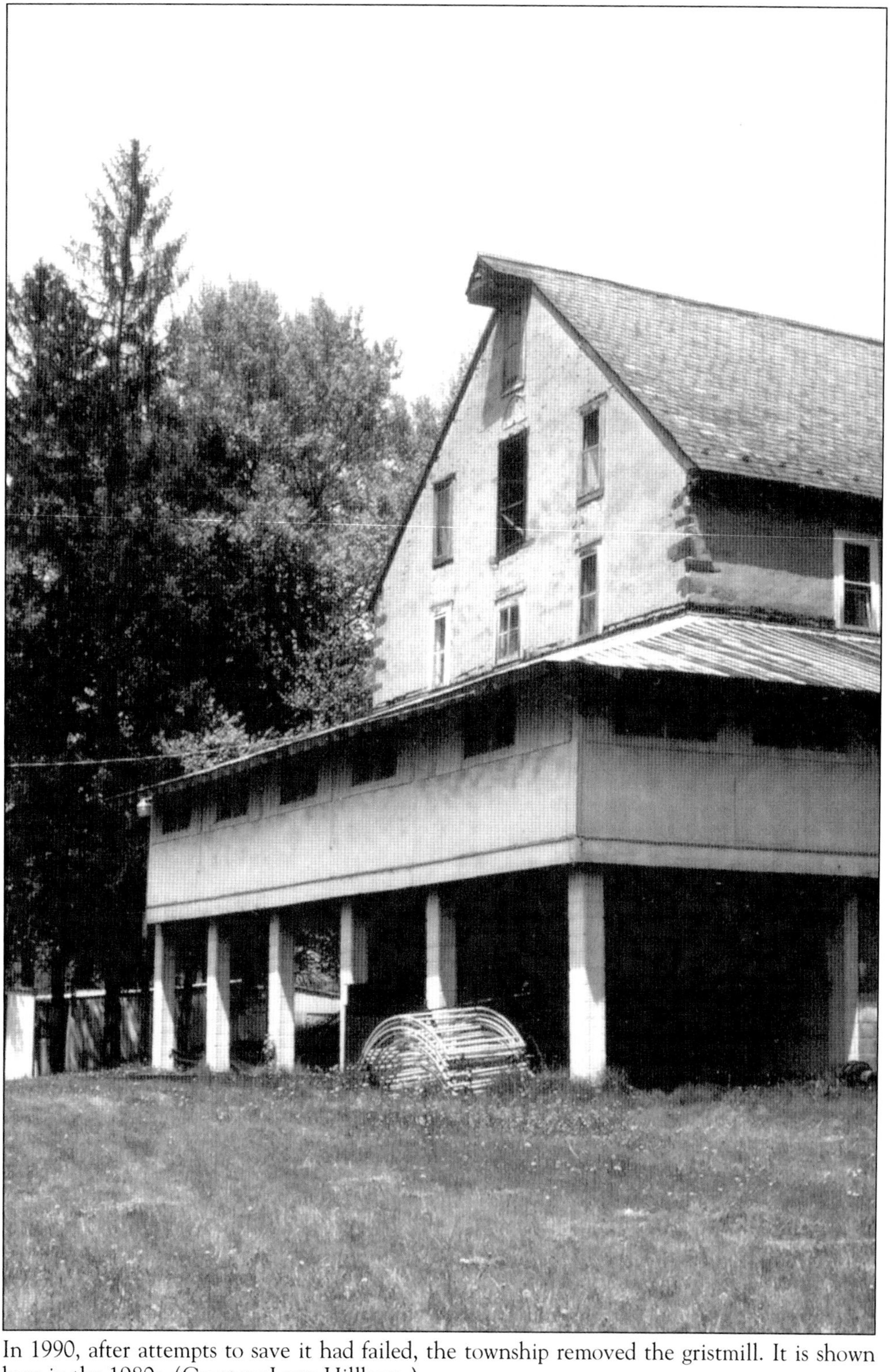

In 1990, after attempts to save it had failed, the township removed the gristmill. It is shown here in the 1980s. (Courtesy Larry Hillborn.)

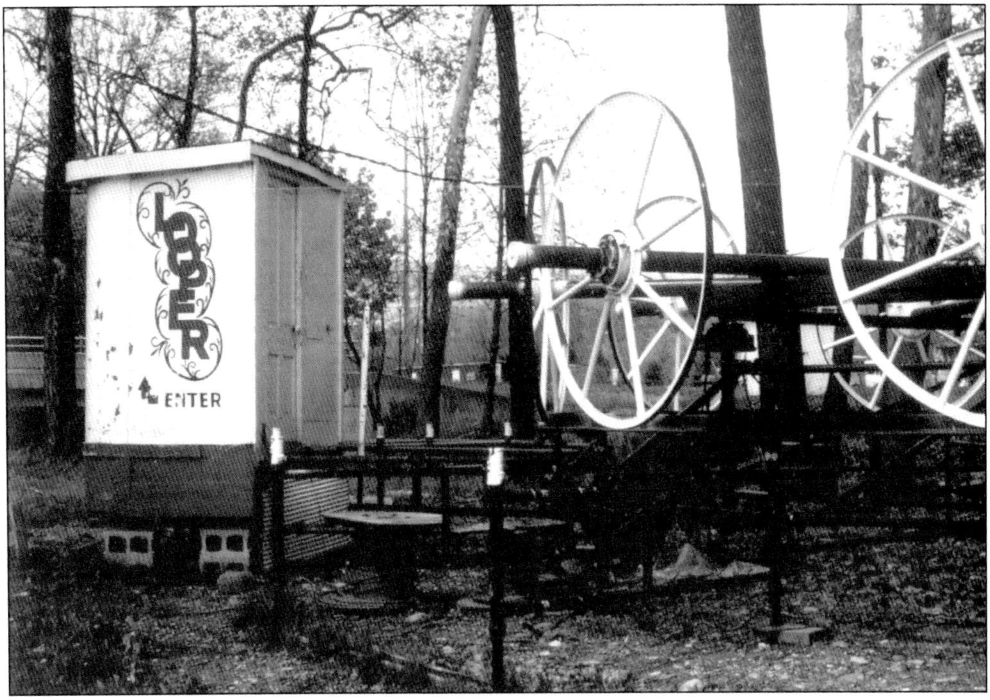

The Looper was added by Saullo Amusements in 1981, when the company leased the park from the township. (Courtesy Larry Hillborn.)

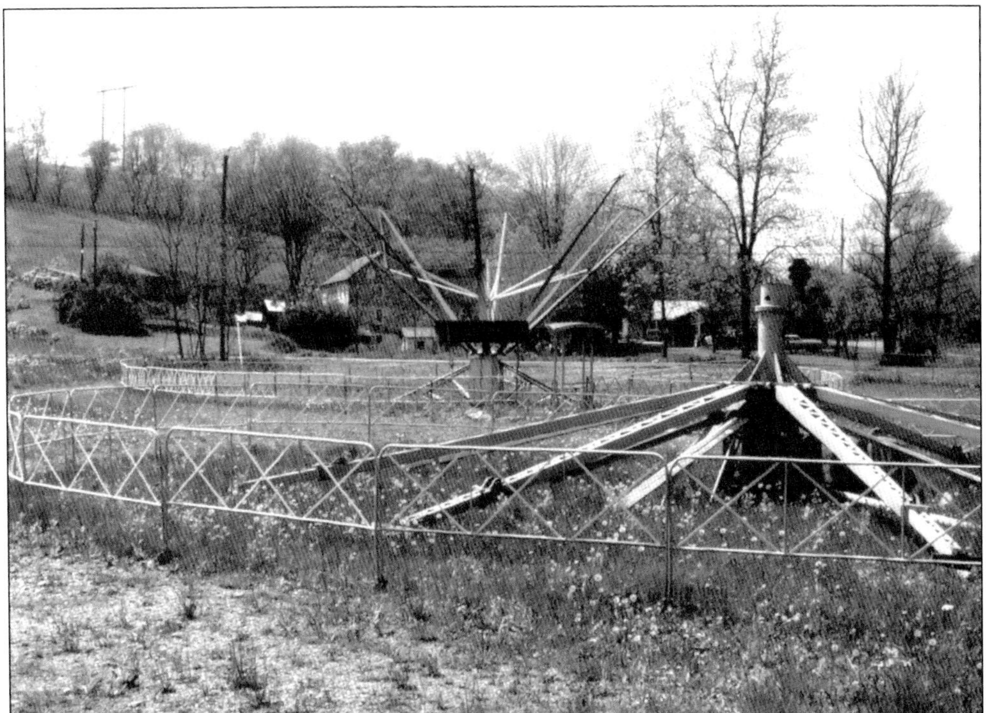

Some of the rides introduced by Saullo Amusements can be seen here. (Courtesy Larry Hillborn.)

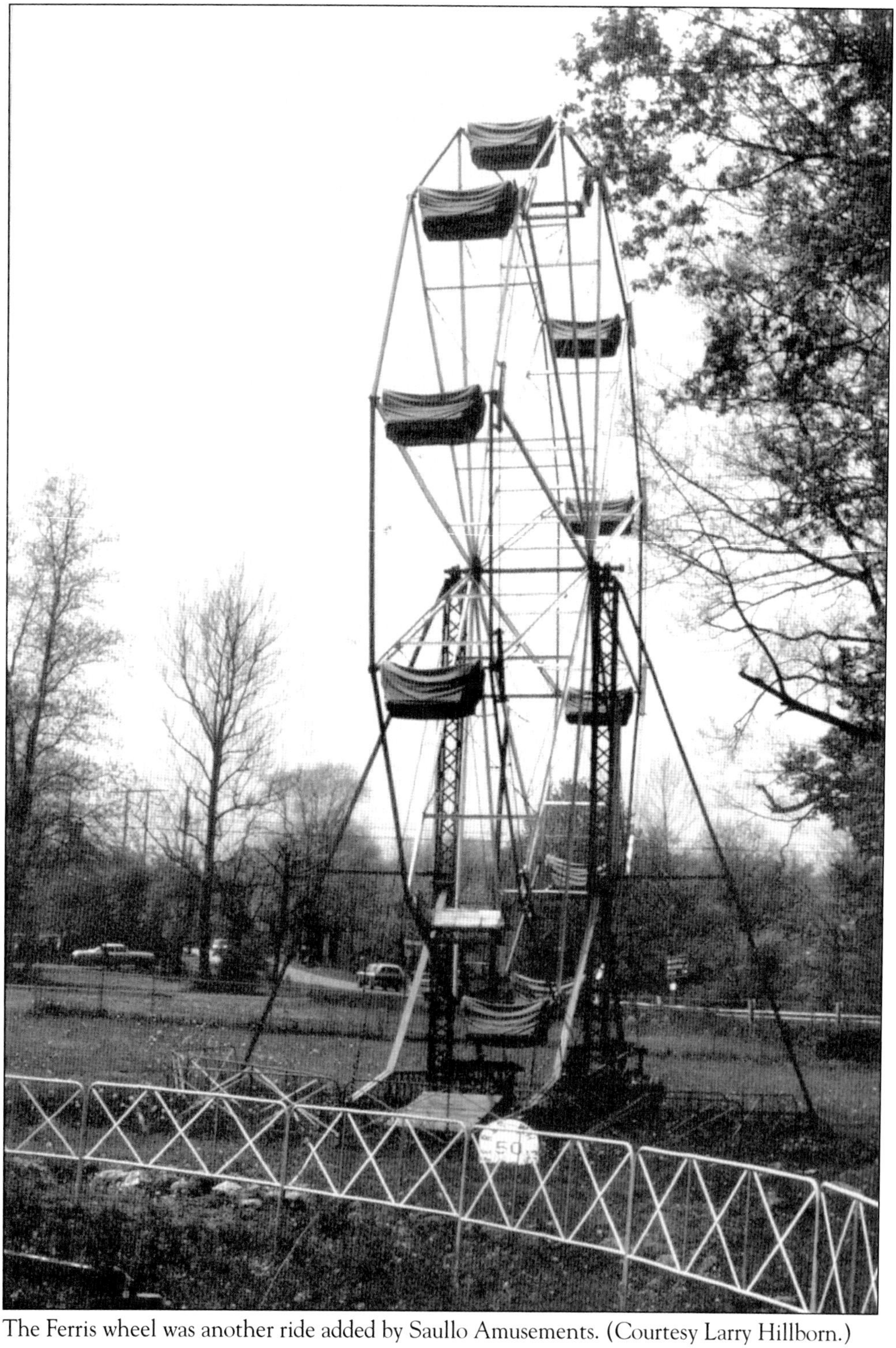

The Ferris wheel was another ride added by Saullo Amusements. (Courtesy Larry Hillborn.)

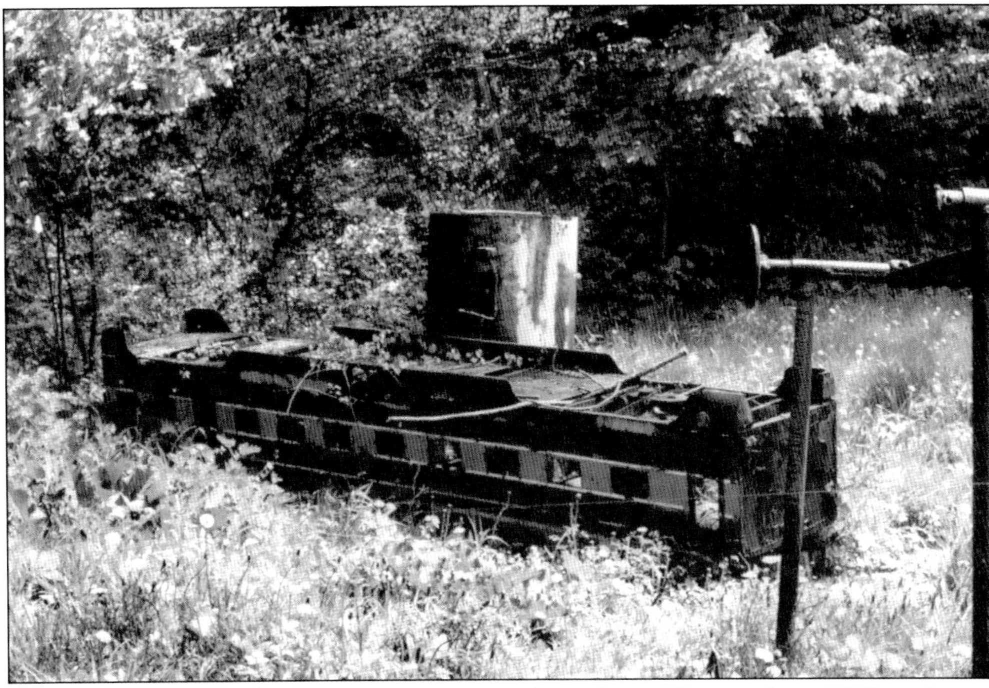

The remains of the Saullo Amusements train are shown here. (Courtesy Larry Hillborn.)

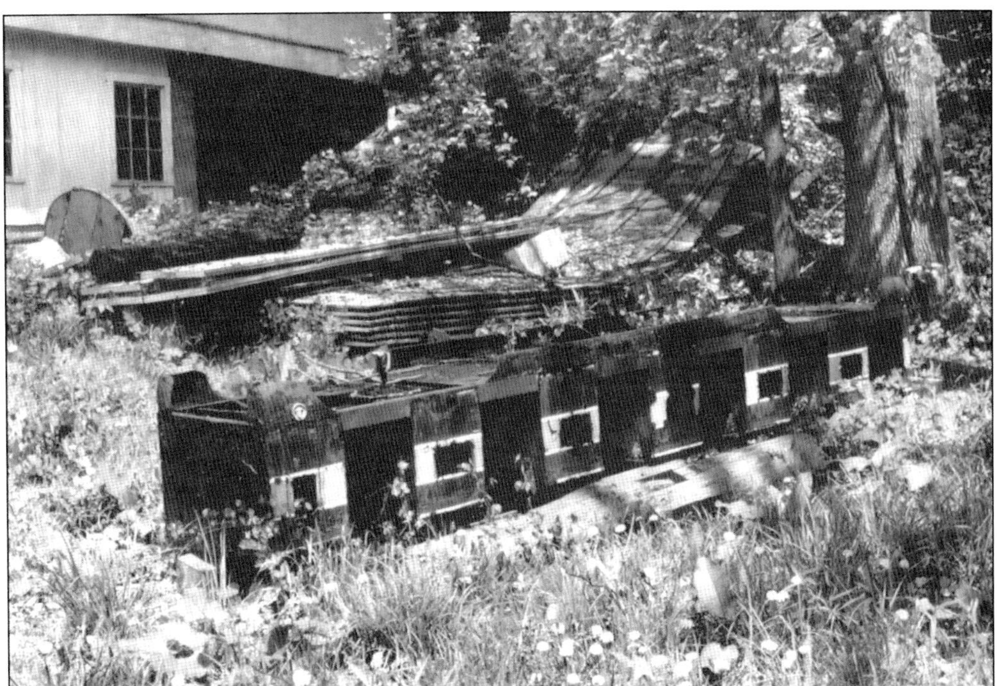

The remains of the train are also visible in this photograph. (Courtesy Larry Hillborn.)

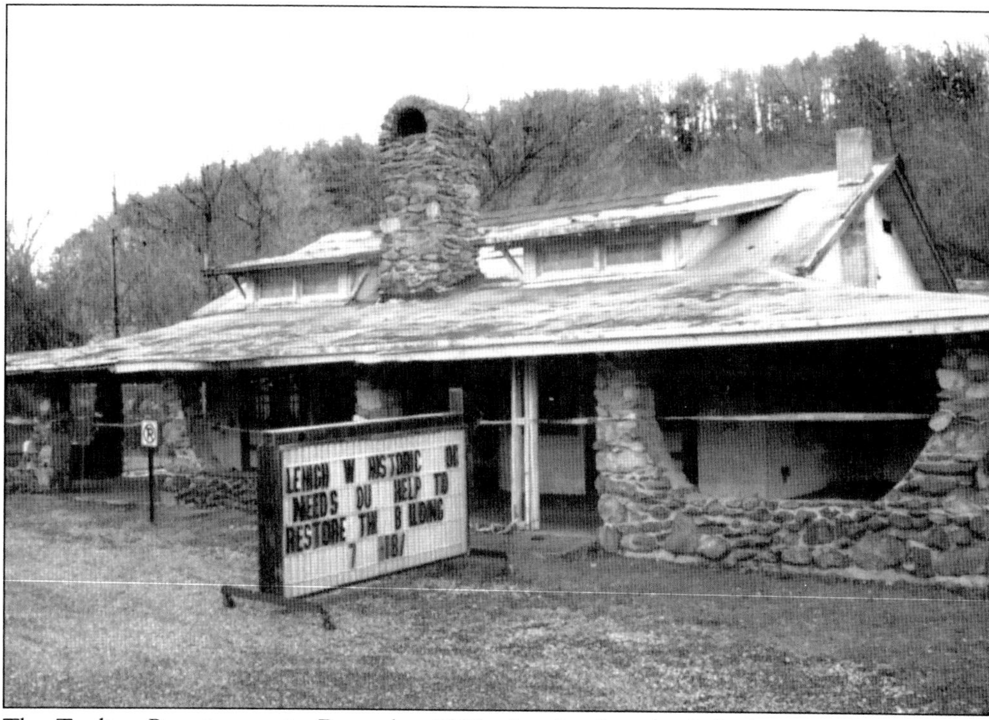

The Trading Post is seen in December 2002, shortly after the Lehigh Township Historical Society entered into a lease for the building. The floor and the walls were in very poor condition because the roof had been leaking for years. (Courtesy the Lehigh Township Historical Society.)

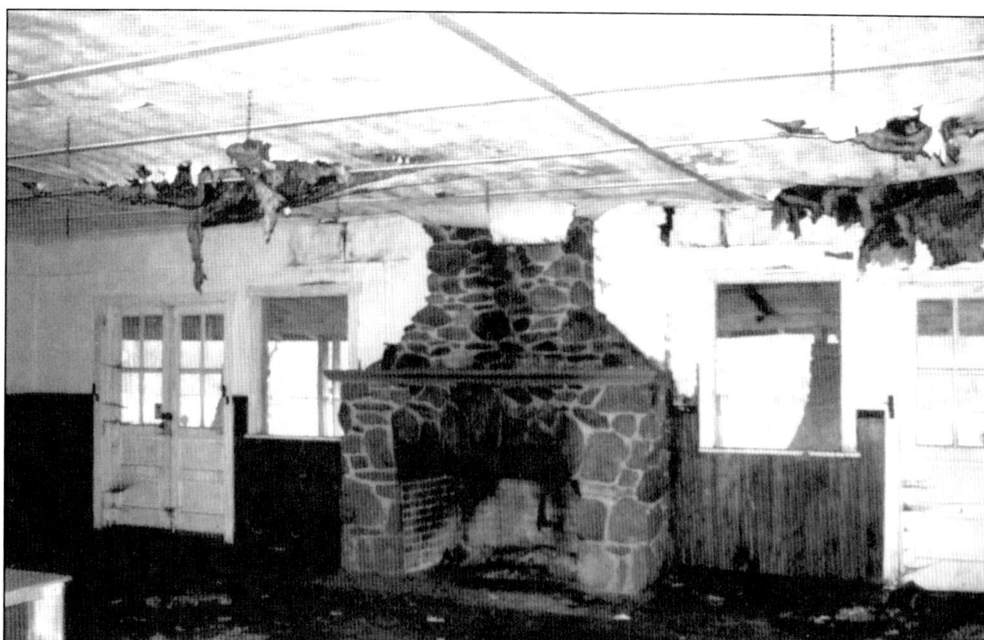

The rotted walls are still hidden by paneling in this interior photograph of the Trading Post, taken in December 2002. (Courtesy the Lehigh Township Historical Society.)

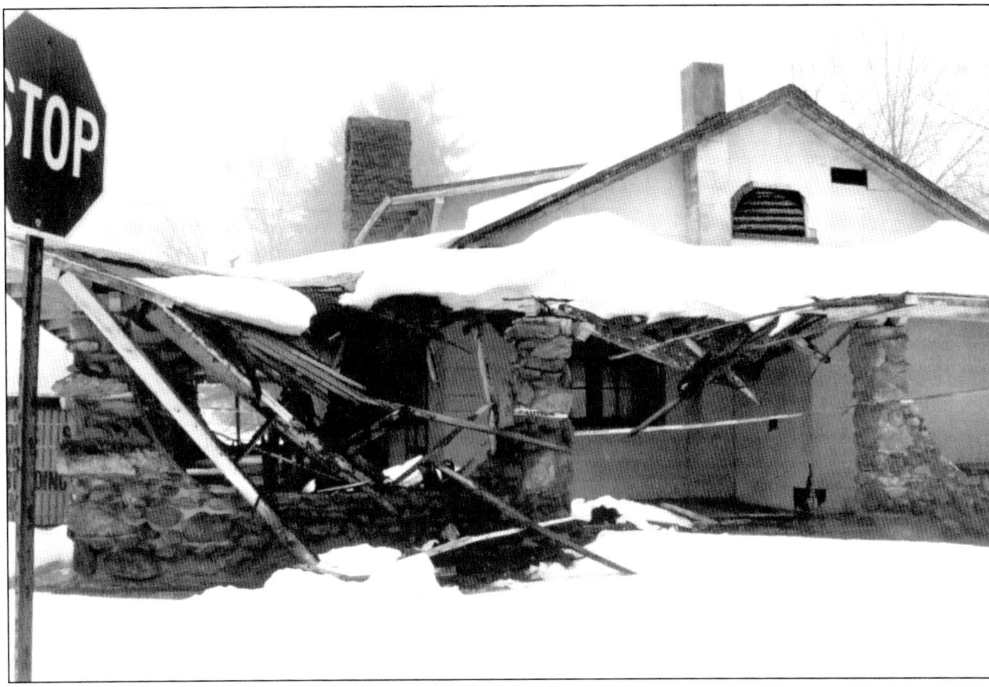

The winter of 2002–2003 was especially hard on the Trading Post. Heavy snowfall caused the collapse of part of the porch roof. (Courtesy the Lehigh Township Historical Society.)

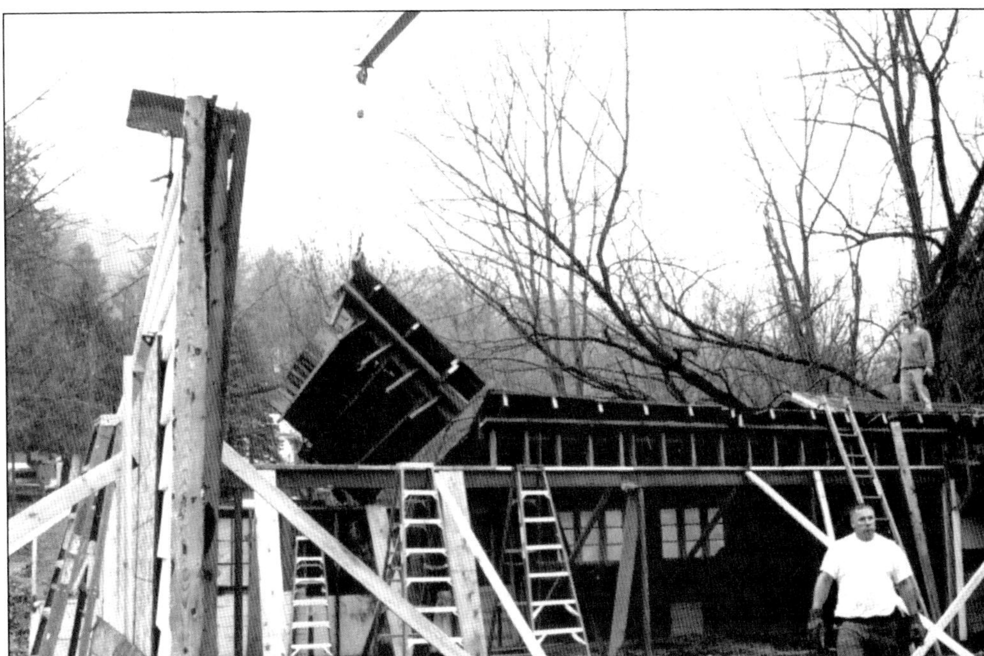

The society decided to have the roof and front wall redone and began removing the roof in November 2003. Here, Frank Guerra of Costa Construction appears on the ground, and Dave Costa is on the roof. (Courtesy the Lehigh Township Historical Society.)

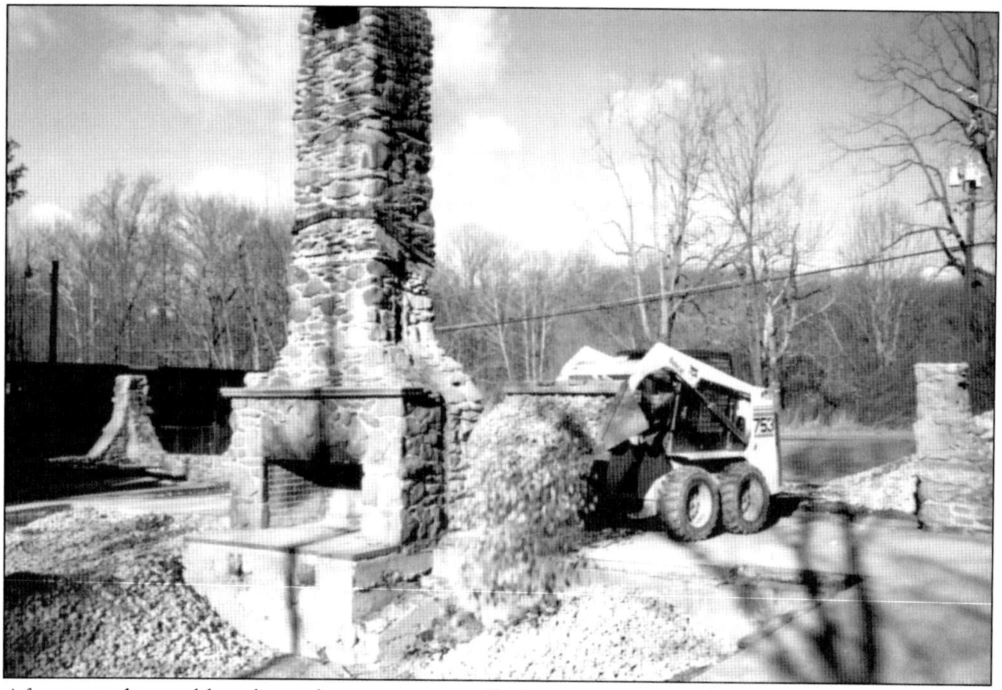

After a windstorm blew down the remaining wall, the society moved forward with reconstruction of the Trading Post, using modern materials designed to look like the original. The first step was to fill in the crawlspace below the floor with concrete. The change was made because of moisture problems in the original structure. (Courtesy the Lehigh Township Historical Society.)

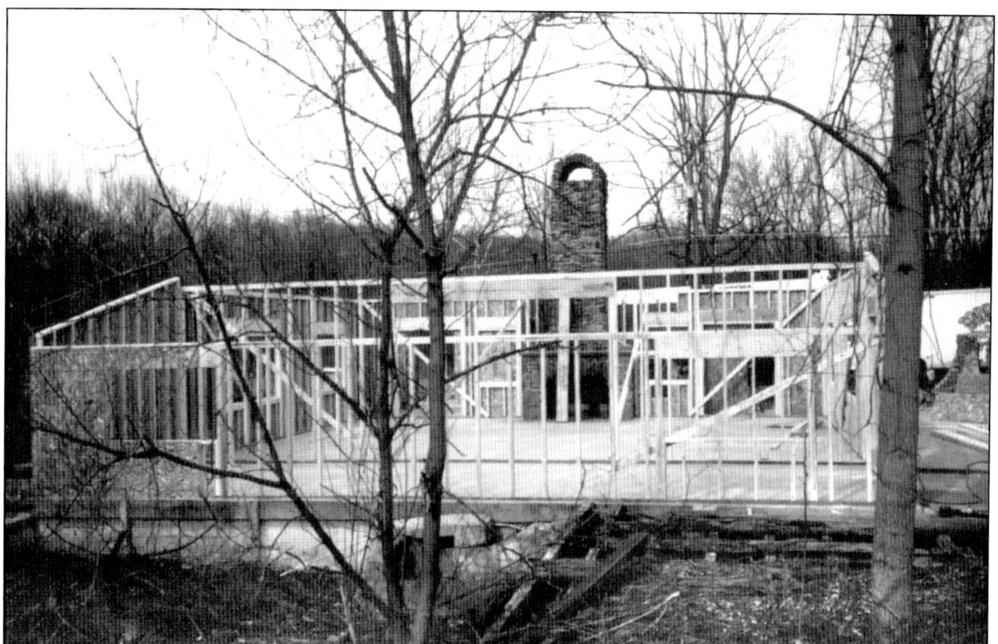

The walls of the Trading Post were rebuilt after the floor was cemented. (Courtesy the Lehigh Township Historical Society.)

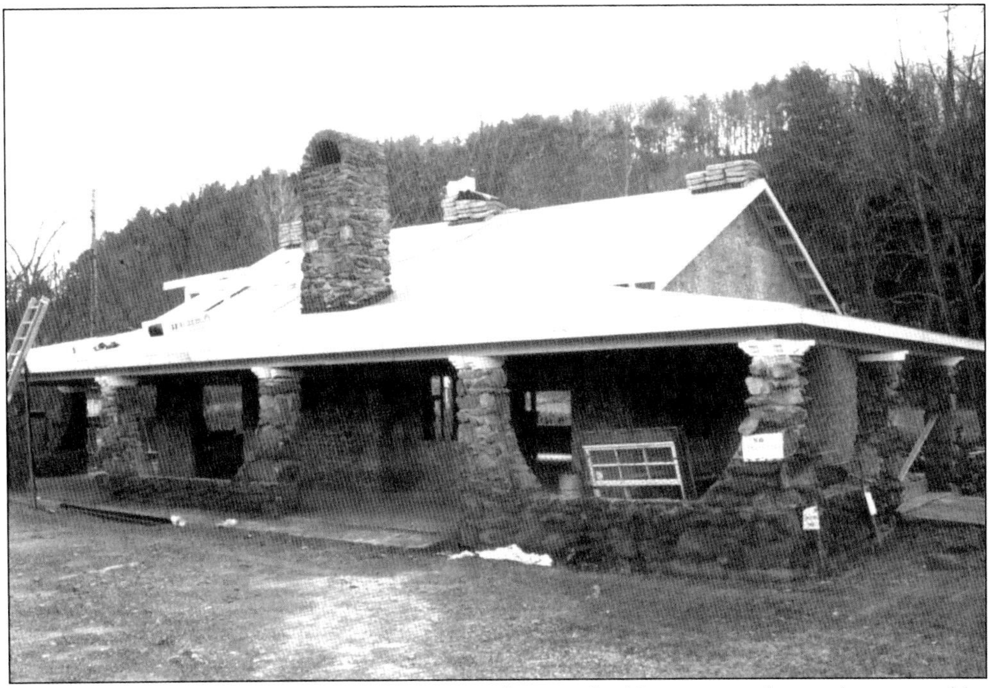

Thanks to the efforts of Costa Construction, the new building was under roof very quickly. The reconstruction would not have been possible without the generosity of Atas International, Alcoa, and Quality Roofing Supply of Allentown, who donated some of the materials. (Courtesy the Lehigh Township Historical Society.)

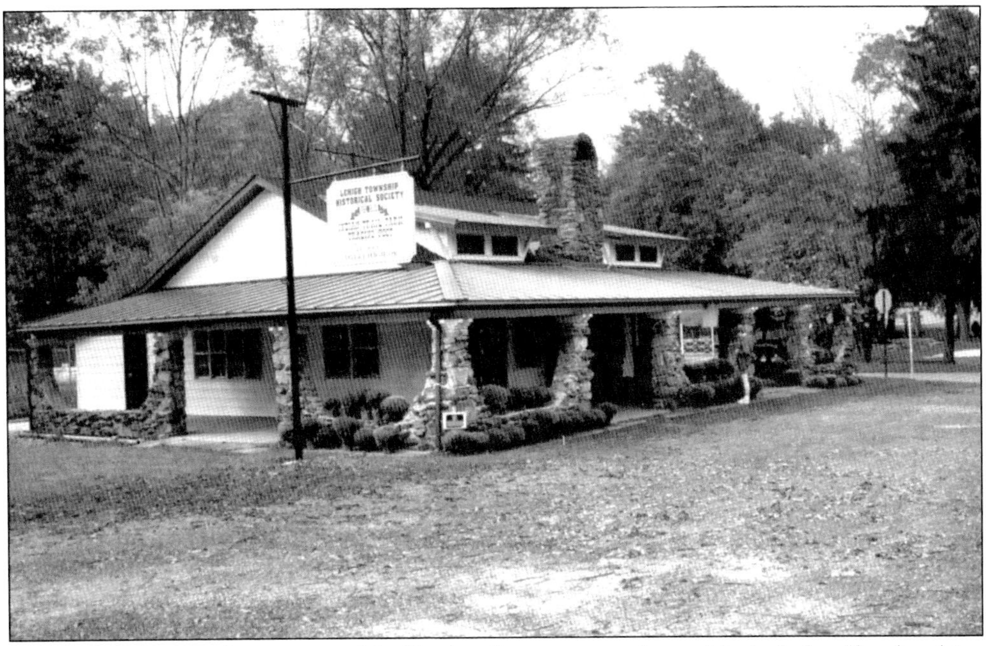

By September 2004, the exterior of the Trading Post was complete, with the help of hardworking volunteers such as Franklin Mummey, Ken Marsh, Wilson Putt, and Chris Satow.

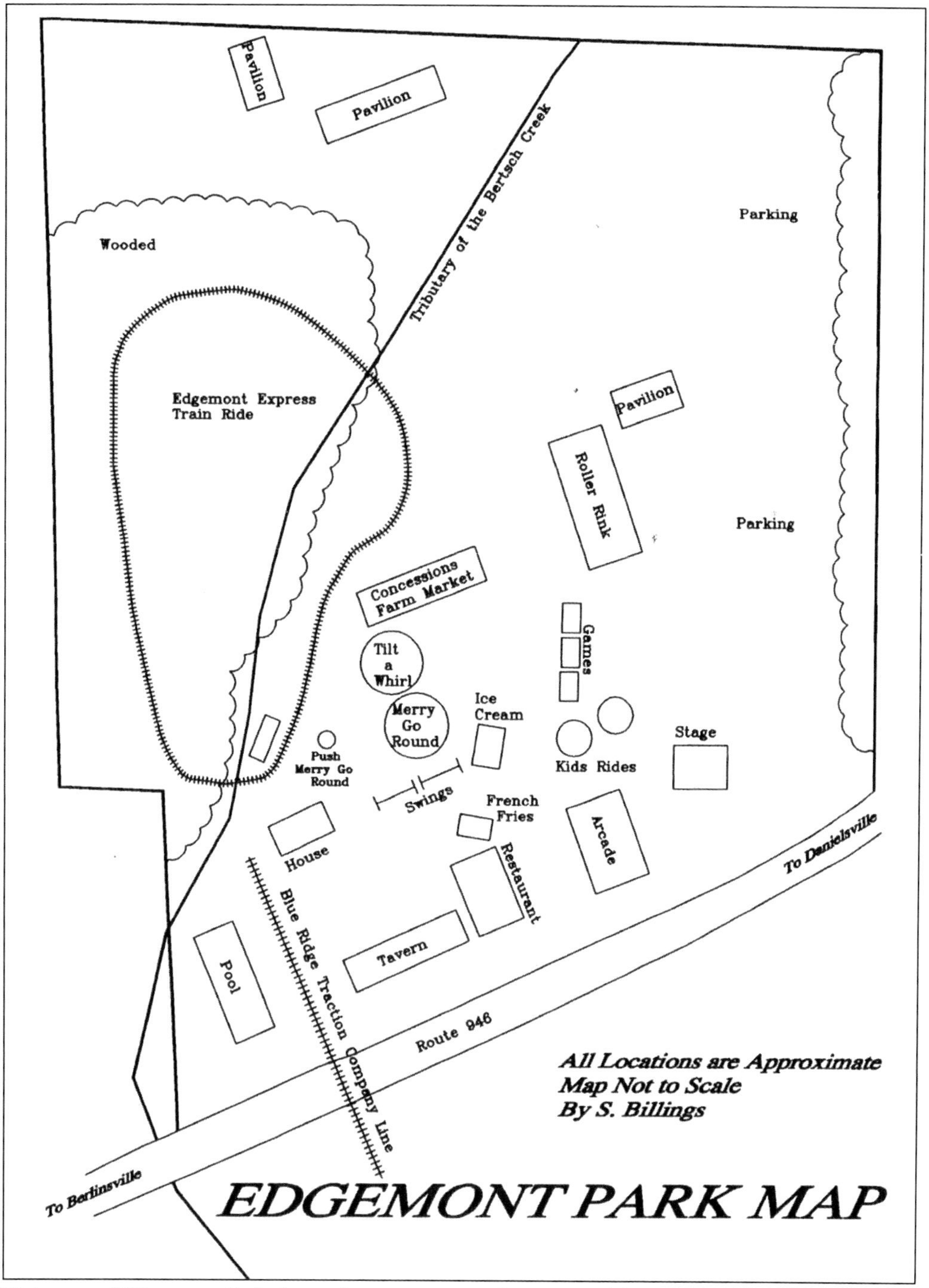

This map of Edgemont Park shows the approximate locations of the rides and buildings, some of which changed and were moved over the years.

Four

Edgemont Park
The Early Years

Edgemont Park was located on Route 946 in the town of Harpers in Lehigh Township, Northampton County, halfway between Berlinsville and Danielsville. William Osterday, Abraham Klose, and Christian Esch owned the land until 1824, when it was sold to Paul Osterday, owner until 1871. It was then sold to Jeremiah and Mary A. Osterday. In 1900, the land was sold again to Irwin A. and Emma Easterday. The property was then acquired by Blue Ridge Traction Company president Jay S. Moyer and his wife, Margaretta. The Moyers sold it to the Blue Ridge Traction Company on January 9, 1909.

The Blue Ridge Traction Company, founded in 1902, started the park as a picnic area along its trolley line. This common practice served as a great way to attract riders, especially on weekends when workers would not be commuting. The location was perfect, being at the line's midpoint. A spur split from its main traction line and traveled directly into the park, which had picnic areas, a baseball field, dance hall, carousel, casino, and children's playground, as well as the promenade. The Blue Ridge Traction Company ended its trolley service on May 30, 1924, but retained ownership of the park until 1930, when it was taken by the E. P. Wilbur Trust Company. The Great Depression heavily affected banks, and the E. P. Wilbur Trust Company went out of business in 1935. All of its assets, including Edgemont, became the property of the Federal Deposit Insurance Corporation (FDIC), which held the park until 1944.

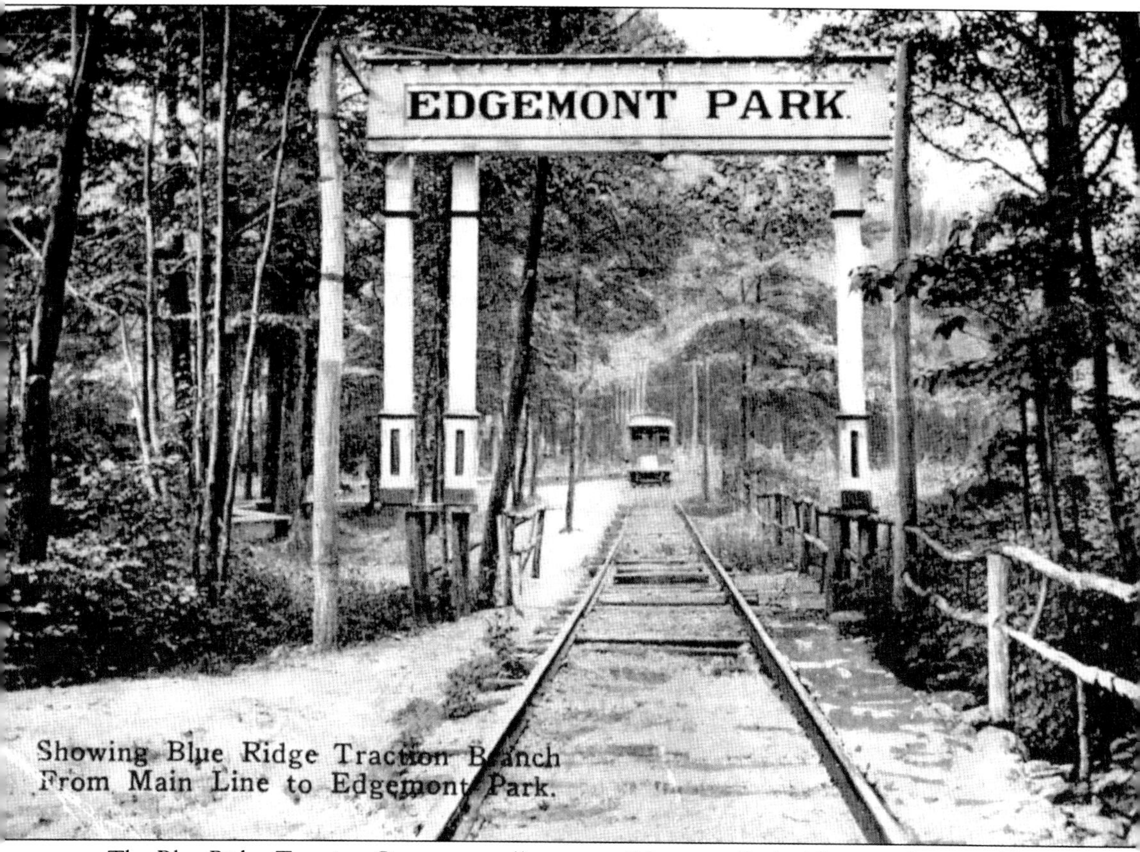

The Blue Ridge Traction Company trolley enters Edgemont Park. (Courtesy Larry Hillborn.)

BLUE RIDGE TRACTION COMPANY

In Effect June 7, 1910 — **TIME TABLE** — Subject to Change without Notice

LEAVE	1	3	5	7	9	11	13	15	17	19	21	23
	A. M.	A. M.	A. M.	A. M.	A. M.	P. M.	P. M.	P. M.	P. M.	P. M.	P. M.	P. M.
DANIELSVILLE ...	5 15	6 30	8 00	9 30	11 00	12 30	2 00	3 30	5 00	7 00	8 30	10 00
EDGEMONT PARK	5 32	6 48	8 18	9 48	11 18	12 48	2 18	3 48	5 18	7 18	8 48	10 18
BERLINSVILLE ...	5 38	6 55	8 25	9 55	11 25	12 55	2 25	3 55	5 25	7 25	8 55	10 25
WALNUTPORT ..... ARRIVE	5 50	7 10	8 40	10 10	11 40	1 10	2 40	4 10	5 40	7 40	9 10	10 40

LEAVE	2	4	6	8	10	12	14	16	18	20	22	24
	A. M.	A. M.	A. M.	A. M.	A. M.	P. M.	P. M.	P. M.	P. M	P. M.	P. M.	P. M.
WALNUTPORT	5 50	7 15	8 45	10 15	11 45	1 15	2 45	4 15	5 45	7 45	9 15	10 45
BERLINSVILLE ...	6 05	7 30	9 00	10 30	12 00	1 30	3 00	4 30	6 00	8 00	9 30	11 00
EDGEMONT PARK	6 12	7 37	9 07	10 37	12 07	1 37	3 07	4 37	6 07	8 07	9 37	11 07
DANIELSVILLE ... ARRIVE	6 30	7 55	9 25	10 55	12 25	1 55	3 25	4 55	6 25	8 25	9 55	11 25

Nos. 1, 2, 3 and 4 do not run on Sundays and Holidays
Nos. 7 and 8 run on Sundays only. Nos. 9 and 10 do not run on Sundays
Nos. 13 and 14 run on Saturdays and Sundays only
Nos. 23 and 24 run on Saturdays only. C. C. MARSH, Superintendent
(OVER) Danielsville, Pa.

According to this 1910 schedule, the Blue Ridge line included four stops—Danielsville, Edgemont Park, Berlinsville, and Walnutport. (Courtesy Larry Hillborn.)

EDGEMONT PARK

This chosen spot for particular people is halfway between the termini of the Road.

On Saturdays, during Park Season, cars run every 45 minutes after 1.15 p. m., direct to the grounds.

Additional cars run for special occasions.

This is The Place for Enjoyment.

There is a man who never drinks,
Nor smokes, nor chews, nor swears;
Who never gambles, never flirts
And shuns all sinful snares...
"He's paralyzed!"

There is a man who never does
A thing that is not right;
His wife can tell just where he is
At morning, noon and night...
"He's dead!"

There is a man not "paralyzed"
And far from being "dead;"
Who enjoys himself at Edgemont
It lengthens life he said...
"He's a live one!"

The Traction Company sells Tickets at Reduced Rates of Fare good only within the Calendar month in which they are issued at the office at Danielsville, Pa.

Packages of convenient size to be quickly handled by the Conductors will be received for transportation at OWNER'S RISK ONLY between points immediately on this line at regular rates of fare in advance.

This advertisement for Edgemont Park was printed on the back of the schedule in the previous view. (Courtesy Larry Hillborn.)

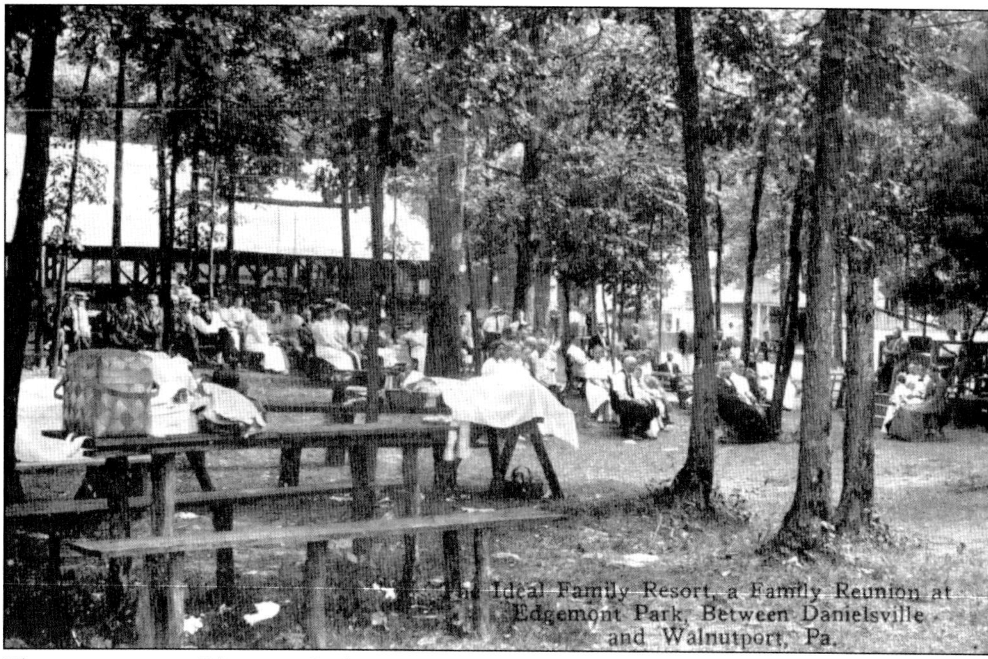

The picnic area at Edgemont Park was quite popular. (Courtesy Larry Hillborn.)

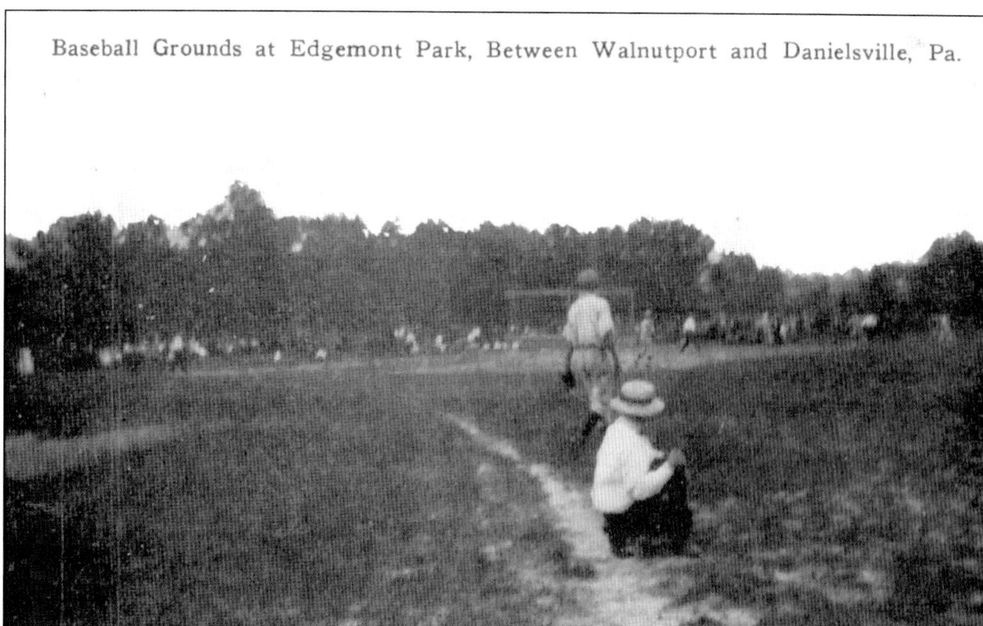

Edgemont Park included a baseball field. (Courtesy Larry Hillborn.)

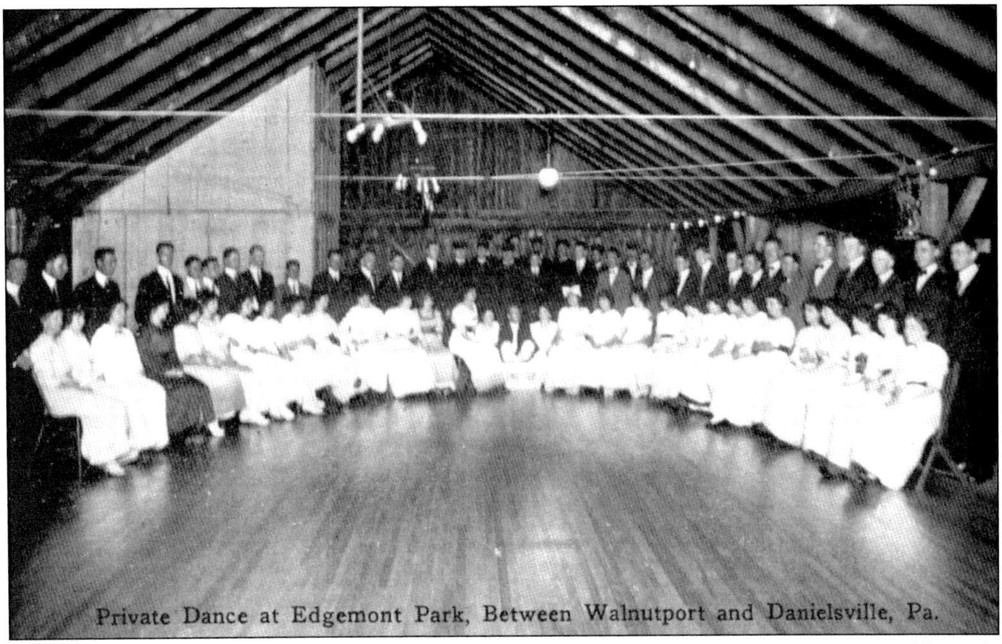

Like its Indian Trail counterpart, Edgemont Park had a dance hall. (Courtesy Larry Hillborn.)

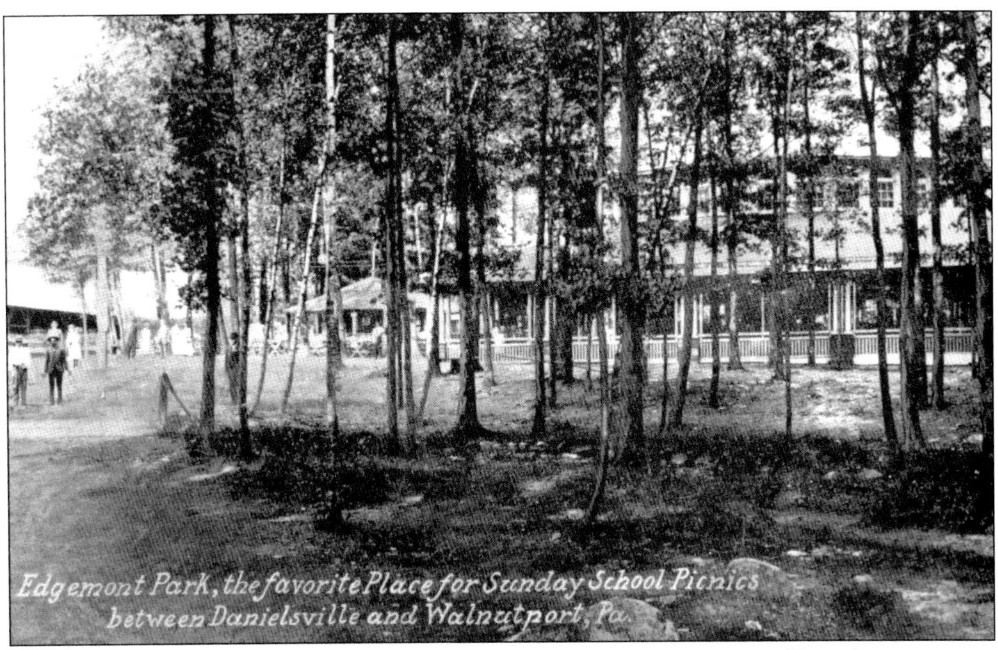

This postcard view of the park was taken around 1910. (Courtesy Larry Hillborn.)

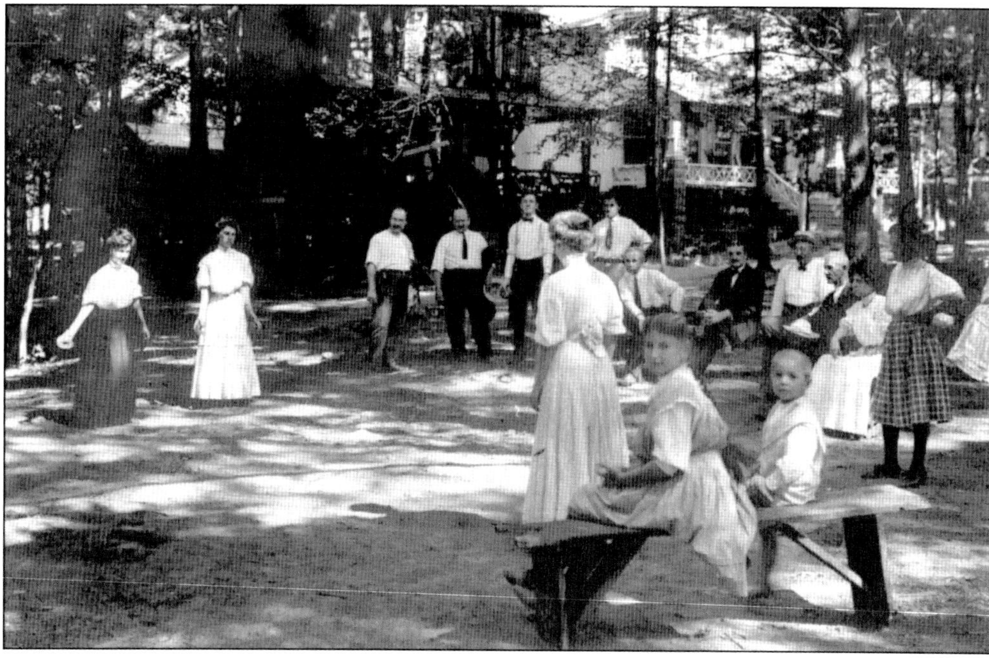

A group enjoys a picnic at Edgemont in this early view. (Courtesy Larry Hillborn.)

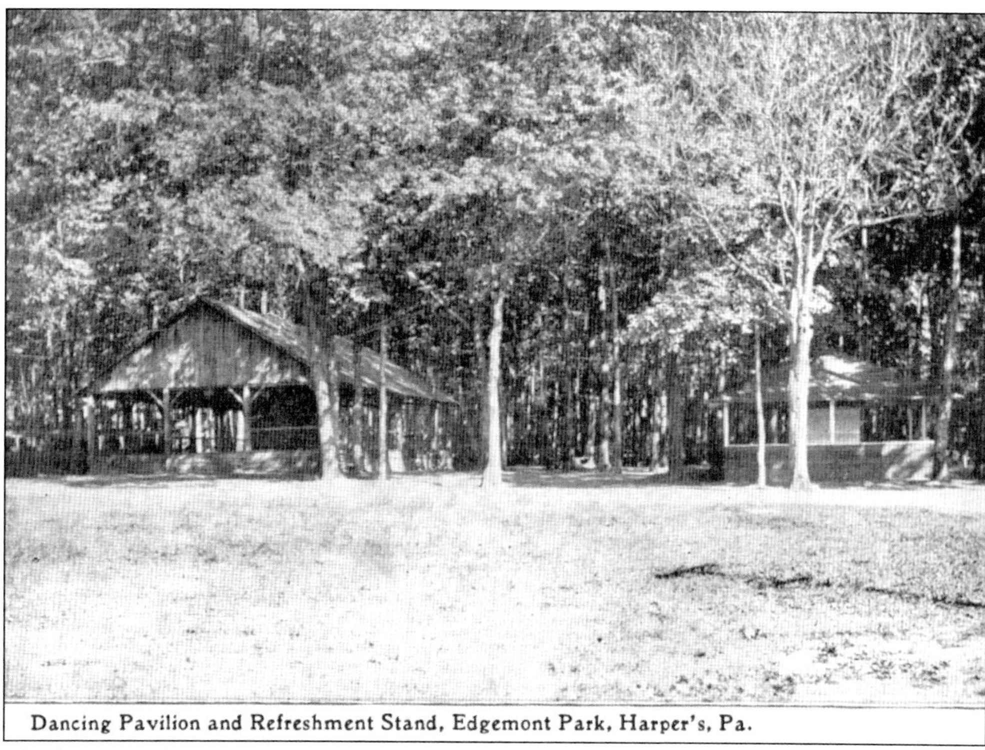

The dance pavilion and refreshment stand are shown here. (Courtesy Larry Hillborn.)

This 1907 postcard shows the promenade at Edgemont Park. (Courtesy Larry Hillborn.)

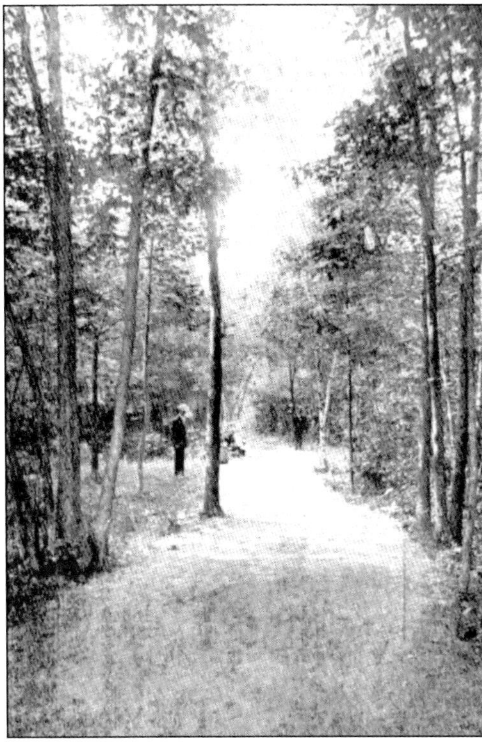

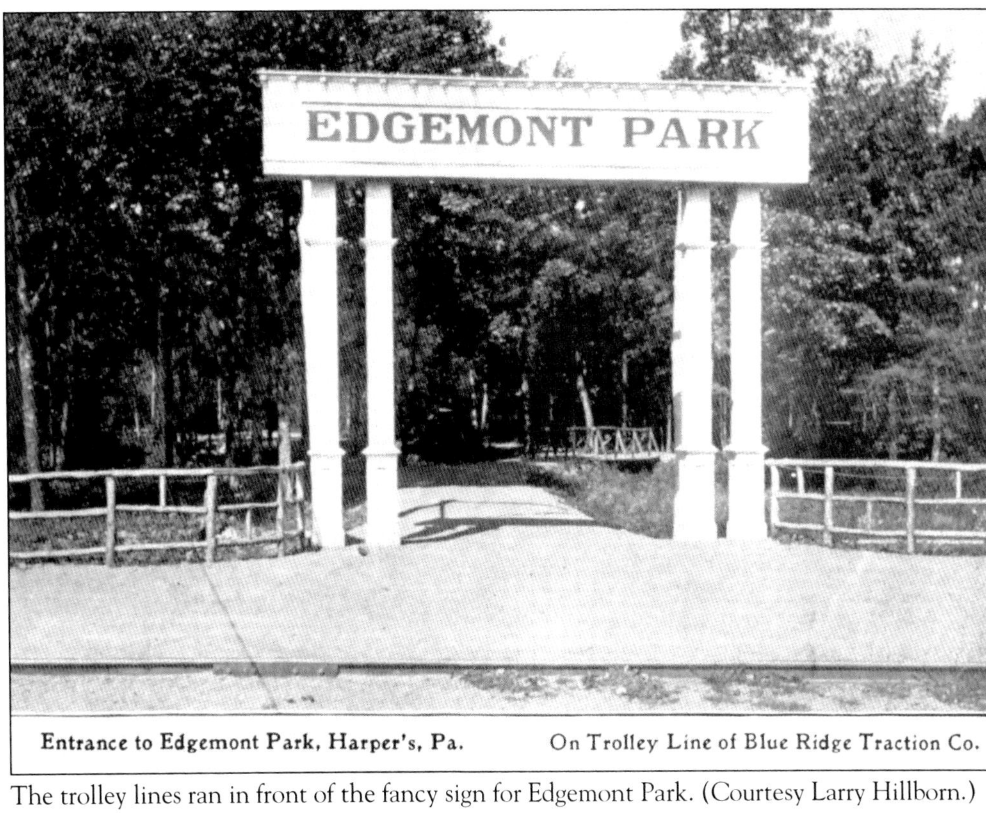

The trolley lines ran in front of the fancy sign for Edgemont Park. (Courtesy Larry Hillborn.)

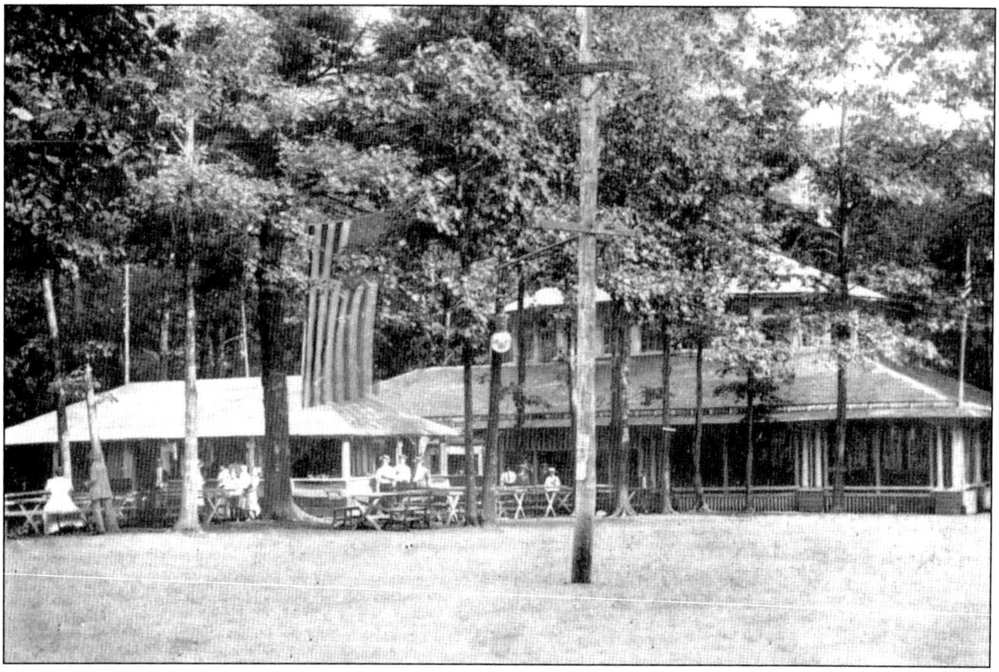

The fate of this carousel is unknown. Note the large flag hanging from the trees. (Courtesy Larry Hillborn.)

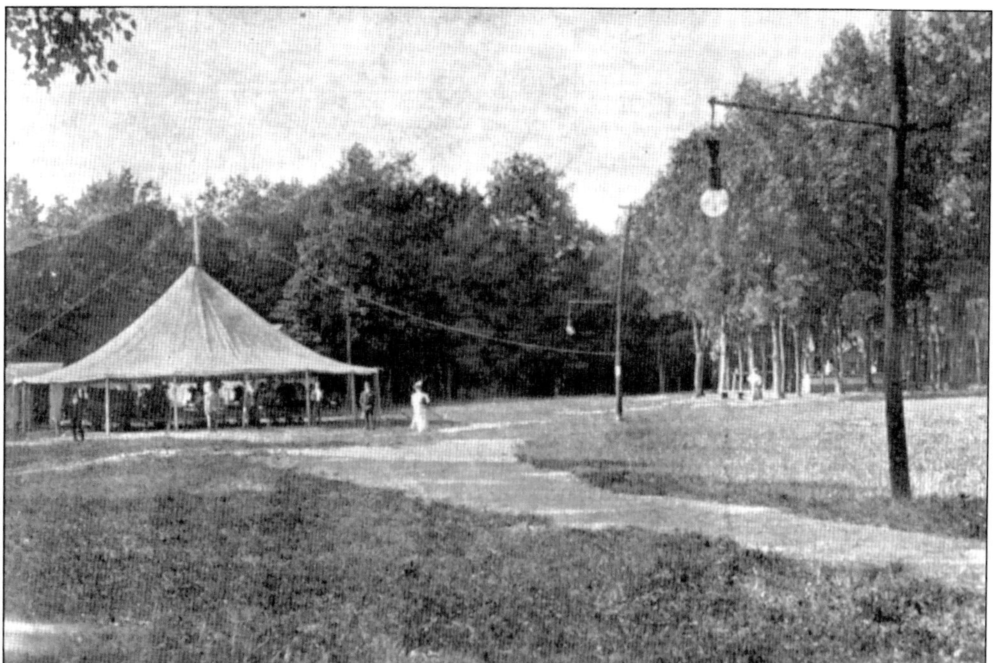

General View Edgemont Park, Harper's, Pa. On Trolley Line of Blue Ridge Traction Co.

The light hanging from the pole to the right may have been powered by the same electricity that ran the trolley. Electric lighting at this time was considered very extravagant. (Courtesy Larry Hillborn.)

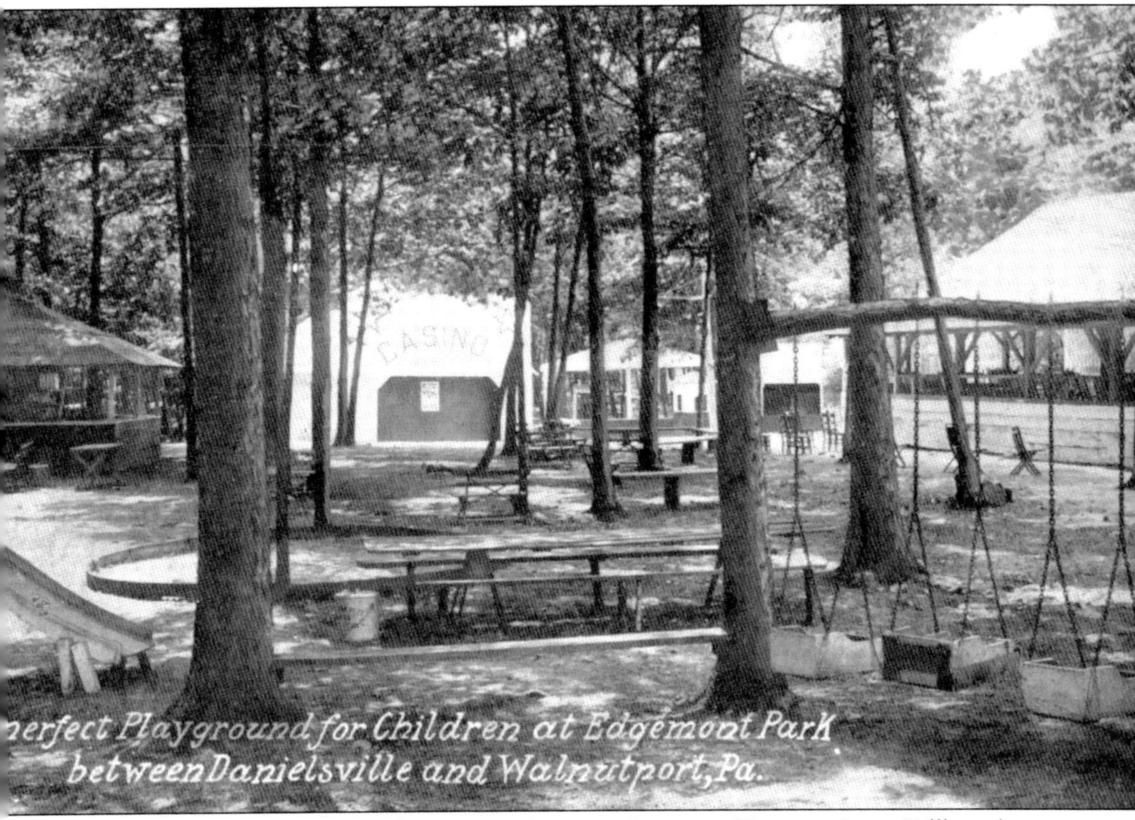

The playground, picnic areas, and casino are shown in this view. (Courtesy Larry Hillborn.)

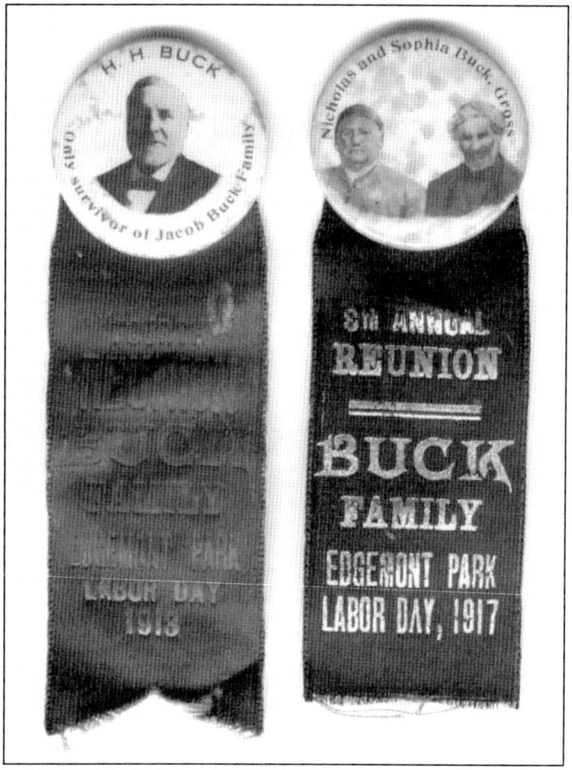

Many families held reunions at both Indian Trail and Edgemont Parks. These pins were distributed at the fourth annual Buck family reunion, held at Edgemont on Labor Day 1913, and the eighth annual reunion, held at Edgemont on Labor Day 1917.

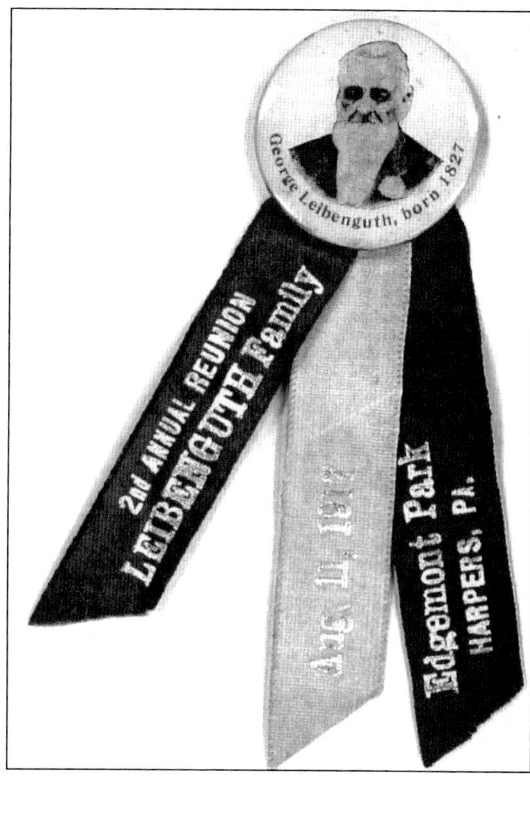

This pin is from the second annual Leibenguth family reunion, held on August 11, 1917, at Edgemont Park.

Members of the Sunday school class of St. John's United Church of Christ in Slatington pose at the Edgemont pool around 1931. From left to right are teacher Helen (Grim) Wert, Laura (Brosious) Scheirer, Virginia Hankee, Mary Catherine (Diefenderfer) Weaver, Ruth Kern, and Joyce Zellner. (Courtesy Laura E. Scheirer.)

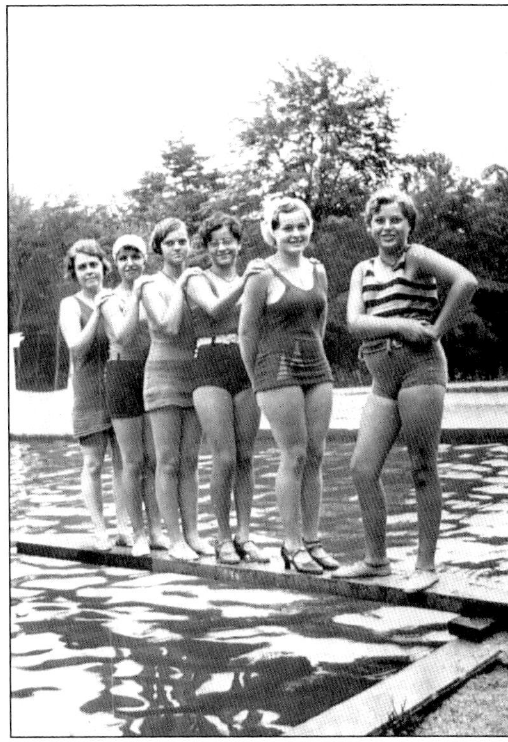

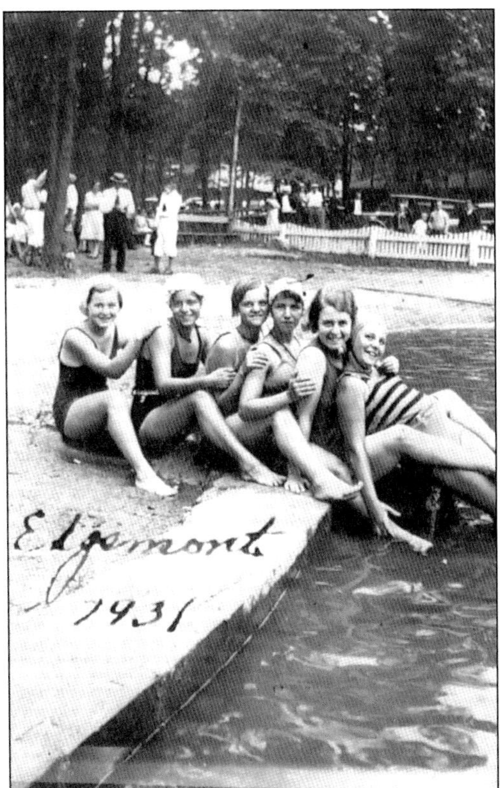

Unlike the one at Indian Trail, the pool at Edgemont Park had a dirt bottom. Members of the St. John's Sunday school class are seen again. (Courtesy Laura E. Scheirer.)

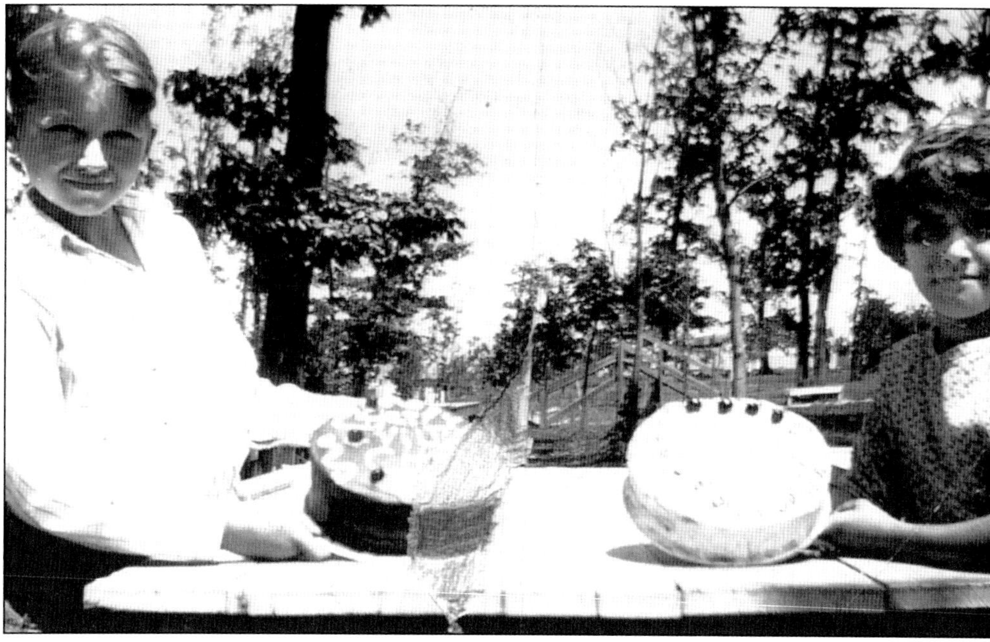

Richard Griffith and Laura (Brosious) Scheirer show off two cakes decorated for a Cherryville Chums picnic. The group, formed in 1904, held annual reunions of Cherryville neighbors at Edgemont Park, Neffs Park, and Indian Trail Park. The group was active for more than 60 years. (Courtesy Laura E. Scheirer.)

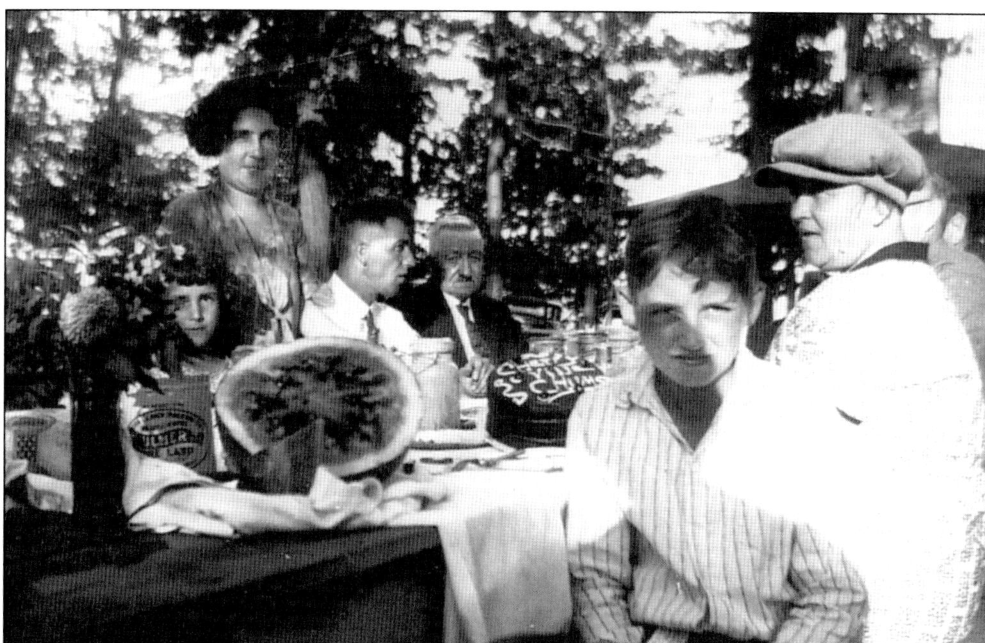

At another Cherryville Chums picnic are, in the back from the left, Laura Brosious, Rilla Brosious, Tobias Brosious, and Richard Mohrey. On the other side are Richard Griffith, Lillie Griffith, Alfred Griffith, and John Griffith. (Courtesy Laura E. Scheirer.)

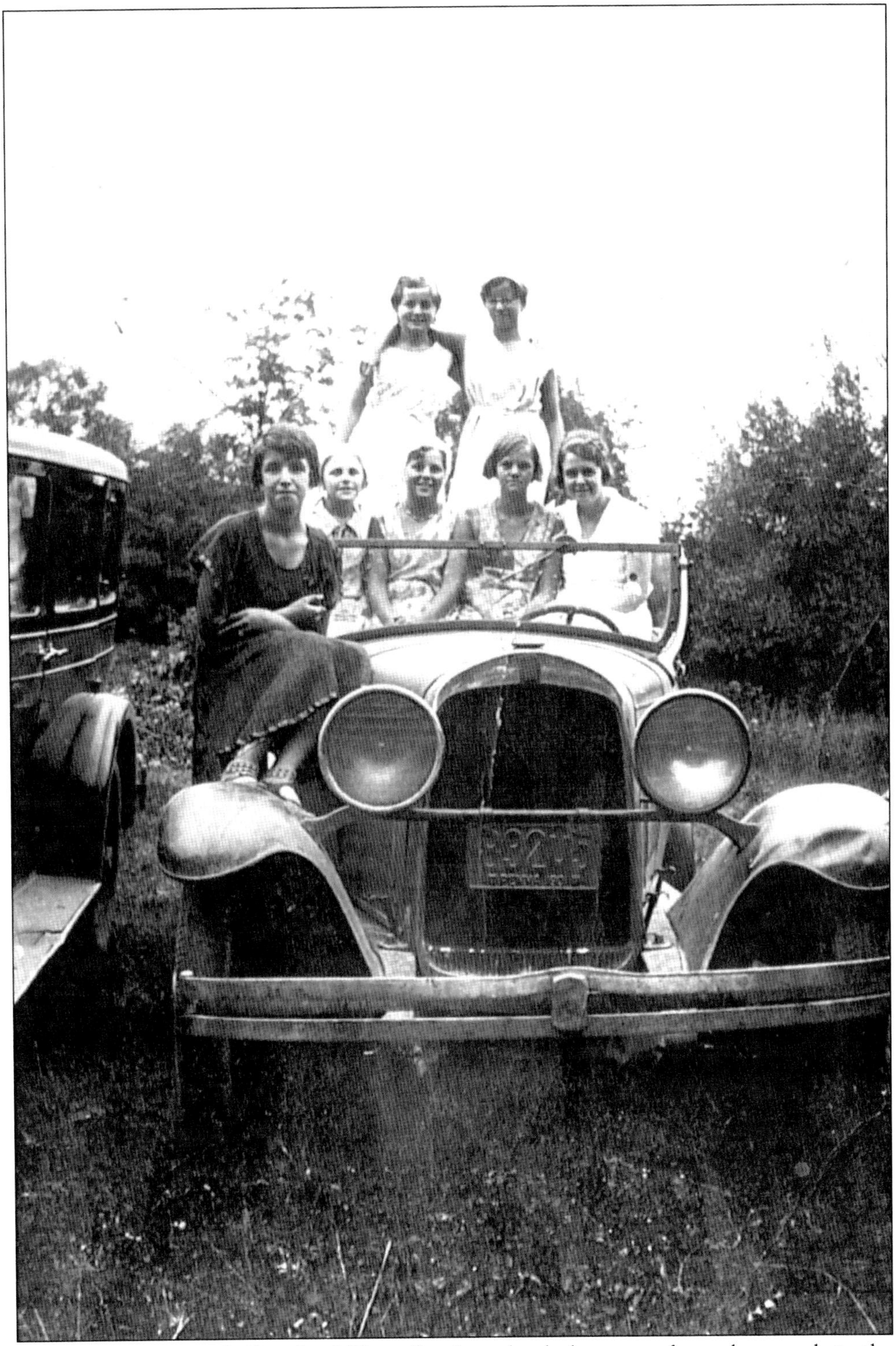

The St. John's United Church of Christ Sunday school class poses for a photograph in the parking area at Edgemont Park. (Courtesy Laura E. Scheirer.)

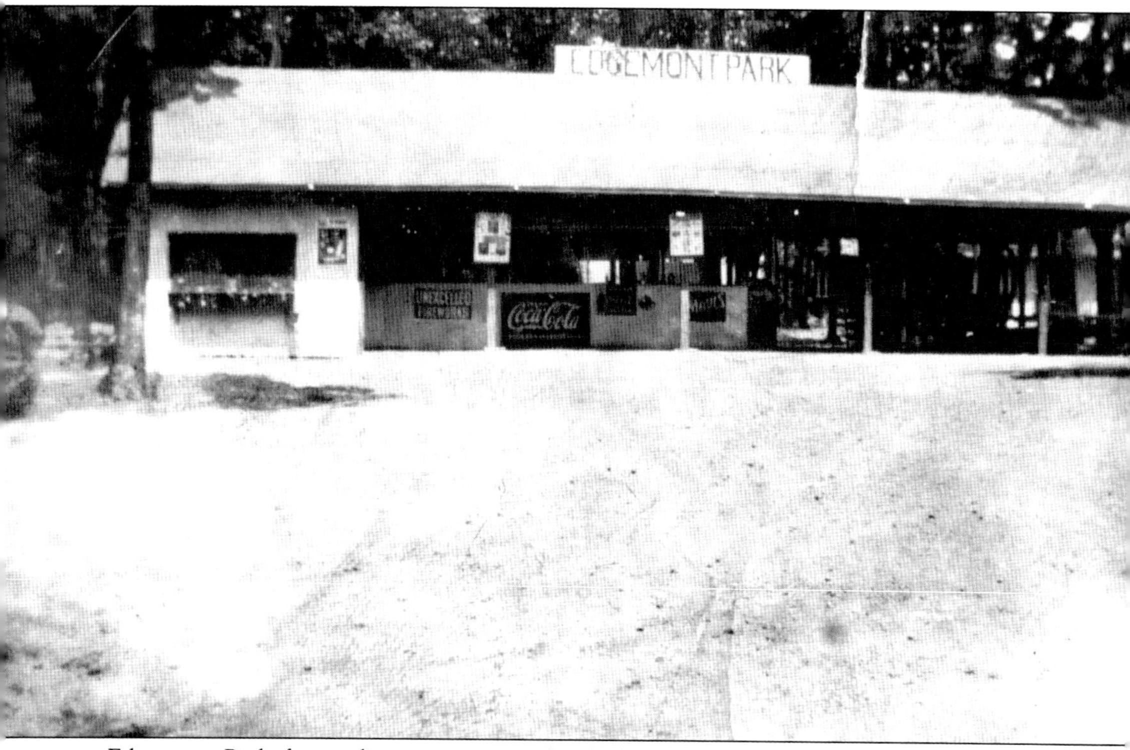

Edgemont Park featured a restaurant and refreshment stand, as seen in this *c.* 1940 view. (Courtesy Alverta and Emily Jones.)

Five

Edgemont Park
The Final Years

In 1944, Clayton A. and Helen A. Buss purchased the park from the Federal Deposit Insurance Corporation and immediately sold it to Bernard A. and Elinora Gallagher. The Gallaghers likely operated the park during the time the FDIC owned it. They owned the park until July 30, 1946, when it was sold to Rollin E. and Anna C. Minnich. The Minniches bought the park after selling the pool and restaurant at Indian Trail Park. During this time, park entertainment was provided by groups such as Harvey Mearns, Wally Gordon and His Boys of Radio, Willis Meyers and His Bar X Ranch Boys, the Circle J Ranch Boys, Mac Quire and His Boys, and Billy Wilson and His Range Romeos. Swimming in the pool was free, but parking cost 50¢. Ethel Reinhard was the lifeguard at the time.

When the Minniches bought the park, it was absent of rides. Subsequently, a group started by Rollin Minnich Jr. purchased rides and brought them to the park. Other group members included Edgar A. Jacoby, Frank Schmidt, Shorty Rimsky, and Quintis Peters.

In 1953, roller-skating began in a small tented rink. On March 10, 1953, the Minniches signed an agreement with Richard W. and Velma H. Morris, allowing them to erect and run a roller rink. A copy of this agreement, signed in the presence of Edgar A. Jacoby and Samuel Spadt, is on file at the Northampton courthouse. On April 30, 1954, a new agreement superceding the first was filed at the courthouse between Edgemont Park Inc. and Richard W. and Velma H. Morris to erect a building to be used as a skating rink of 61.3 by 132 feet. Designed for open air, the building had large windows that could be opened. The door faced the park to take advantage of its location.

Interestingly enough, a week after that agreement was signed—on May 6, 1954—the park was sold to Edgemont Park Inc. Paul Deschler served as president of the company and Ralph W. Barthold as its secretary. Under this ownership, the park also included a grocery store, according to an October 1956 sign proclaiming, "Edgemont Park Grocery will be closed for remodeling."

The amusement park was sold at sheriff's sale on November 16, 1959, to Joseph A. and Katherine Cerrone and Carmine J. and Rose Senneca. The rides at this time included the merry-go-round, train, tilt-a-whirl, kids' tilt-a-whirl, and kids' fire engines. Sally Star was a popular park entertainer during these years.

The park was sold again on June 1, 1963, to Richard W. and Velma H. Morris, the last people to own it in entirety. When the park closed around 1965, the rides were sold off. The merry-go-round was likely purchased by Stephen Andruzak and moved to Lancaster County, where the horses and animals were sold for $80 each and the structure itself was converted into a display room for Andruzak's stained-glass business. The ice-cream stand, which had been operated by John Scherer, was sold for $1,000 to Julia Smith, who had run the park French fry stand for its final five years. The stand, known as Edgemont Rest, operated on Route 946, a few hundred yards from the park, until 1999.

On June 4, 1963, the Morrises sold the roller rink and 6.71 acres surrounding it to T. James Martin, who sold it to Midland Farms on May 31, 1966. The building was used as a garment factory and a storage building for a number of years. On February 8, 1980, the Edgemont Park Roller Rink Corporation, run by Tony and Betty Bastin, purchased and restored the rink. It was sold in August 1996 to the current owners, Kenneth E. and Kristen K. Moyer, who have kept the facility in operation.

The rest of the park was sold off in pieces over the next few years. The Edgemont Tavern, with 1.47 acres of land, was purchased by James O. and Ruth A. Redline on February 6, 1967. The Redlines operated the tavern until they sold it to Daniel M. Farkus on September 11, 1990. The tavern remained in business until 2003, when the liquor license was sold. Barbara A. Razzano bought the building on November 6, 2003, and is converting it into Edgemont Park Antiques.

The arcade, with 0.48 acres of land, was sold to Anthony Stampone Jr. and Marion Stampone on May 1, 1965, with the stipulation that it not be used for an auction or furniture business. It was then sold to Daniel Thibault on August 28, 1973. The building was used as a dance studio for a number of years before being purchased by its current owners, Kevin R. and Colleen A. Redline, who operate Redline and Redline Wood Working. The market-concession building, with 1.51 acres of land, was sold to Daniel S. and Nettie M. Miller in 1965 and has remained in the Miller family since. Daniel Miller and his son Wilson ran the auction there before Wilson's son Glen D. Miller assumed operation. His other son, Brian Miller, now owns the building, where he ran a gym from 1992 to 2003. An office for his indoor-air and water-purification business now occupies the building.

A total of 10.1 acres, which included the pool and the train area, was sold to Ralph J. Longenbach on June 28, 1966. On May 9, 1975, Frank P. Yost purchased the property. He later sold it to Kenneth E. and Kristen K. Moyer, who currently reside in the house located on the rear of the property. The small house, with 0.21 acres, was sold to Midland Farms on June 20, 1969, and then to Ethel McMahon on March 24, 1975. On October 31, 1977, it was purchased by Paul Rokowski and then owned by Anthony S. Henits. He sold it to Stephen E. and Alyce M. Unger, who currently live there.

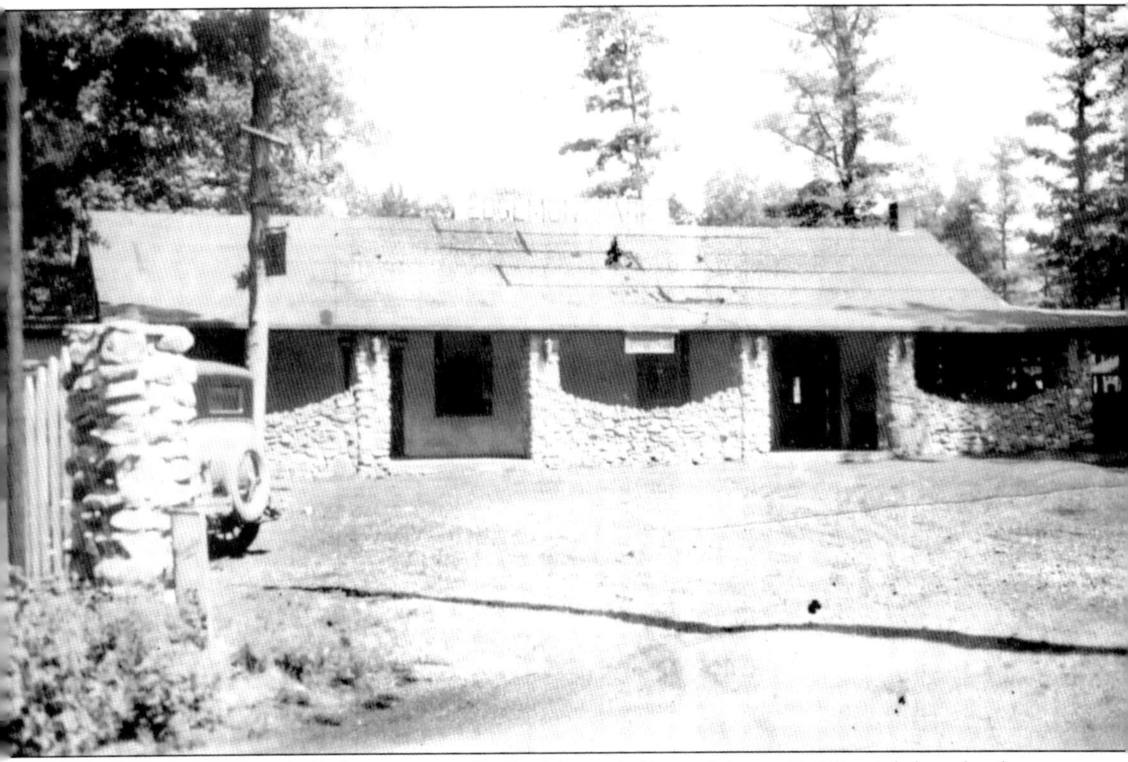

The tavern is seen in 1946, the year that Rollin Minnich Sr. and Anna C. Minnich bought the park. (Courtesy Shirley Szoke.)

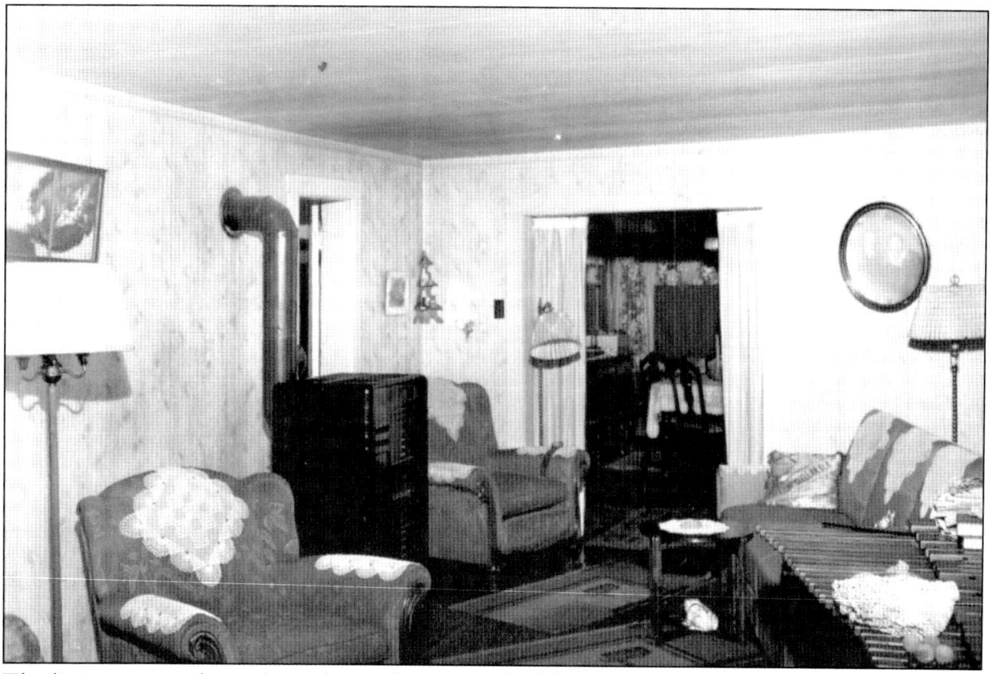

The living area at the park was located at one end of the tavern building. This view reveals how it looked when the Minniches resided there. (Courtesy Shirley Szoke.)

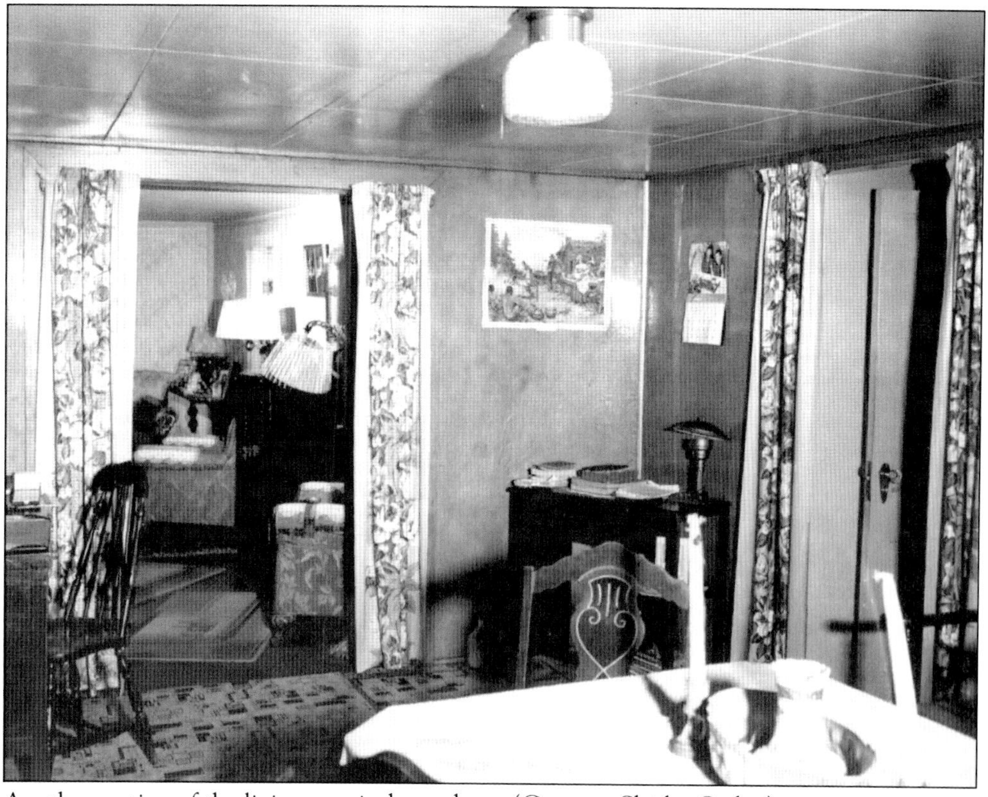

Another section of the living area is shown here. (Courtesy Shirley Szoke.)

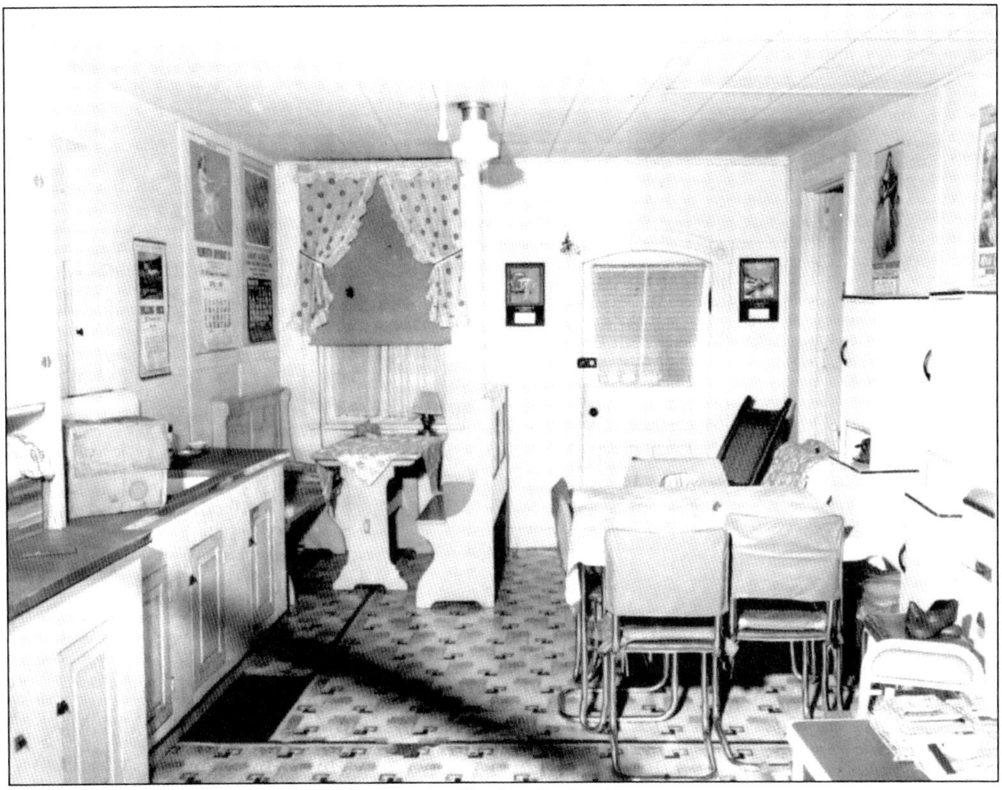

This is the Minniches' kitchen. (Courtesy Shirley Szoke.)

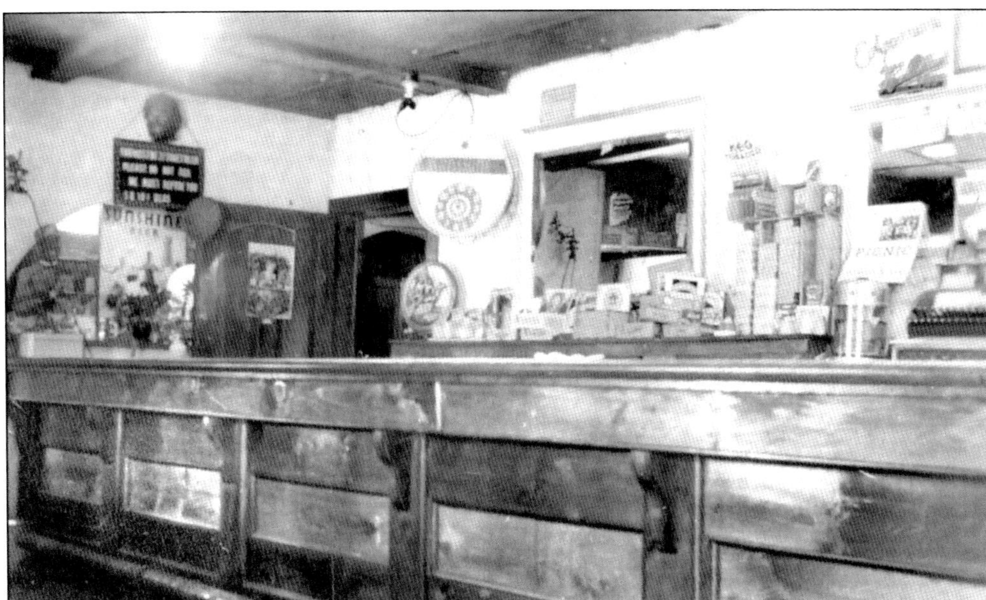

The sign at the end of the tavern bar promotes Sunshine beer. (Courtesy Shirley Szoke.)

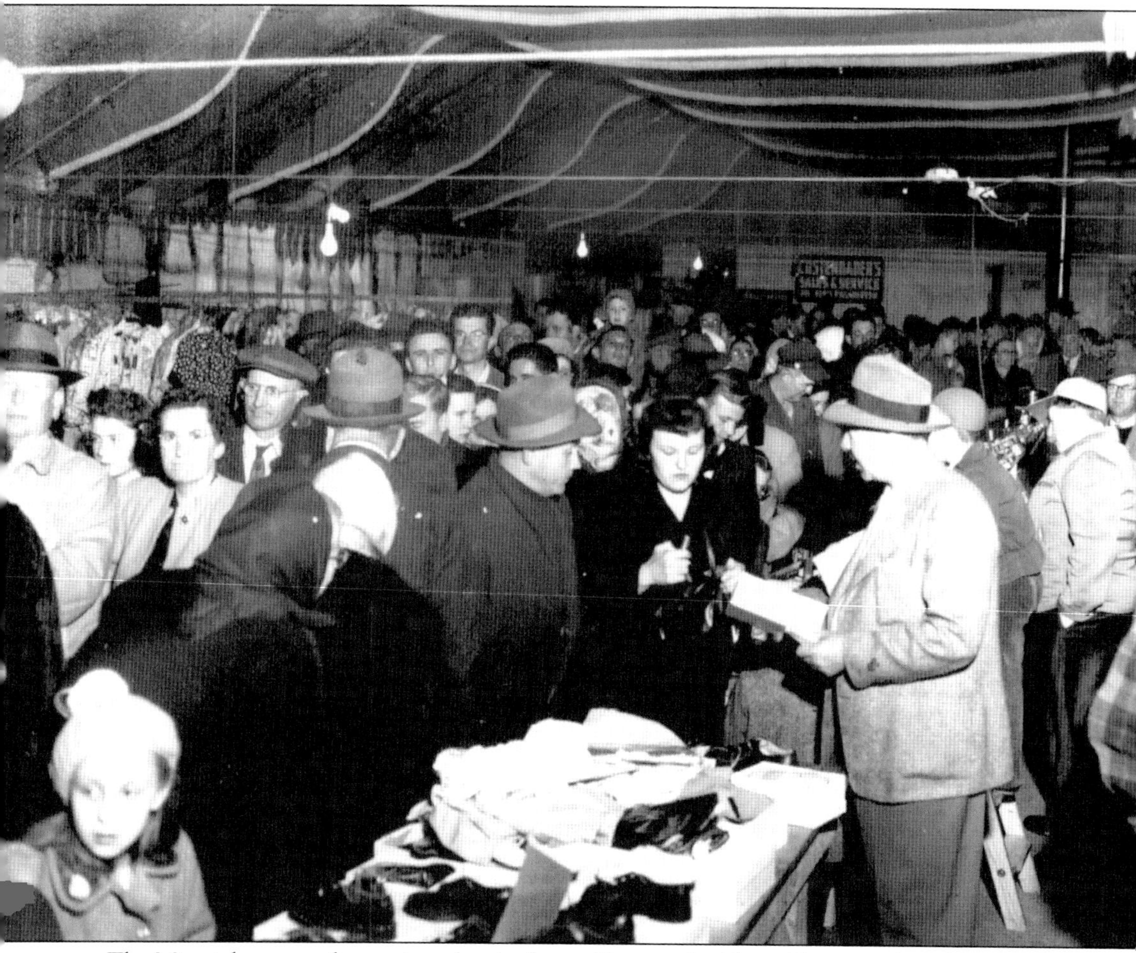

The Minniches ran a farmers' market in the park's main building. Shoes are for sale on the table in the center of the photograph. (Courtesy Shirley Szoke.)

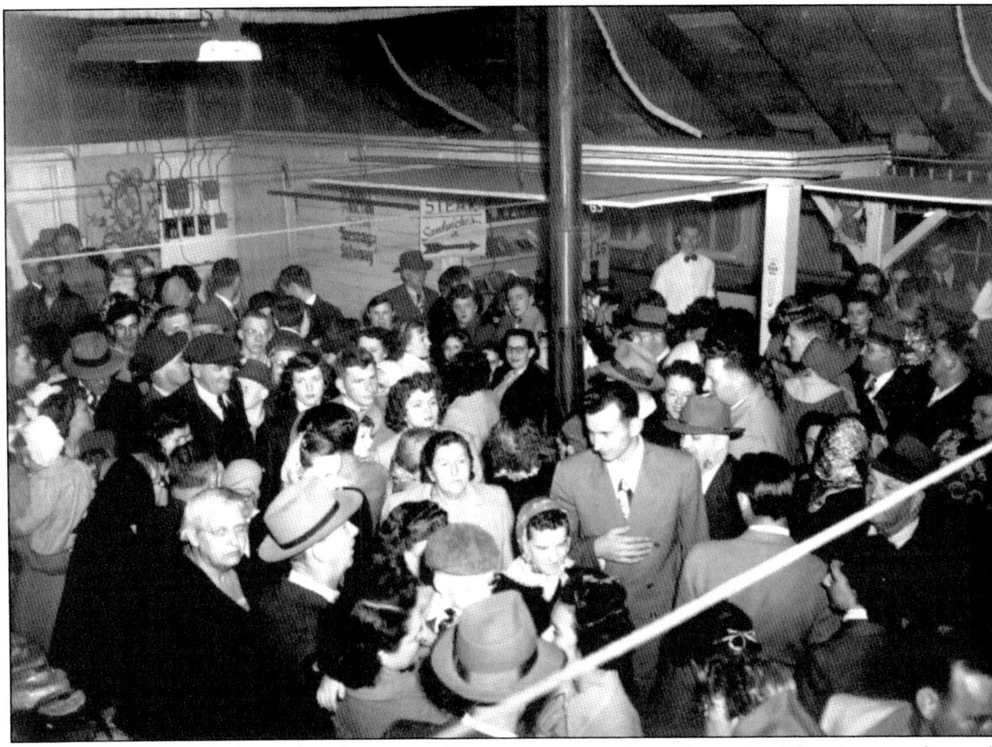

The market sold steak sandwiches, served by a man wearing a bow tie. The sign on the wall states that the market auction is open on Tuesday and Saturday. (Courtesy Shirley Szoke.)

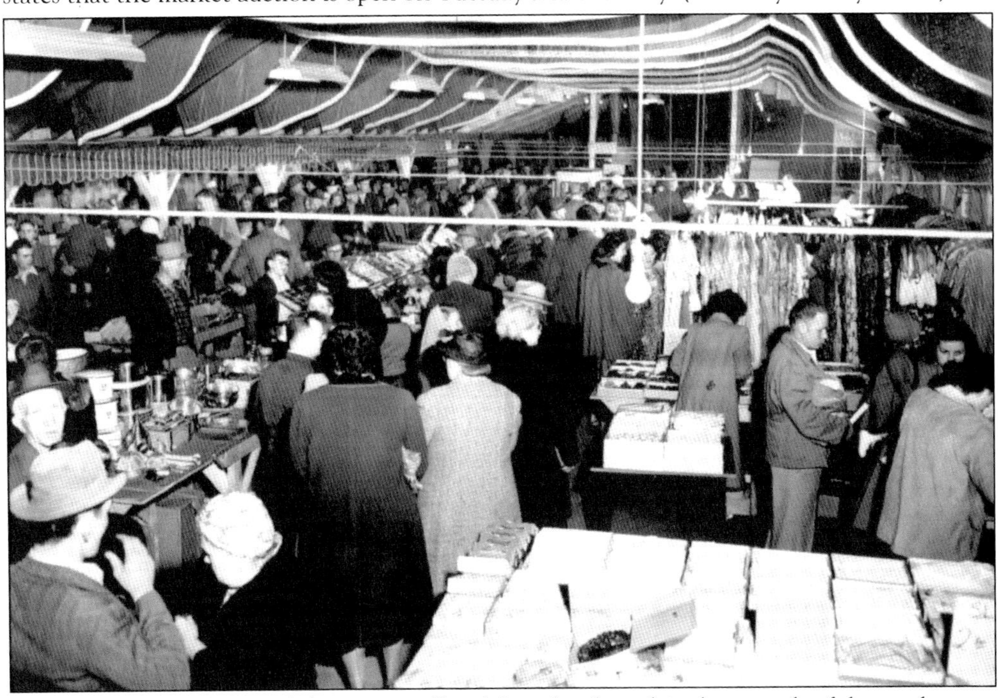

Pots and pans, clothes, and shoes were offered for sale when this photograph of the market was taken. (Courtesy Shirley Szoke.)

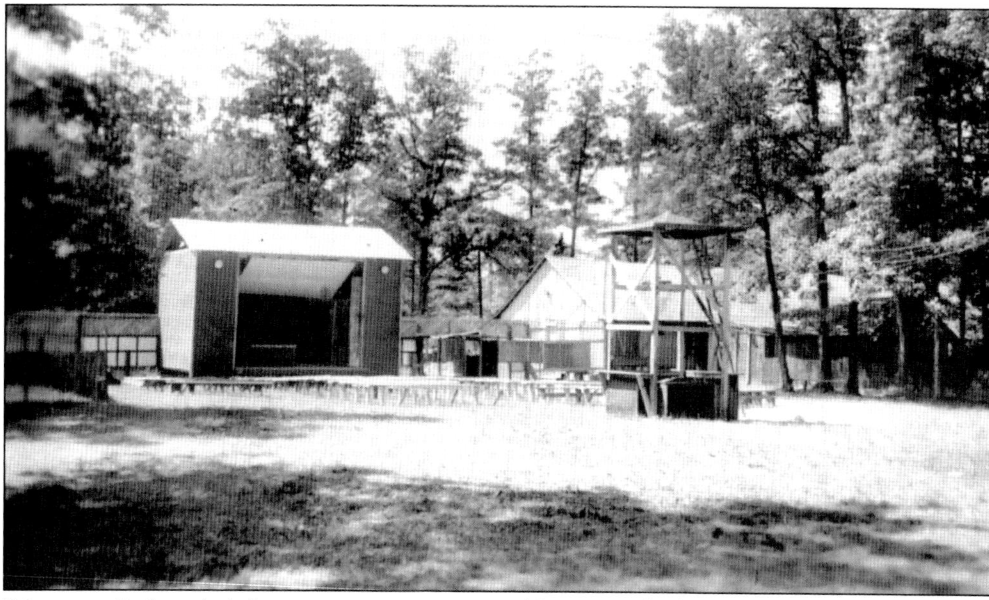

Edgemont Park included an entertainment stage. (Courtesy Shirley Szoke.)

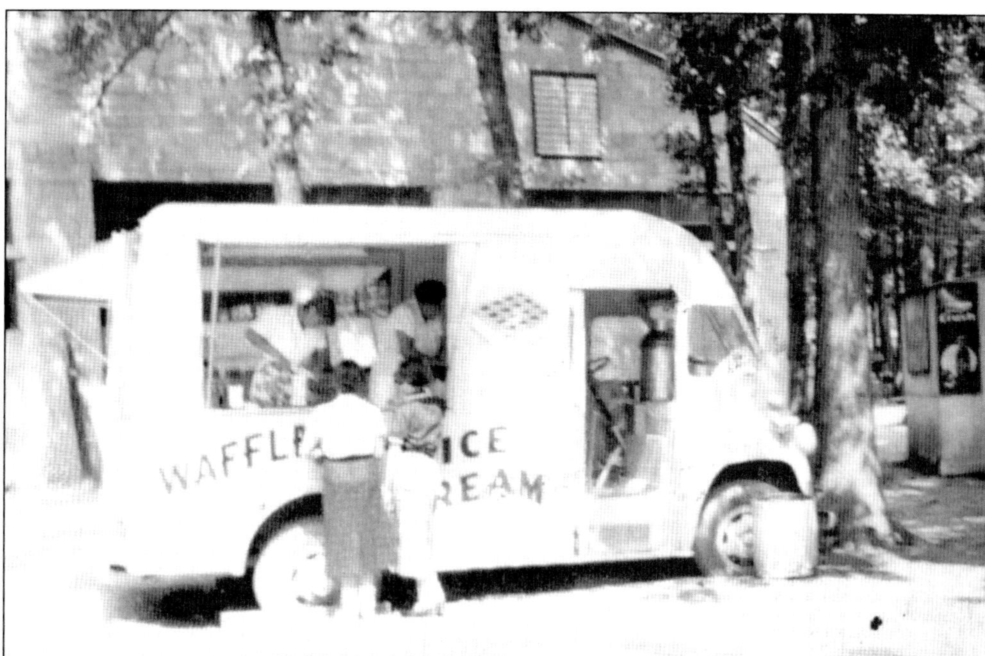

Rollin Minnich Jr. purchased an ice-cream truck, seen parked in front of the roller rink. (Courtesy Shirley Szoke.)

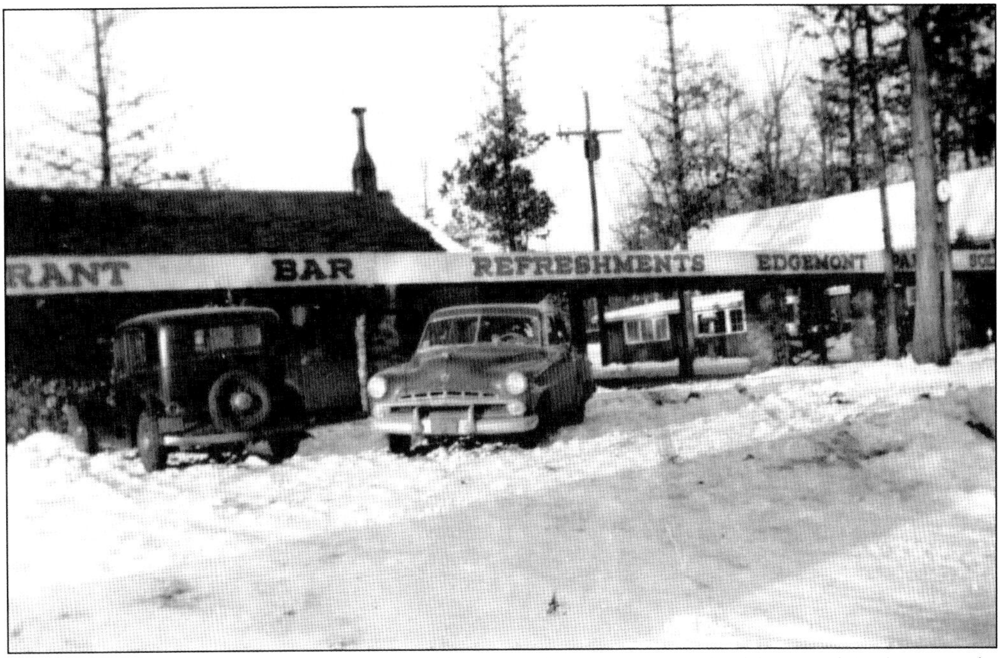

Snow blankets the area surrounding the Edgemont Park Restaurant building in this photograph, taken on January 11, 1954. (Courtesy Rollin Minnich Jr.)

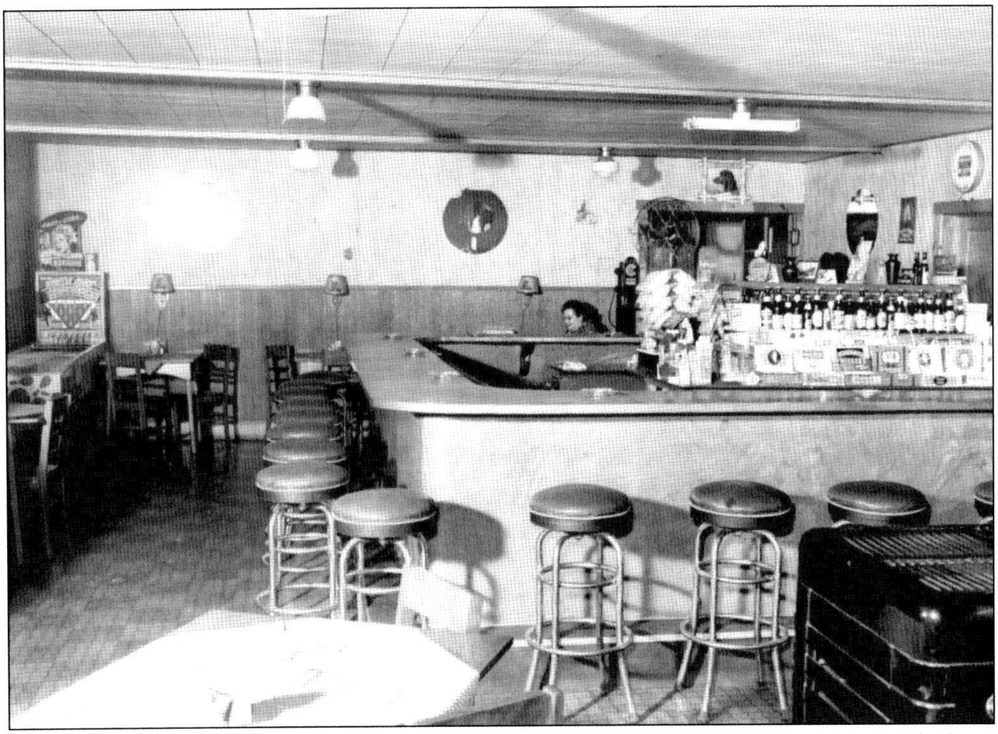

After the Minniches purchased the park, they renovated the bar. (Courtesy Shirley Szoke.)

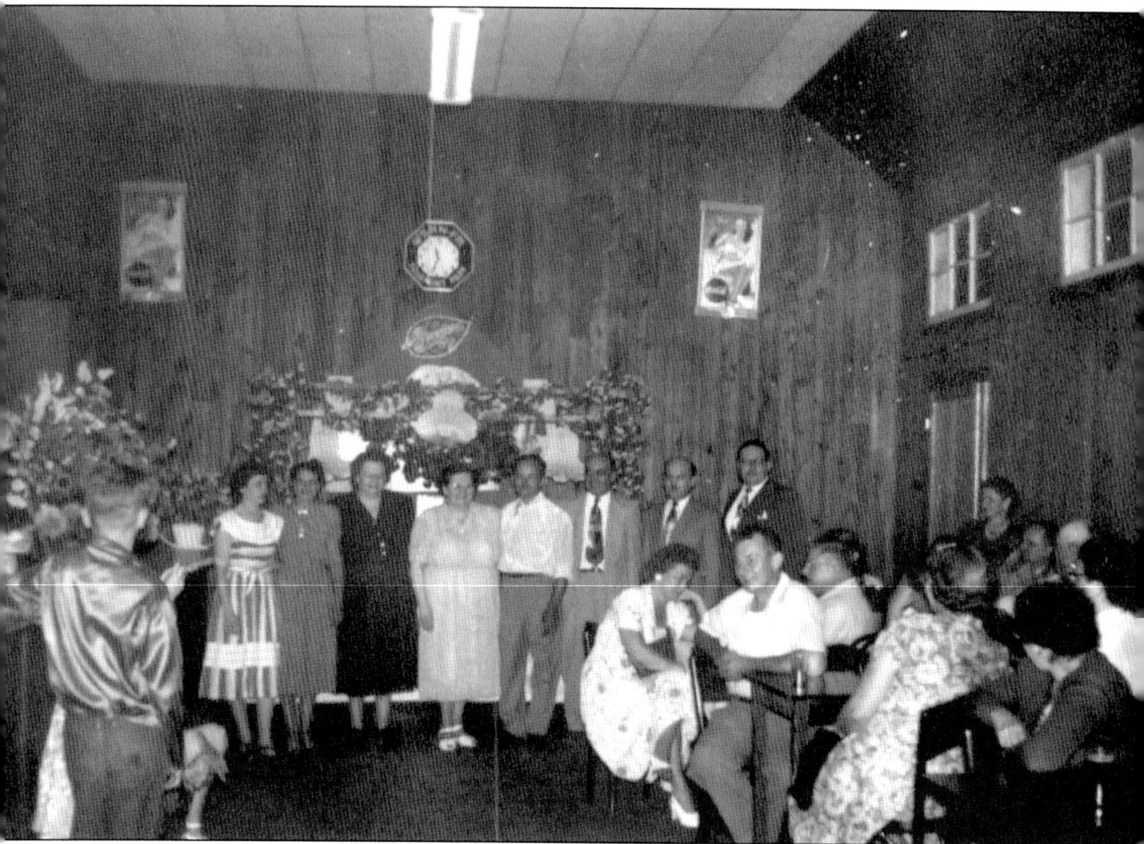

In this interior view of the restaurant, Rollin Minnich Sr. and Anna Minnich celebrate their wedding anniversary. (Courtesy Shirley Szoke.)

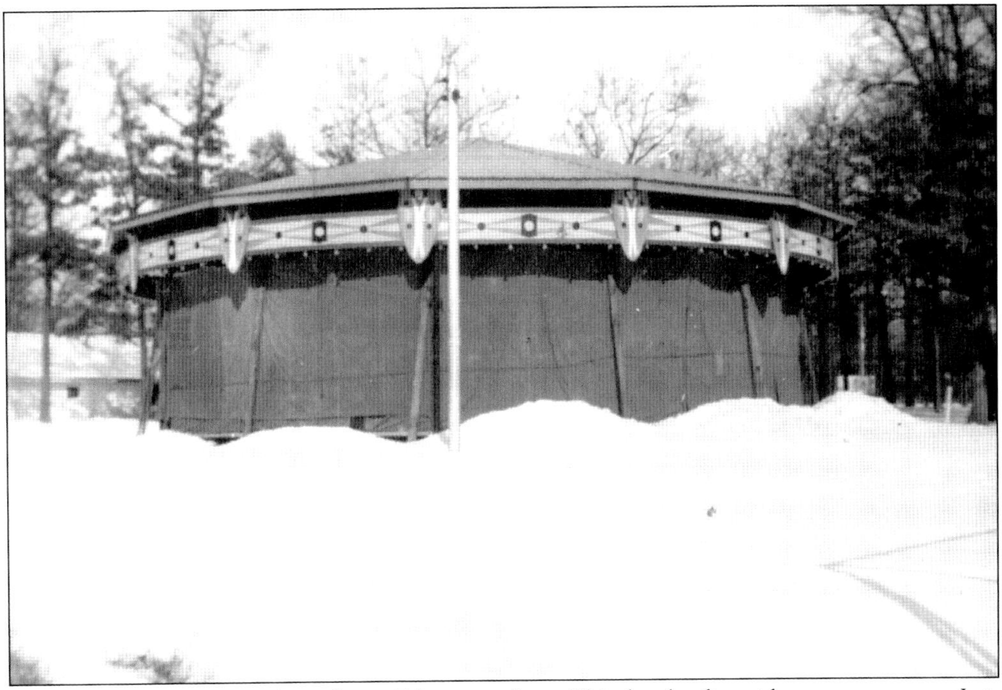

The merry-go-round was brought to Edgemont from Ohio by the five ride group partners. It is shown here closed up on January 11, 1954. (Courtesy Rollin Minnich Jr.)

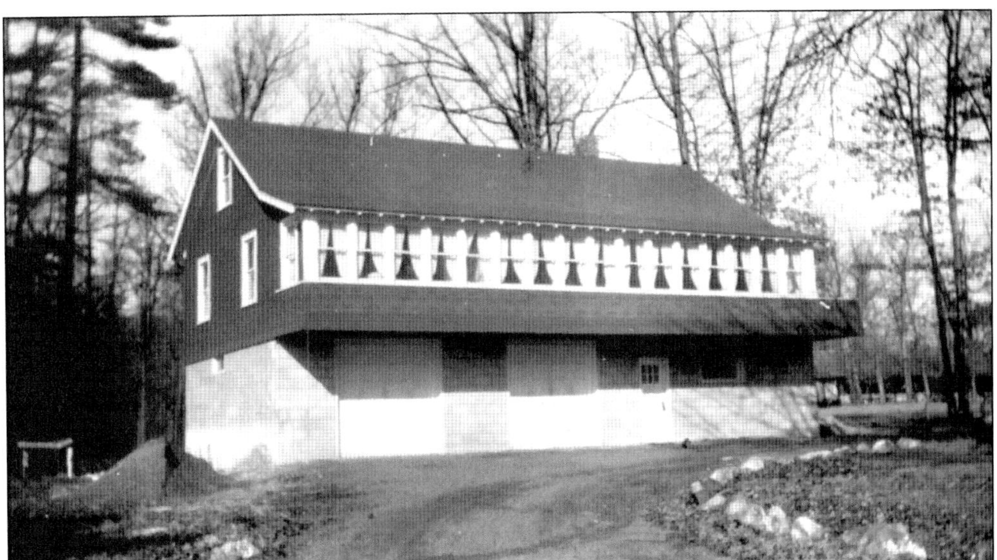

This building, located behind the tavern-restaurant, was constructed by the Gallaghers for Elinora's parents, who stayed in the house even after the Minniches bought the park. When Rollin Minnich Jr. returned from World War II, he and his wife, Belle, lived there. (Courtesy Rollin Minnich Jr.)

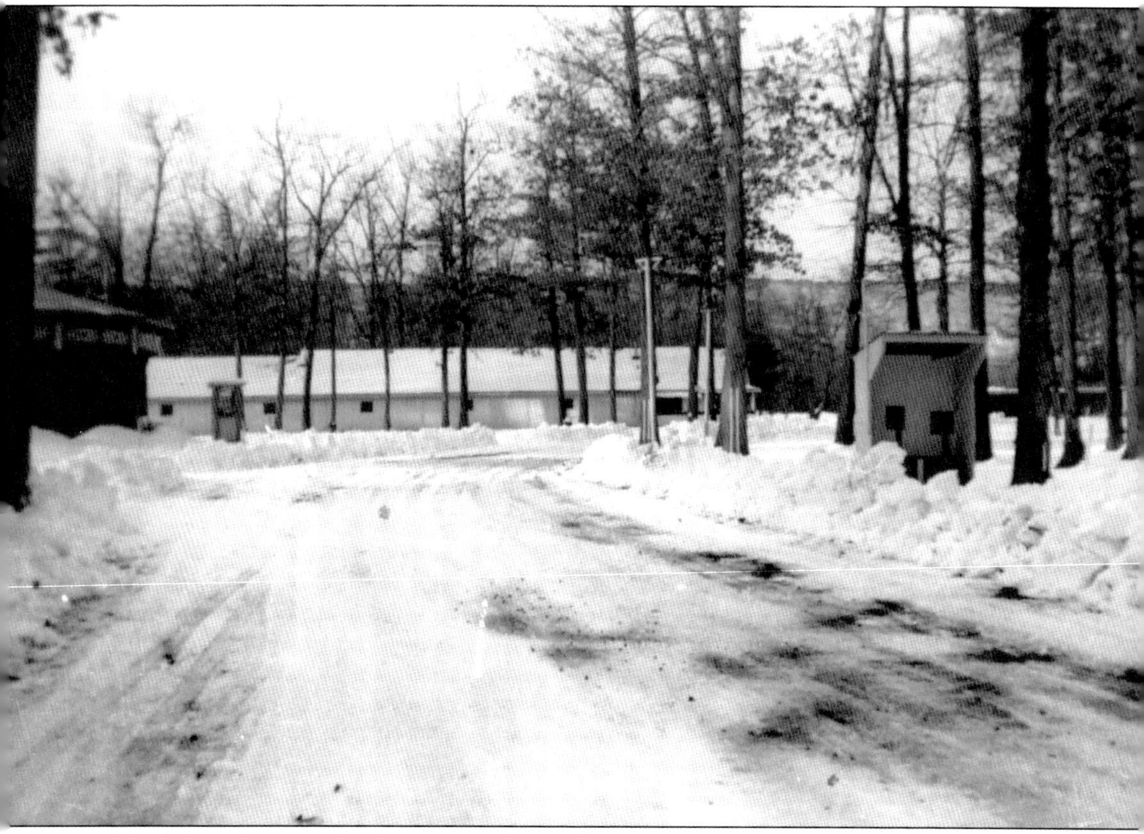

The Minniches ran the farmers' market and auction, as well as park concessions, from this building, shown in the snow on January 11, 1954. (Courtesy Rollin Minnich Jr.)

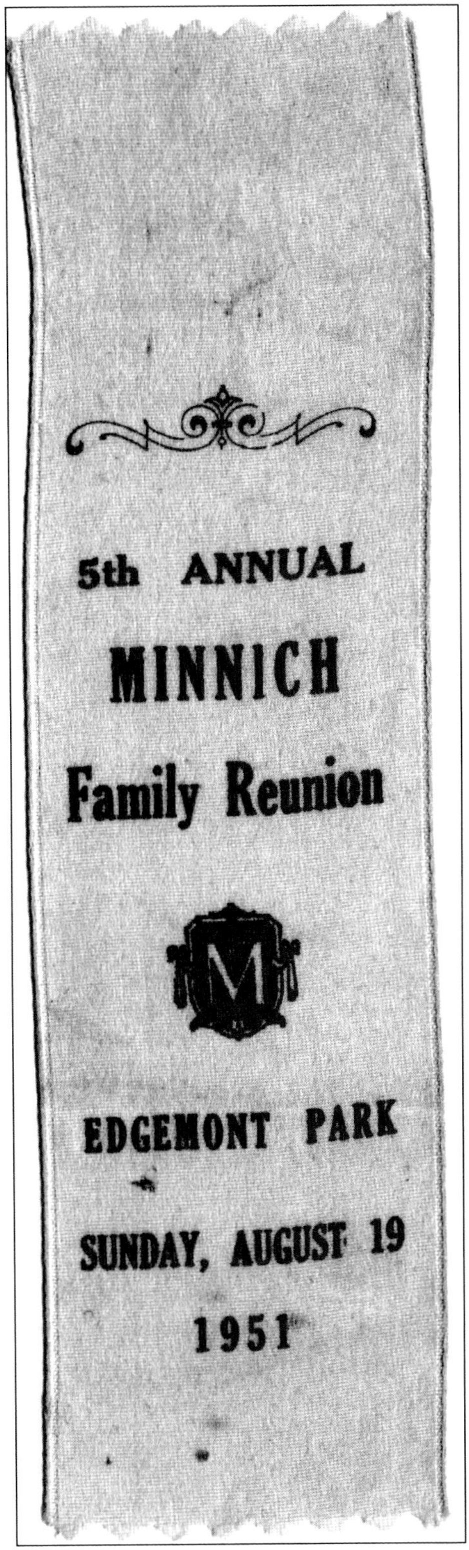

This ribbon is a memento from the fifth annual Minnich family reunion, held on August 19, 1951. (Courtesy Rollin Minnich Jr.)

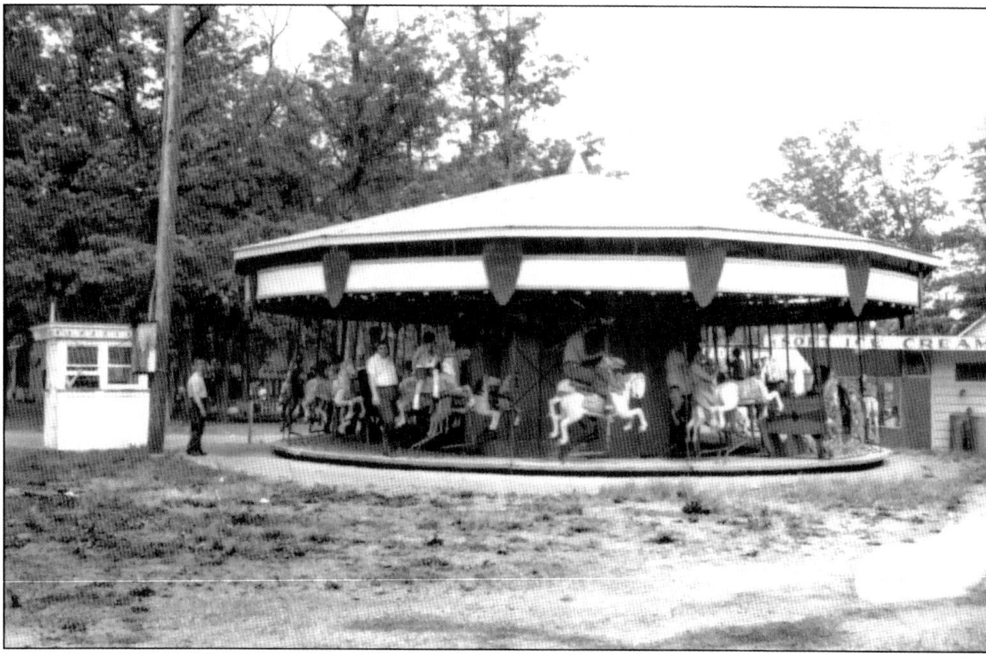

William Beck photographed many local scenes, including this one of the merry-go-round at Edgemont, while running the Route 45 drive-in movie theater now known as Becky's. The ice-cream stand can be seen to the right, and the ticket booth is to the left. (Courtesy the William Beck family.)

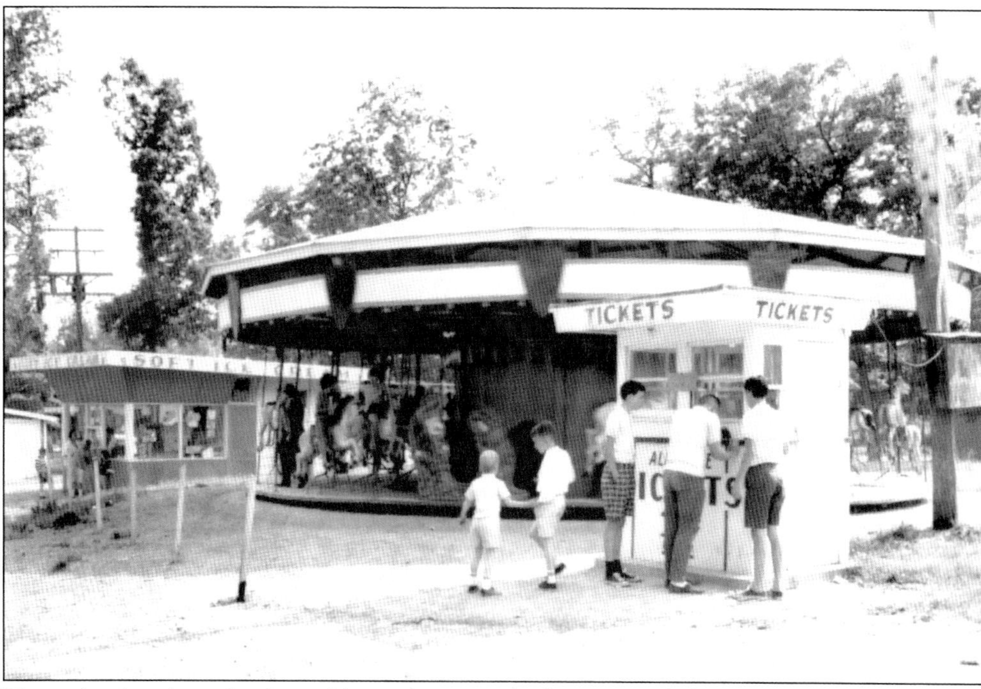

The ticket booth is clearly visible in this view, looking toward the restaurant and merry-go-round from the auction house. The ice-cream stand appears to the left of the merry-go-round. Gloria Newhard worked at the stand in 1957 and 1958. (Courtesy the William Beck family.)

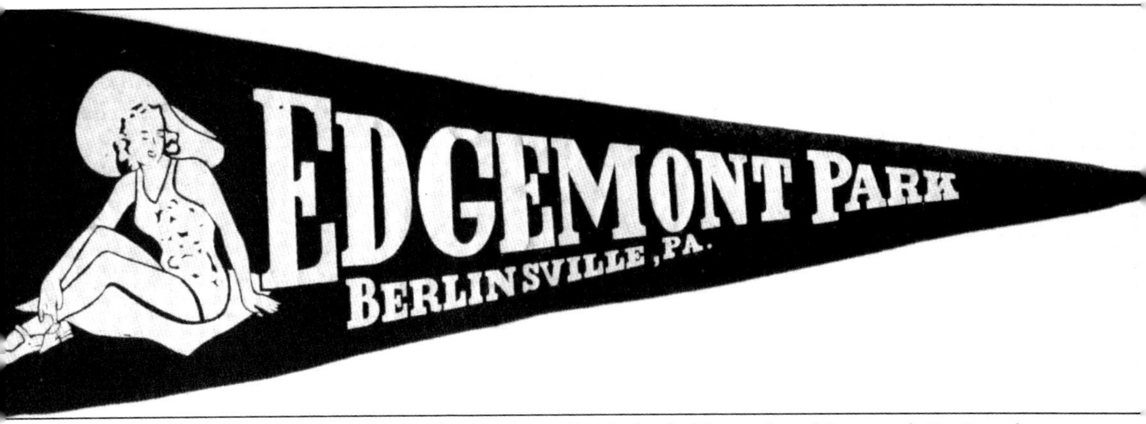

This Edgemont Park pennant was donated to the Lehigh Township Historical Society by Stephen and Alyce Unger.

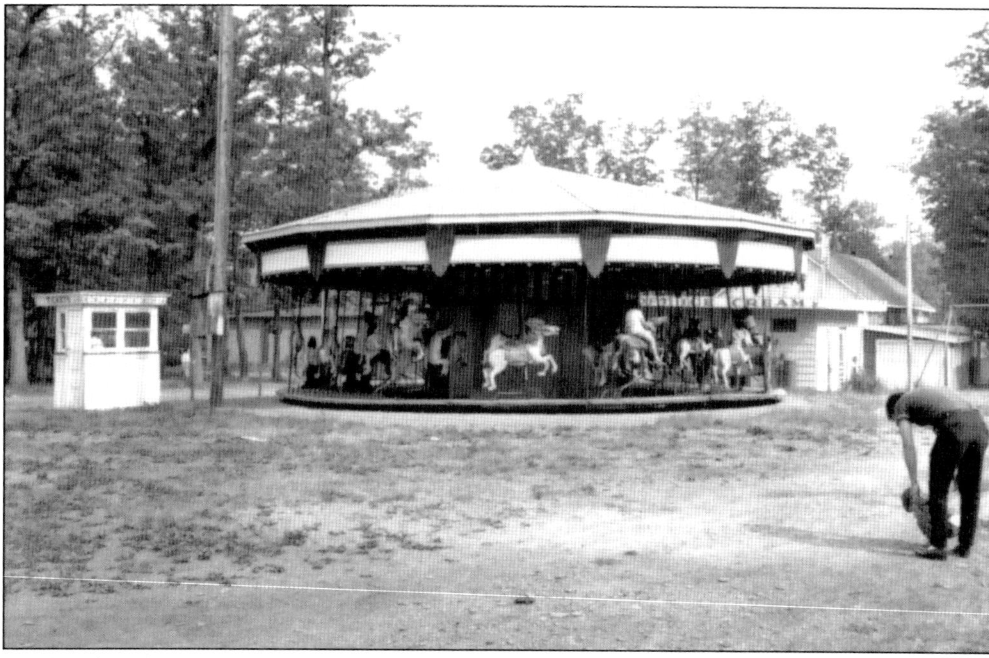

Frank Schmidt operated the merry-go-round, seen in this photograph taken by William Beck. (Courtesy the William Beck family.)

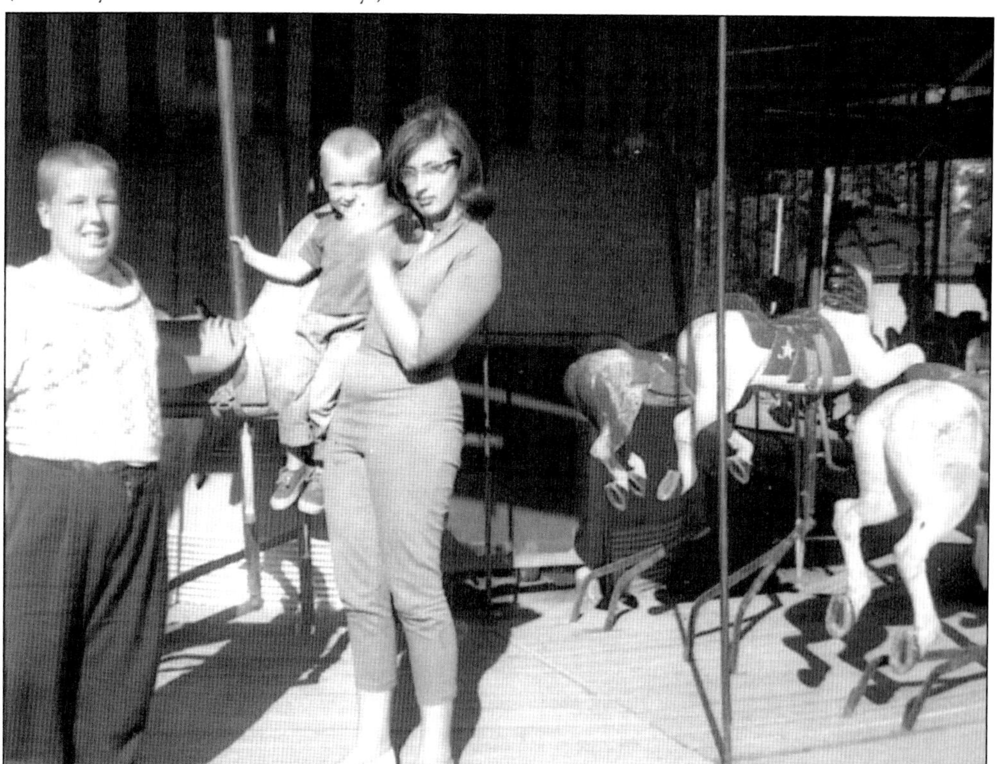

Edward Arey and Linda Hohl, holding Daniel Arey, stand in front of the merry-go-round in 1964. (Courtesy Kenneth and Kristine Moyer.)

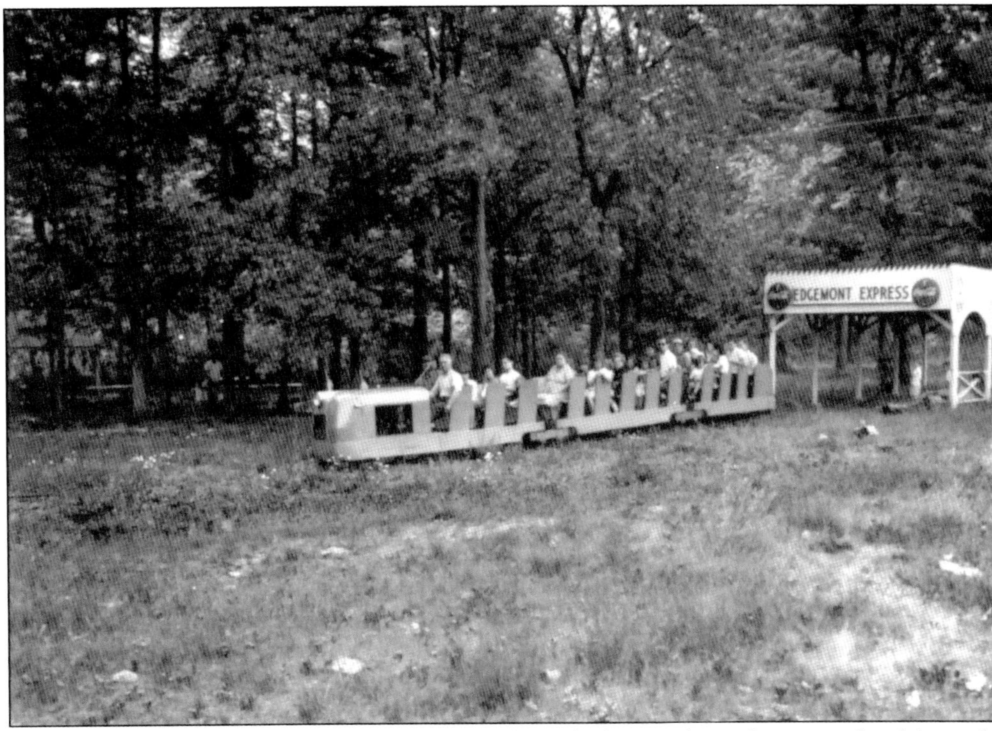

The Edgemont Express carried riders on a loop through the woods on the west side of the park. (Courtesy the William Beck family.)

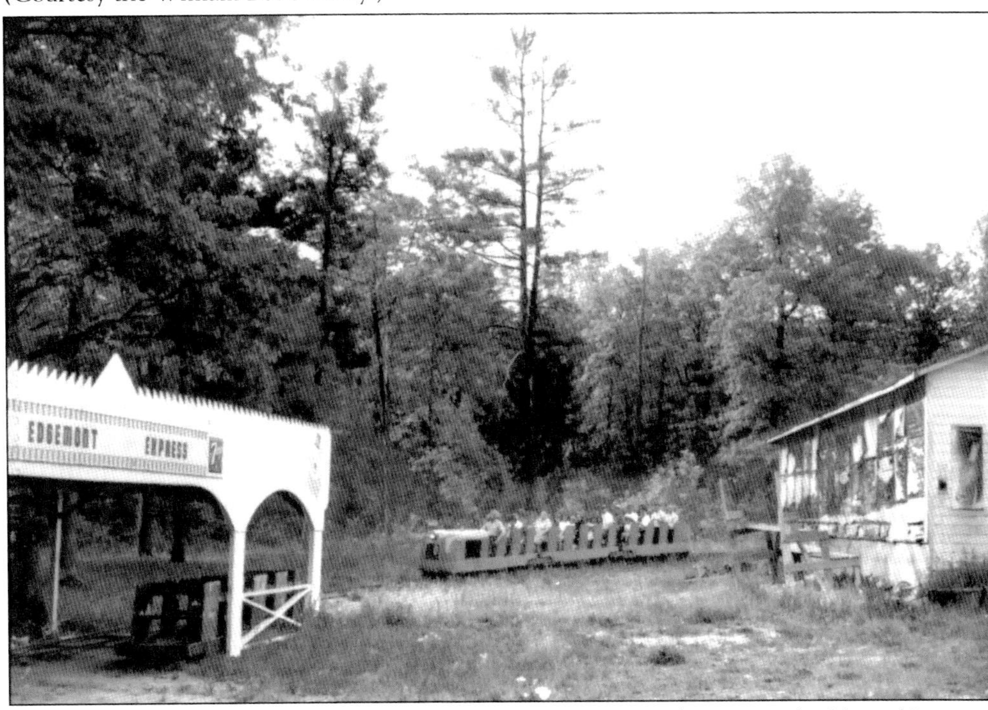

Operated by Shorty Rimsky, the Edgemont Express train passes the auction building. (Courtesy the William Beck family.)

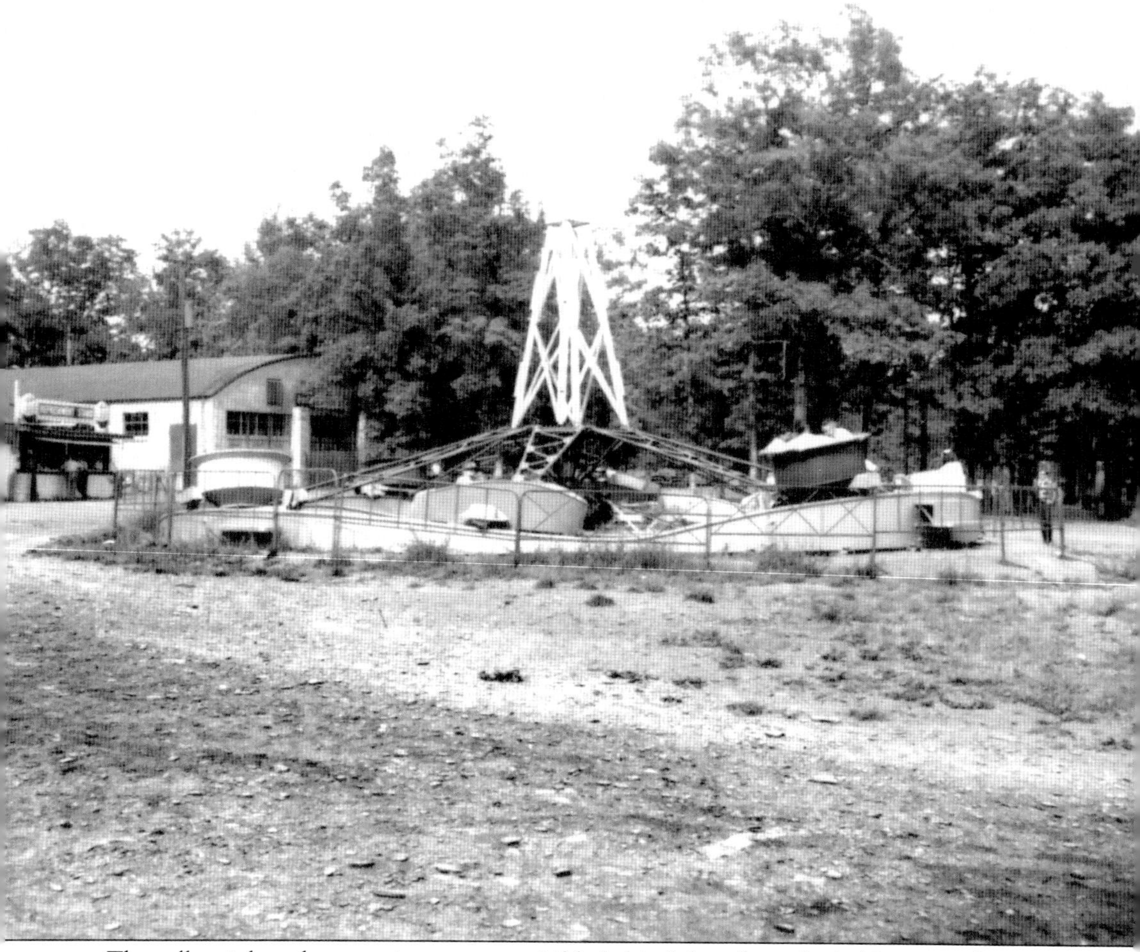

The roller rink and concession area are visible behind the tilt-a-whirl. (Courtesy the William Beck family.)

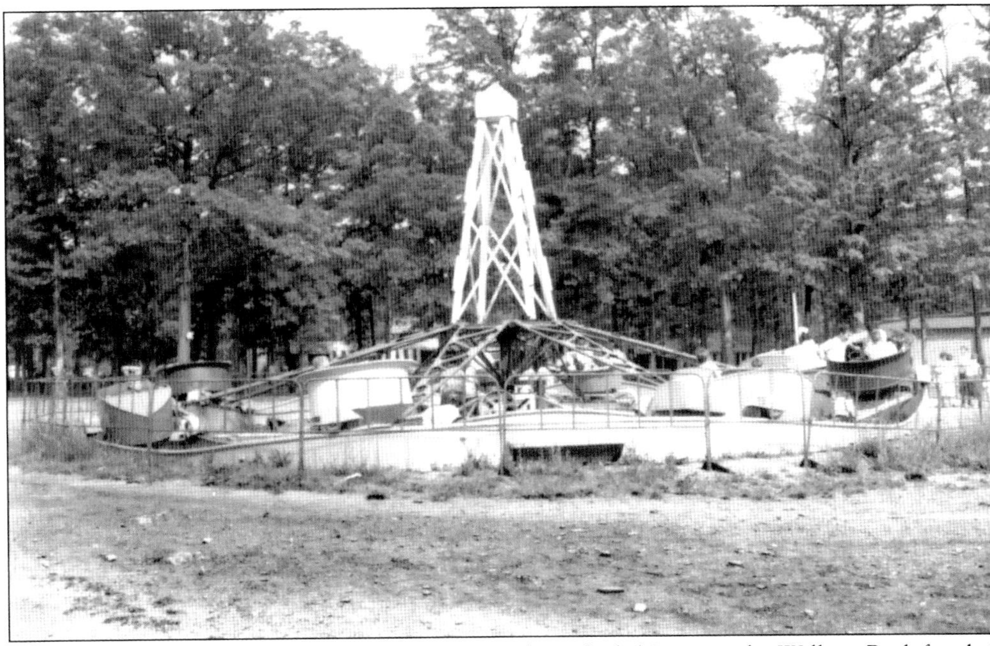

In this view, tall trees create a background for the tilt-a-whirl. (Courtesy the William Beck family.)

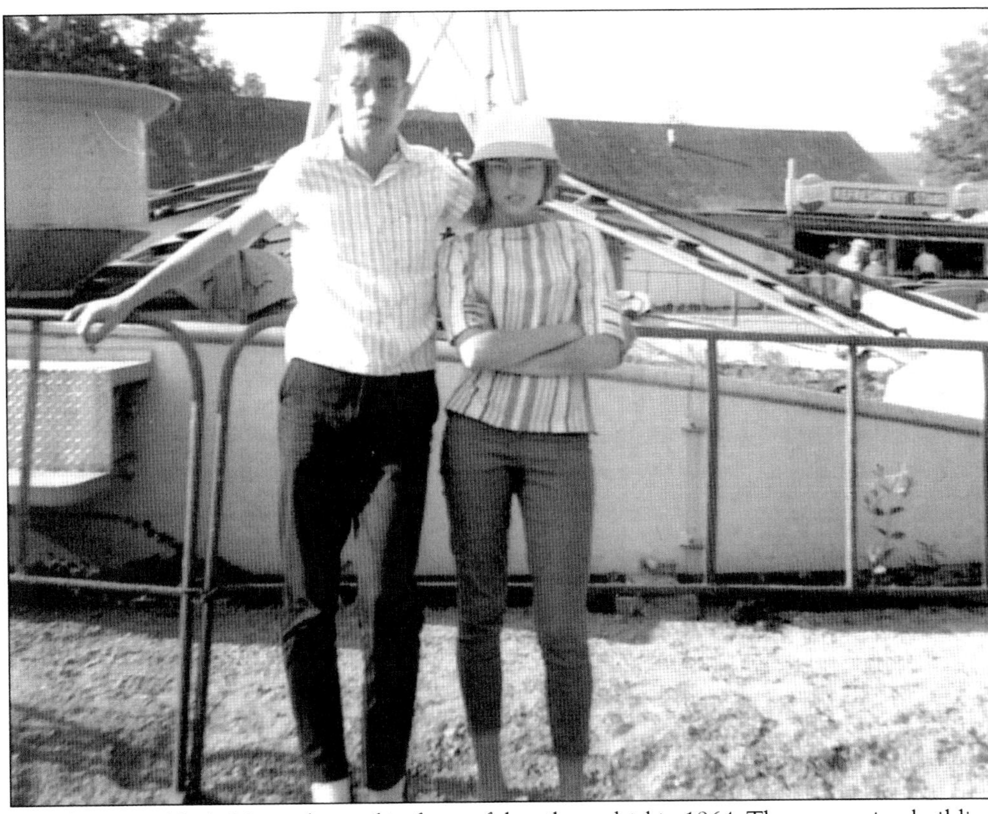

David Arey and Judy Minnich stand in front of the tilt-a-whirl in 1964. The concession building can be seen in the far right. (Courtesy Kenneth and Kristine Moyer.)

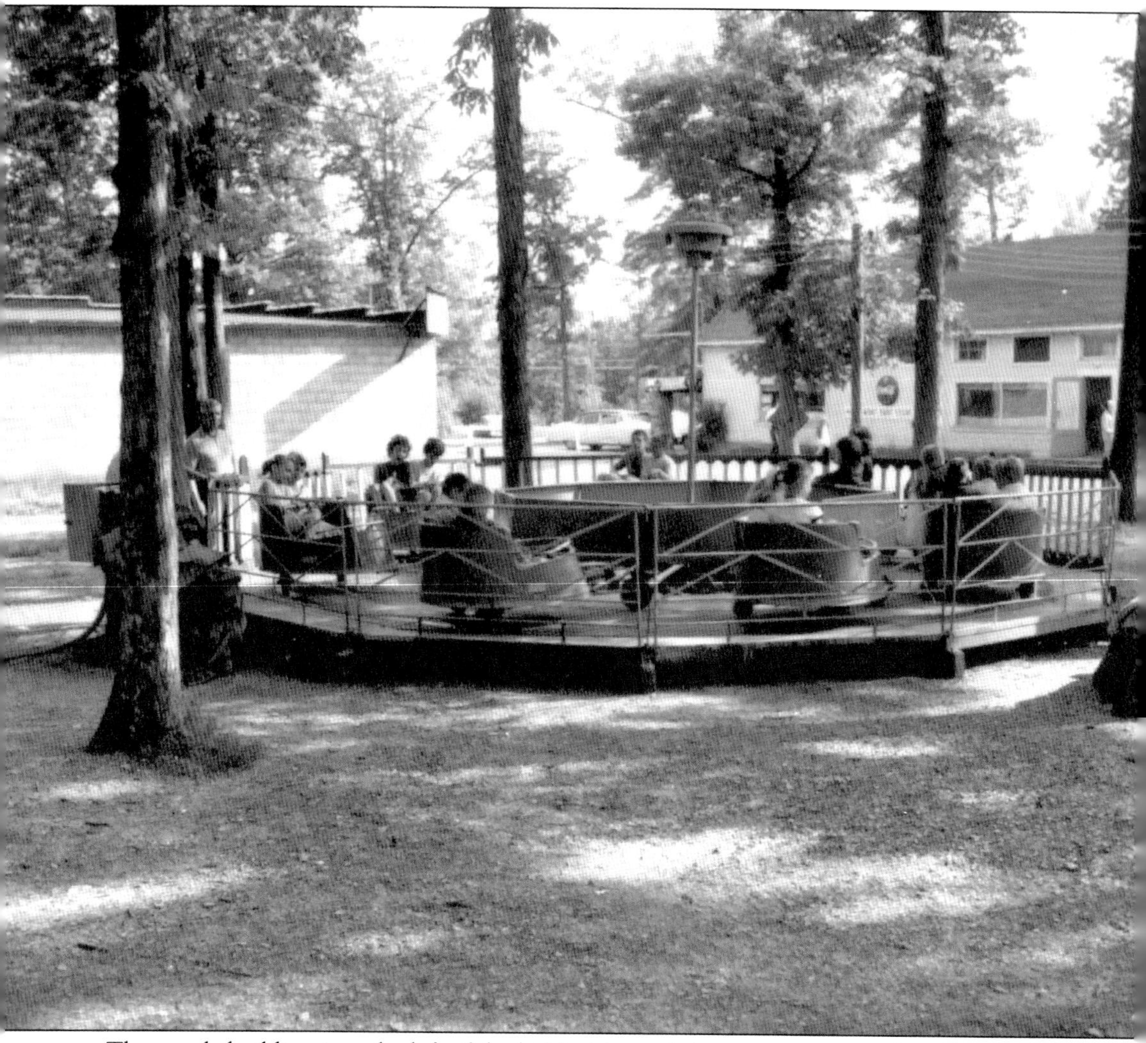

The arcade building is to the left of the kids' whip, and the restaurant is to the right. (Courtesy the William Beck family.)

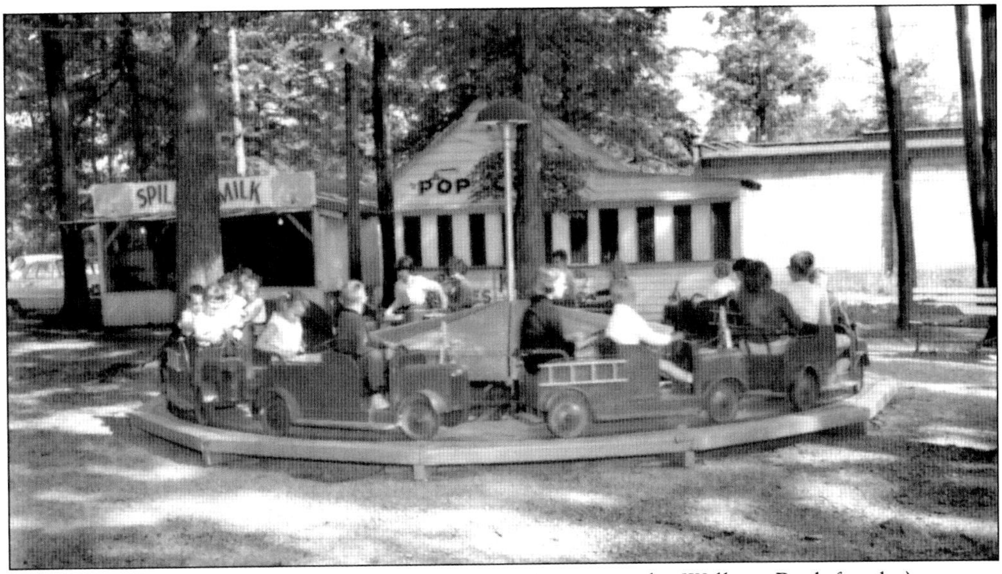

Games are visible behind the kids' fire truck ride. (Courtesy the William Beck family.)

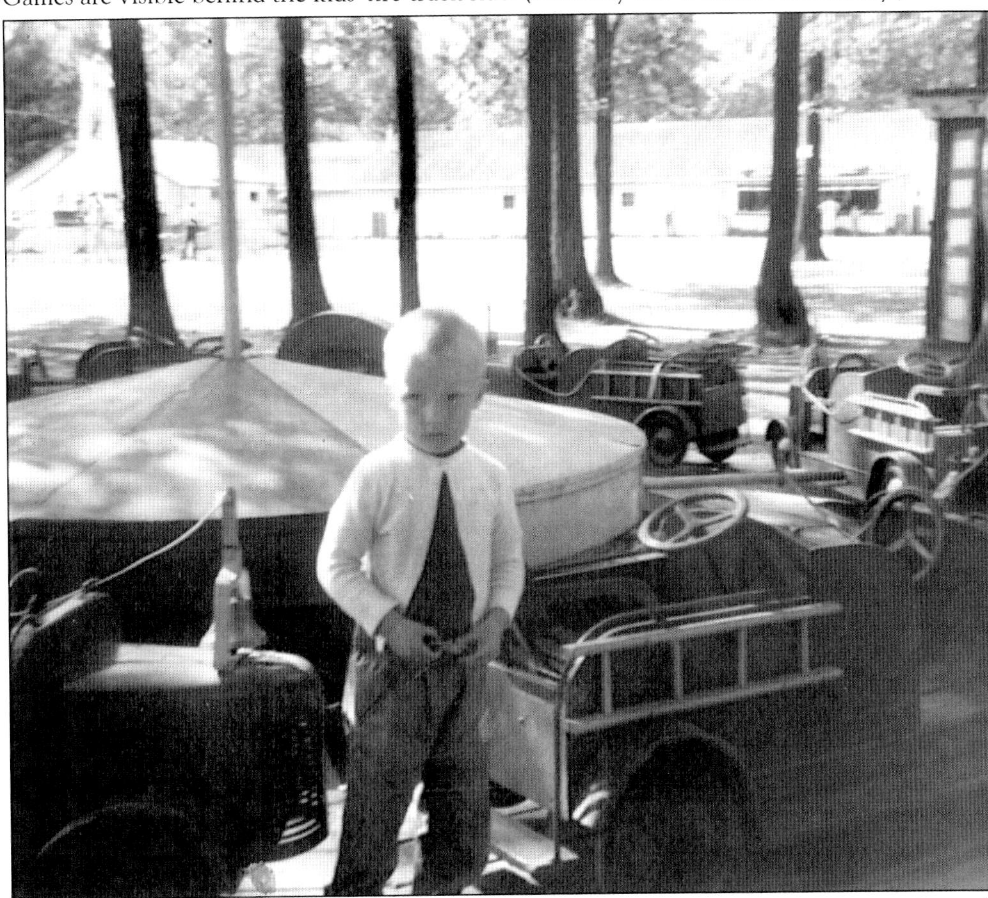

Daniel Arey stands in front of the kids' fire trucks in this 1964 photograph. (Courtesy Kenneth and Kristine Moyer.)

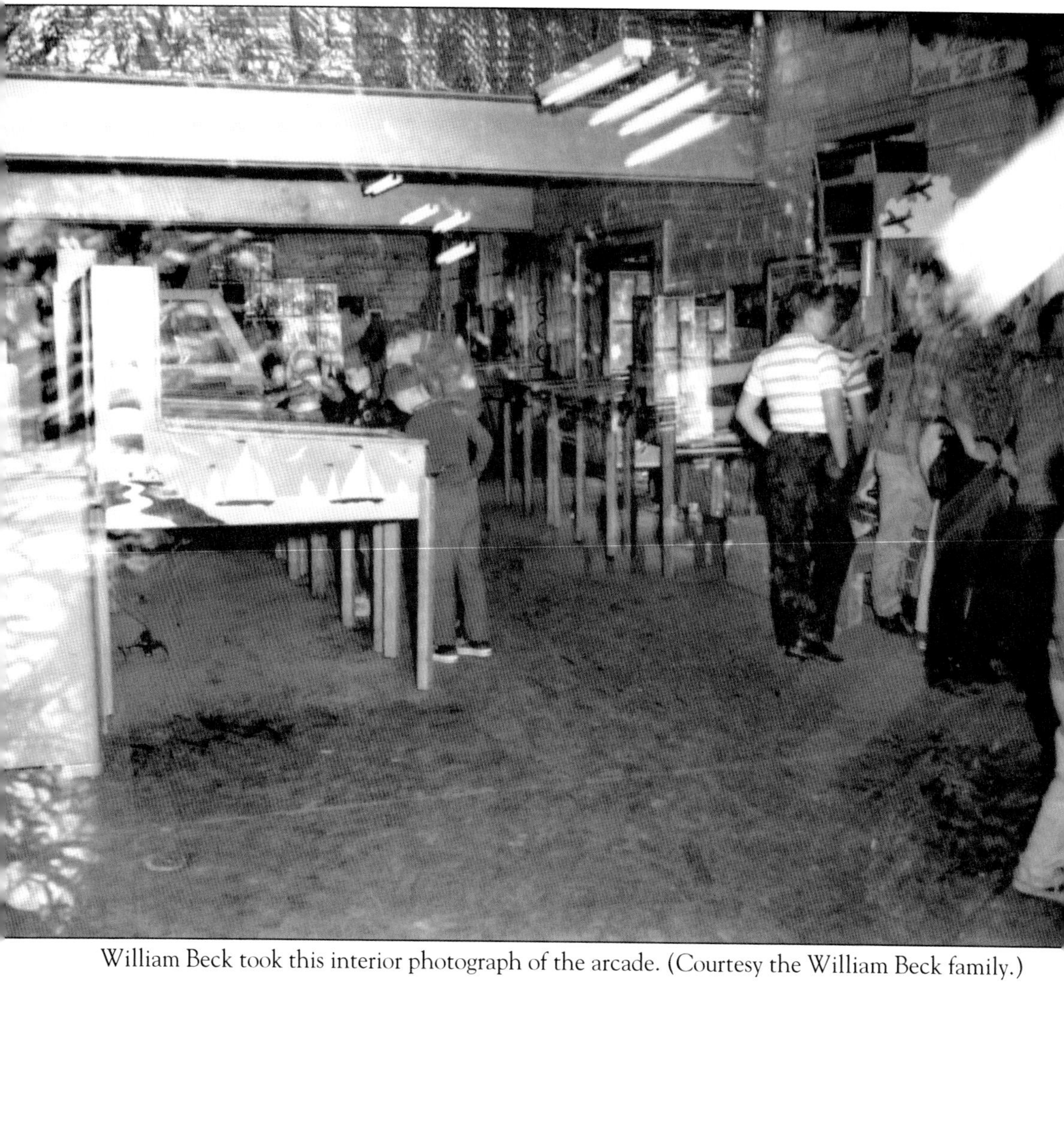

William Beck took this interior photograph of the arcade. (Courtesy the William Beck family.)

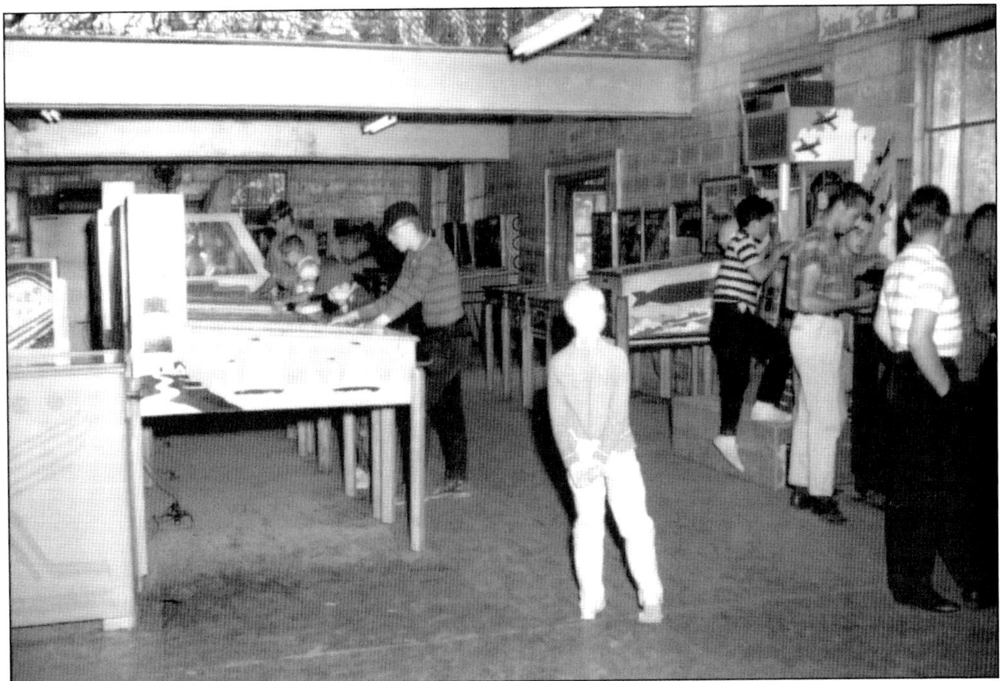

The games are more easily seen in this William Beck view of the arcade interior. (Courtesy the William Beck family.)

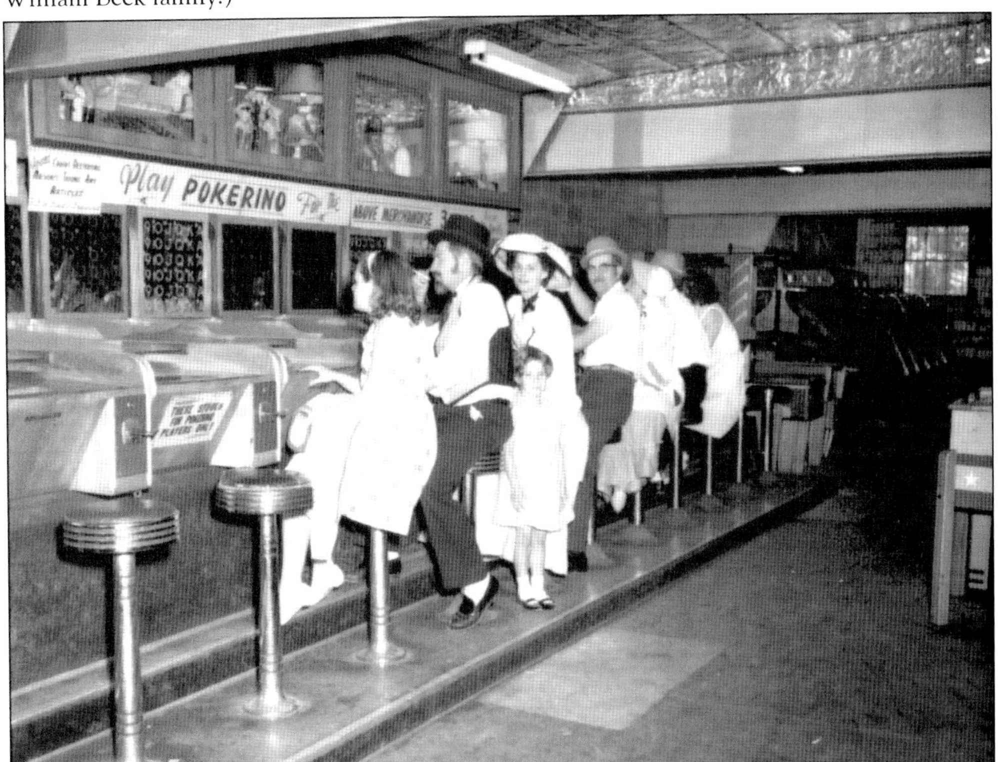

People gather at the Pokerino game in the arcade. (Courtesy the William Beck family.)

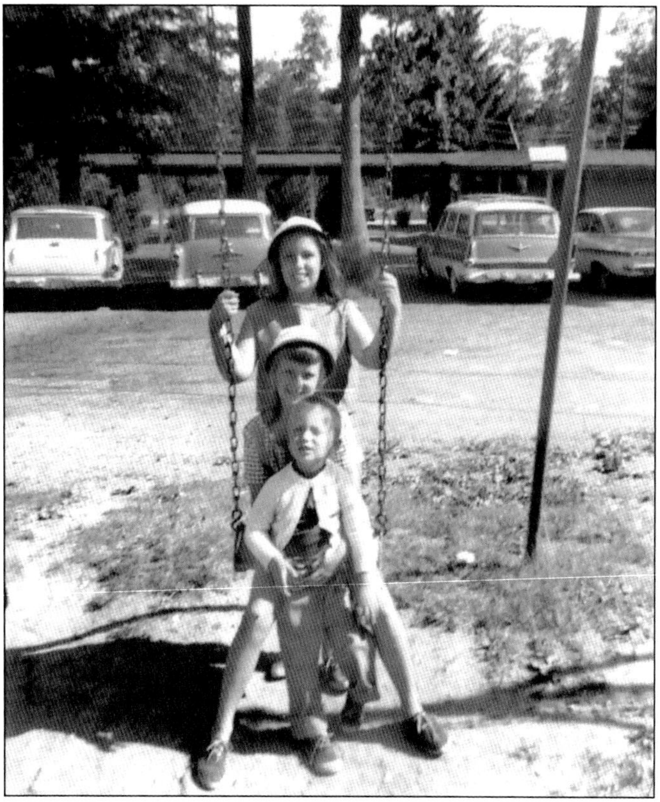

Kathleen Arey (top), Kristine Moyer, and Daniel Arey pose on a swing behind the restaurant in 1964. (Courtesy Kenneth and Kristine Moyer.)

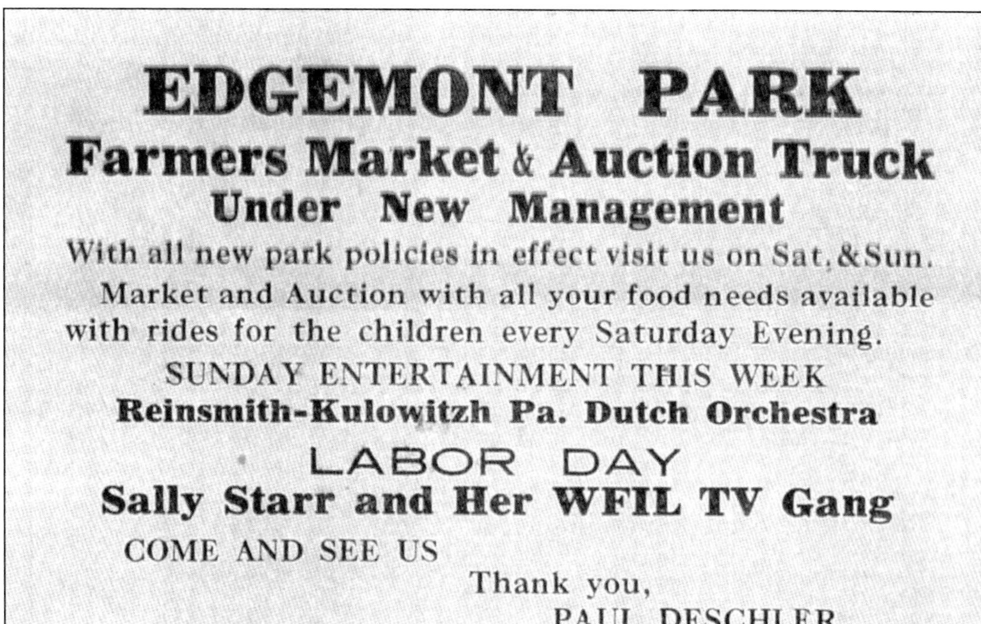

EDGEMONT PARK

Farmers Market & Auction Truck

Under New Management

With all new park policies in effect visit us on Sat.&Sun.
Market and Auction with all your food needs available with rides for the children every Saturday Evening.

SUNDAY ENTERTAINMENT THIS WEEK

Reinsmith-Kulowitzh Pa. Dutch Orchestra

LABOR DAY

Sally Starr and Her WFIL TV Gang

COME AND SEE US

Thank you,
PAUL DESCHLER

This flyer advertises the farmers' market and entertainment at the park while under the ownership of Paul Deschler. (Courtesy Stephen and Alyce Unger.)

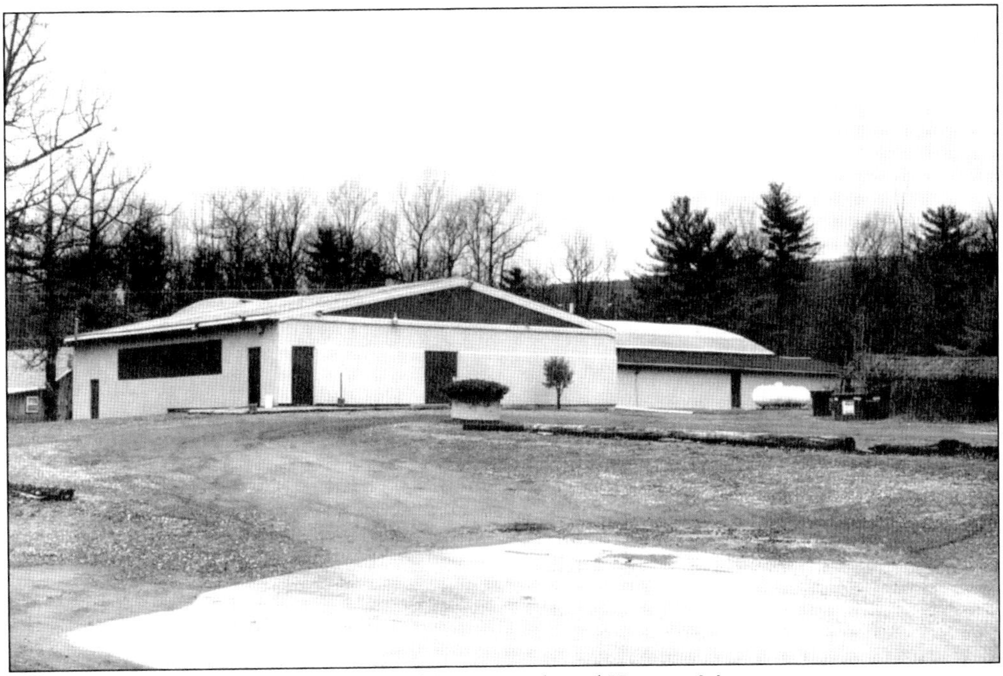

The rink, shown here in 2004, is owned by Kenneth and Kristine Moyer.

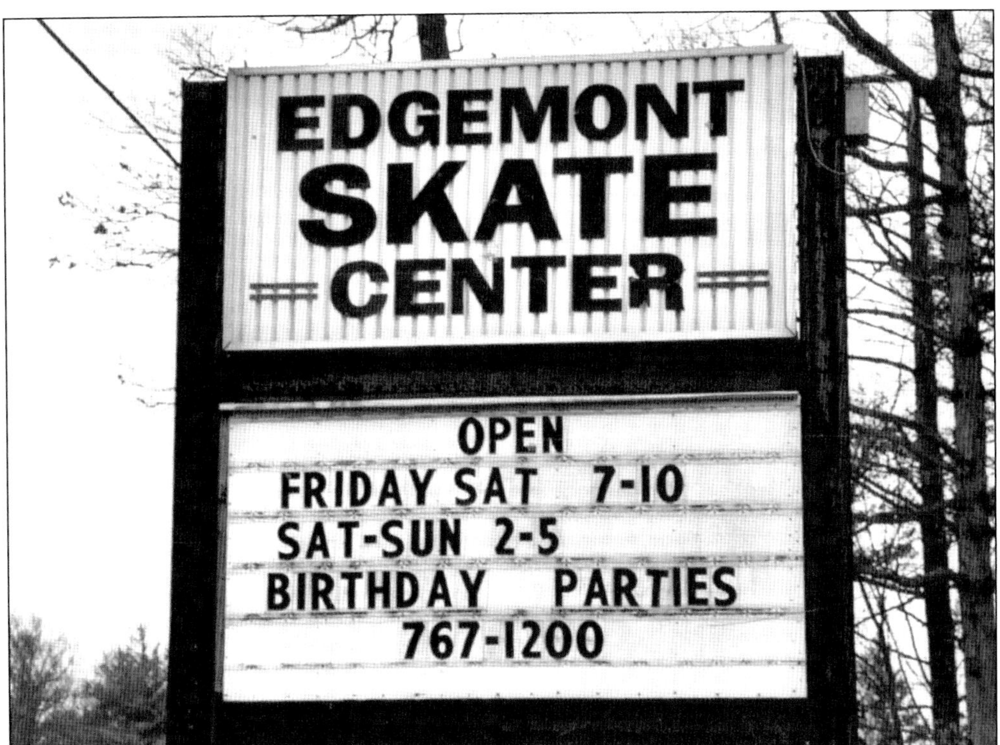

This sign advertises the roller rink, which is still in operation.

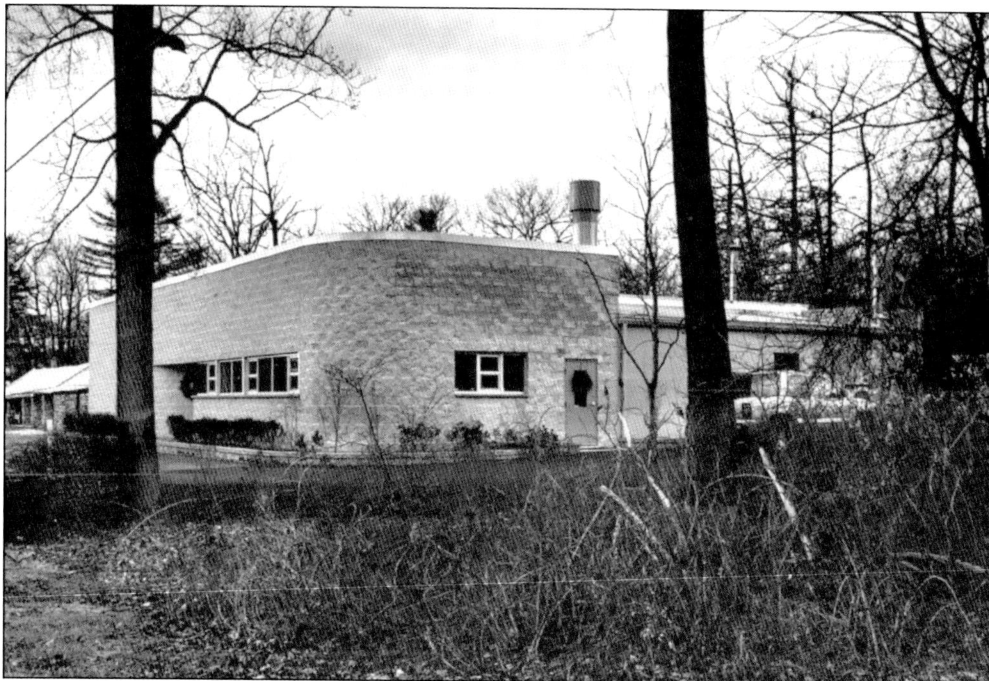

The arcade acquired a whole new look when Redline and Redline Wood Working remodeled it, as evidenced in this photograph.

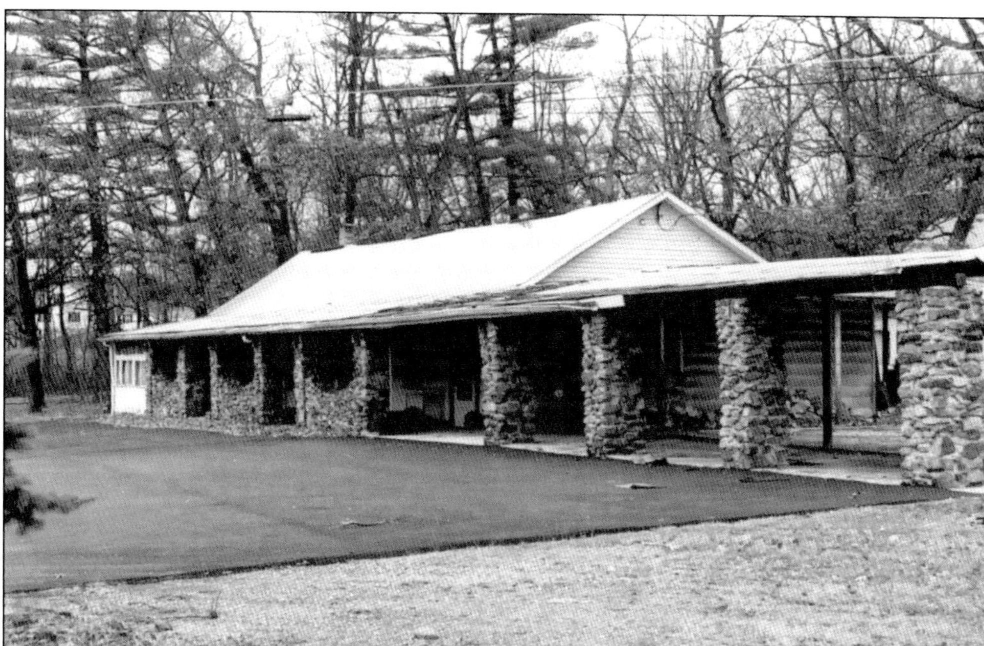

The tavern is shown in 2004, after it was sold to Barbara Razzano, who is converting it into Edgemont Park Antiques.

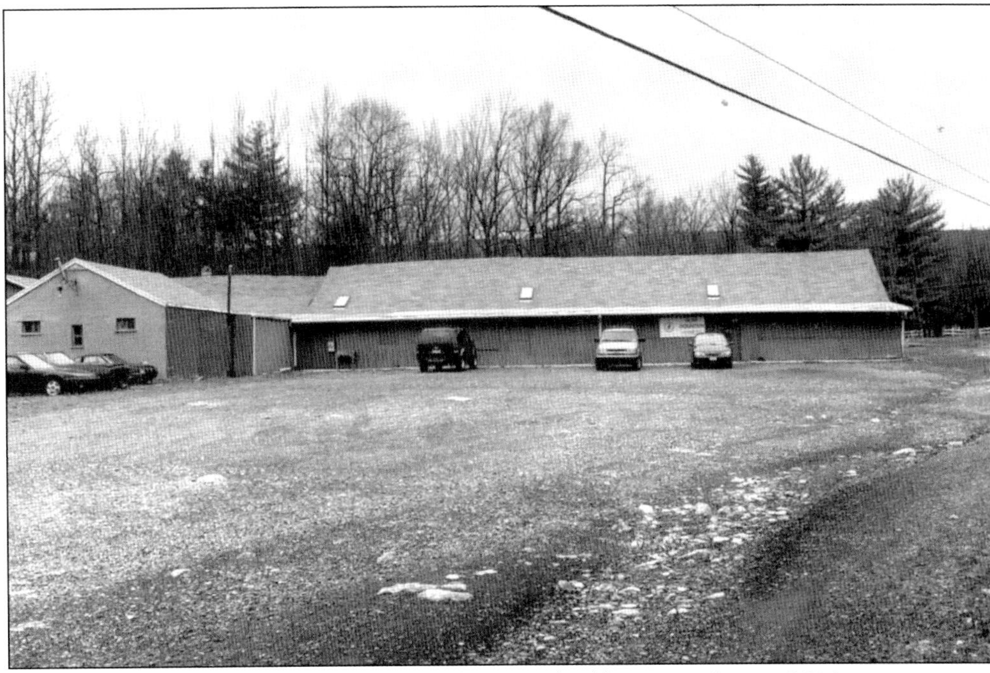

This photograph of the farmers' market and auction building was taken in 2004.

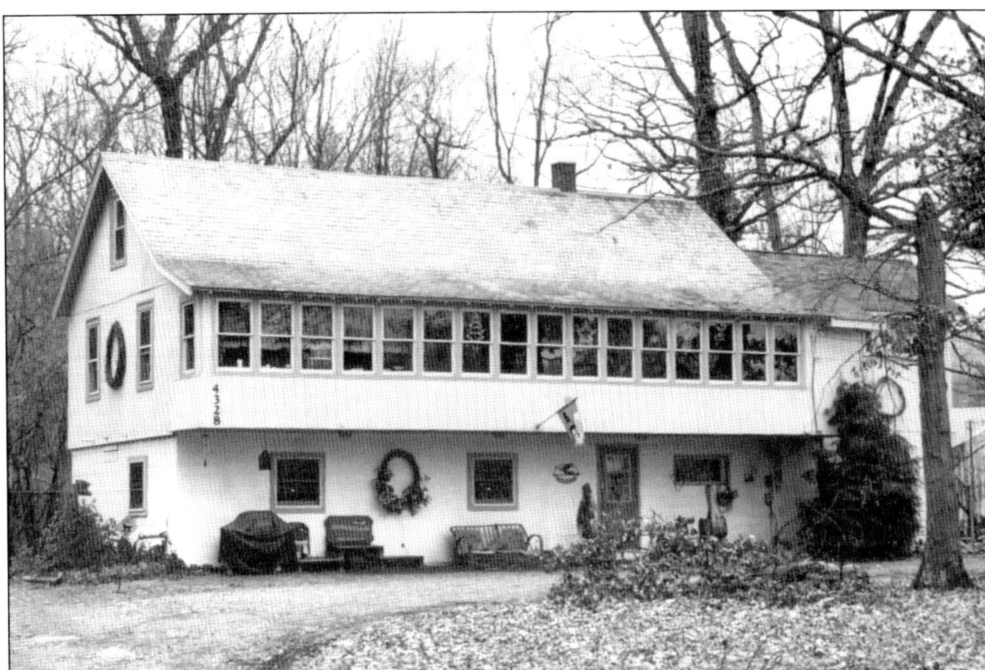

The house built by the Gallaghers remains a residence.

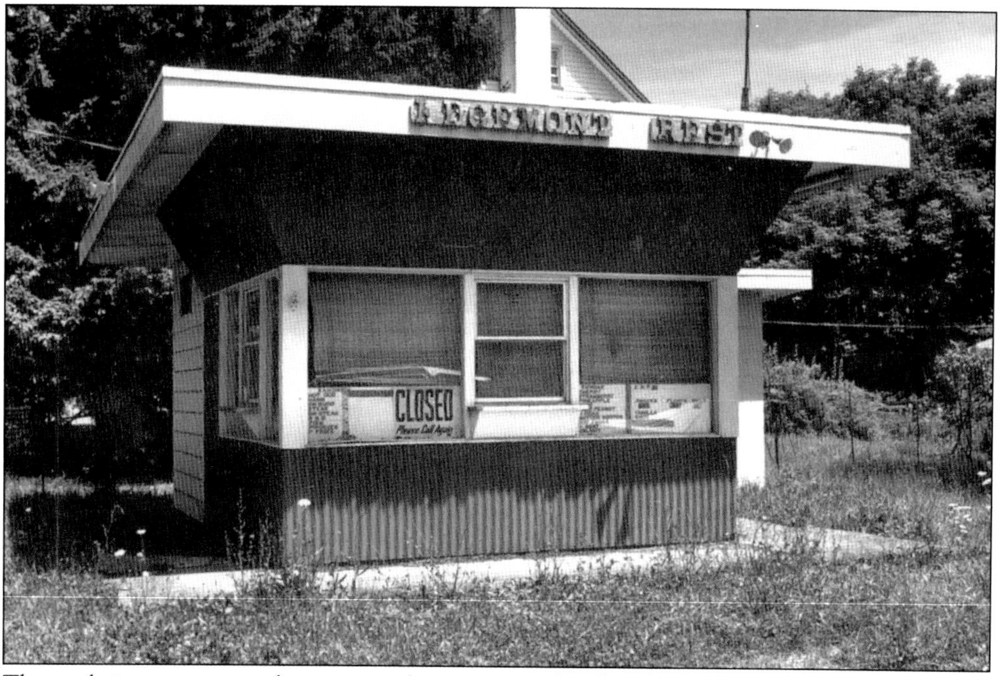

The park ice-cream stand was moved to a site a few hundred yards up Route 946. After purchasing it around 1965, Julia Smith operated the stand at this location until 1999.

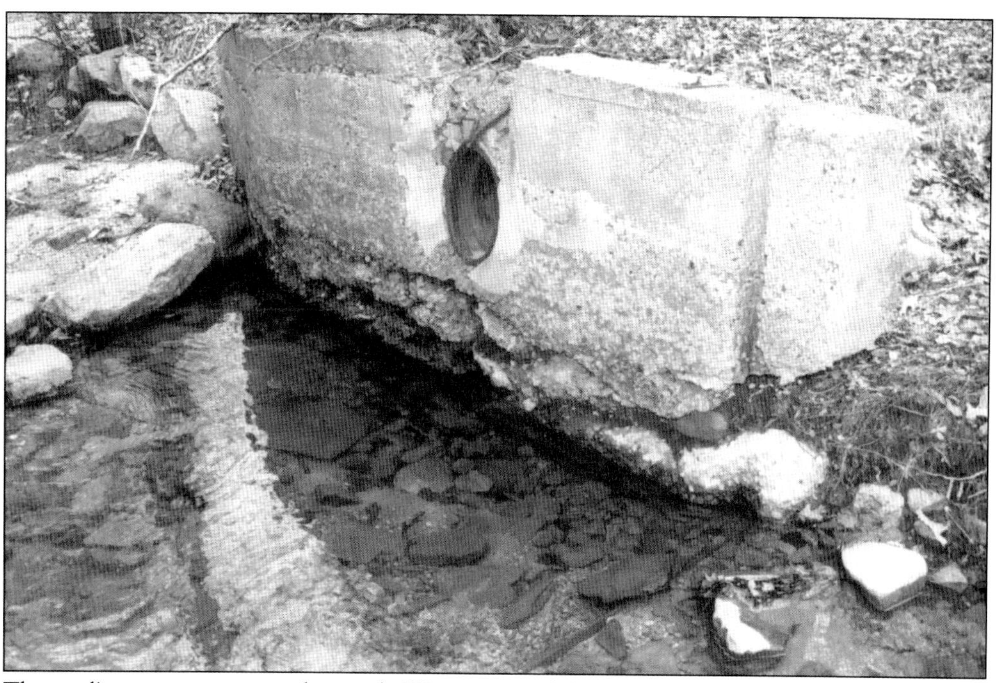

The pool's water source was the creek. Water entered the pool through this pipe.

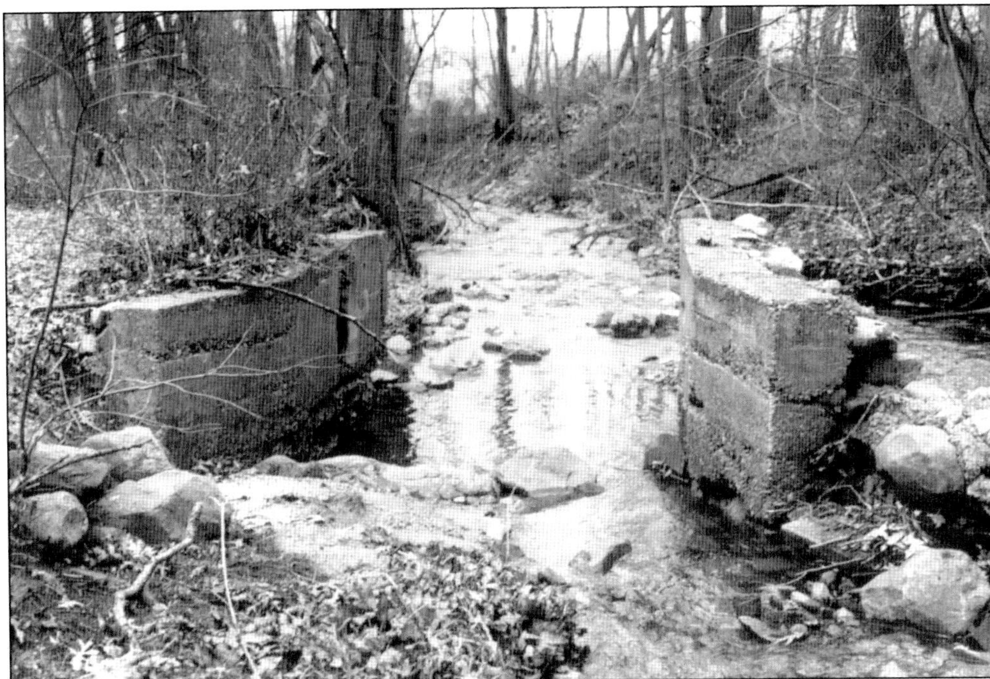

The creek ran between these two wing walls, and when dammed, the water flowed into the pool. A pipe at the other end of the pool drained water back out into the creek.

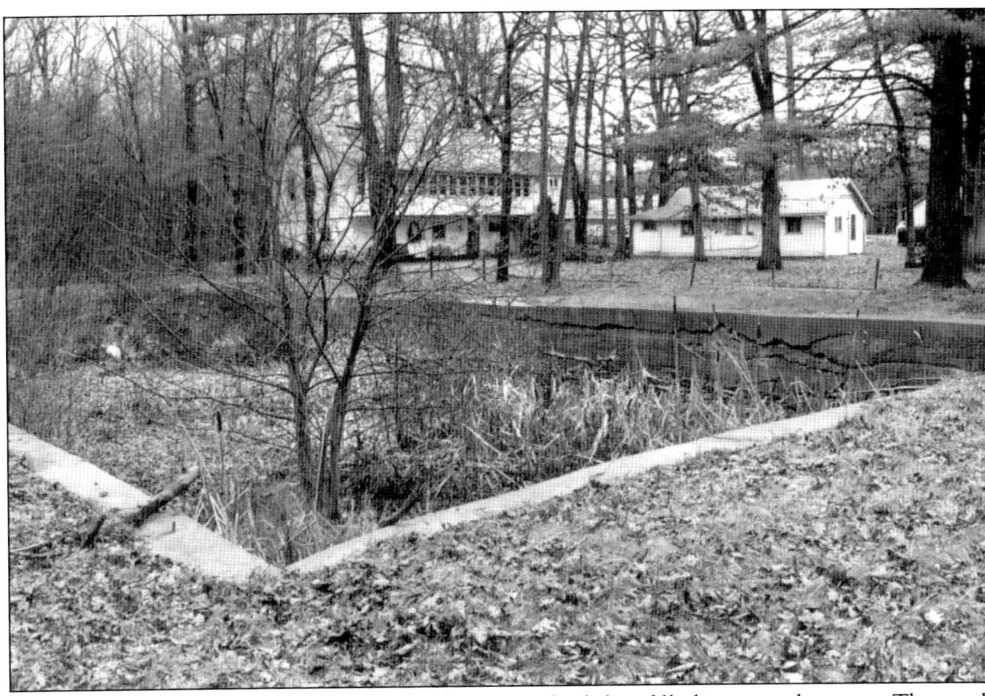

The pool, shown here in 2004, had a dirt bottom, which has filled in over the years. The small cottage in front of the house was built by the Minniches for Belle Minnich's parents, who never moved in. It then became a break area for park workers. It even included a slot machine.

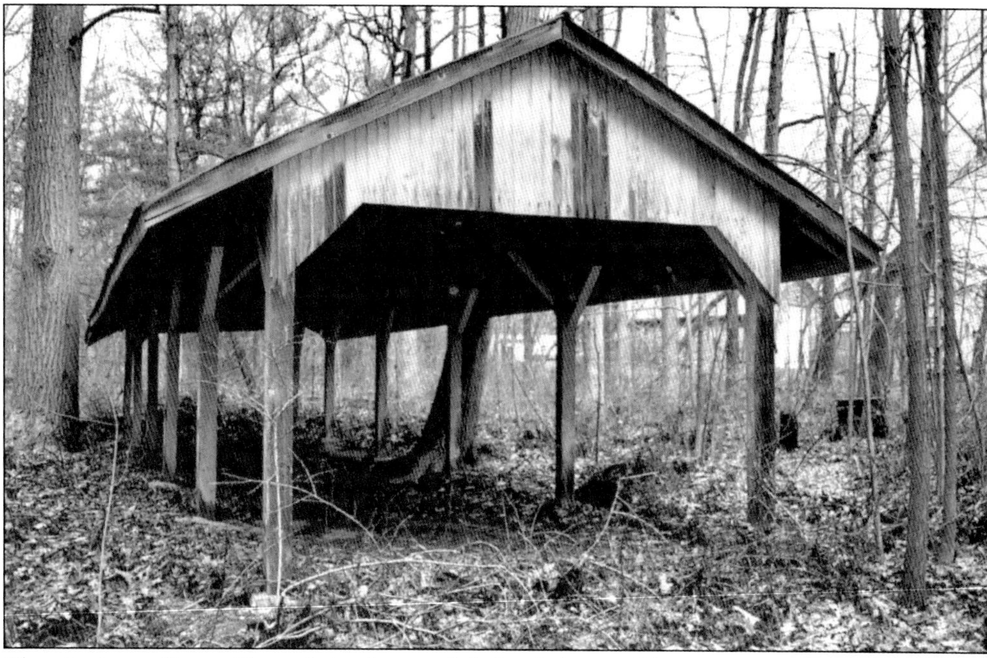

The picnic pavilion still stands in the woods behind the small house.

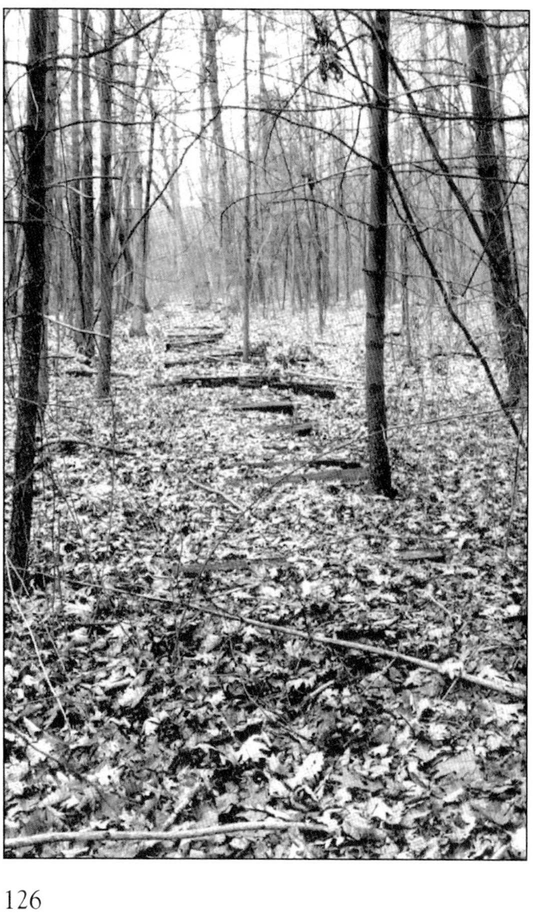

Railroad ties, pictured in 2004, serve as evidence of the train's movement around the grounds.

This 2004 photograph shows the remnants of a ride similar to a maypole.

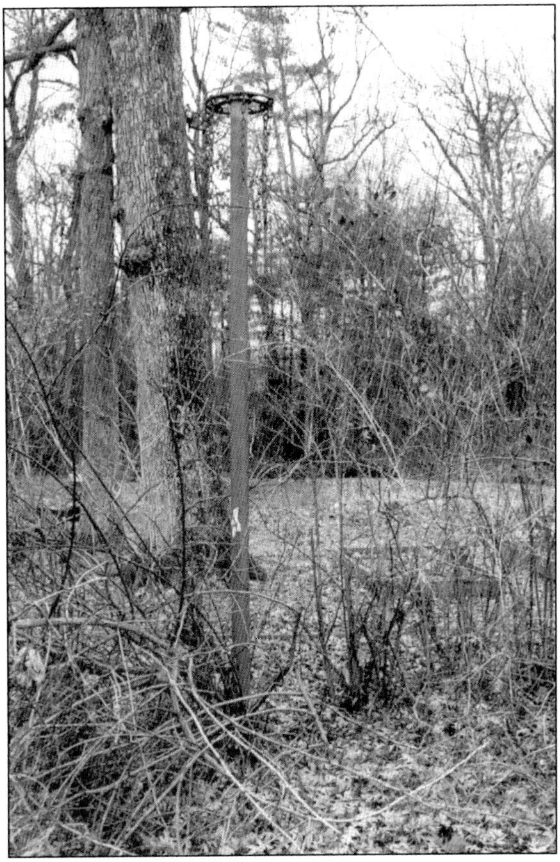

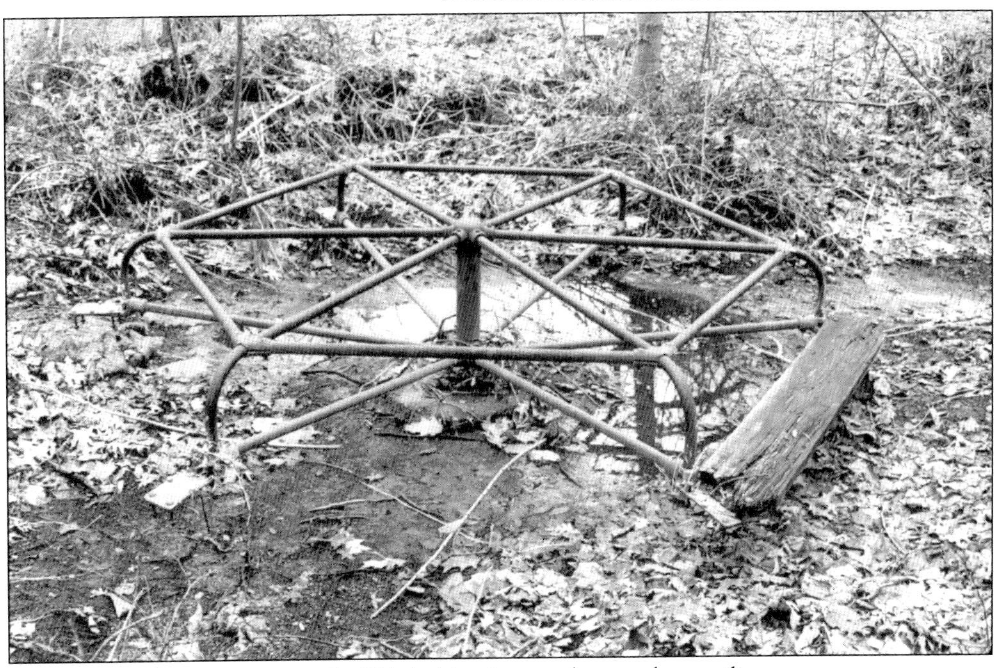

The small push merry-go-round still inhabits the woods near the pavilion.

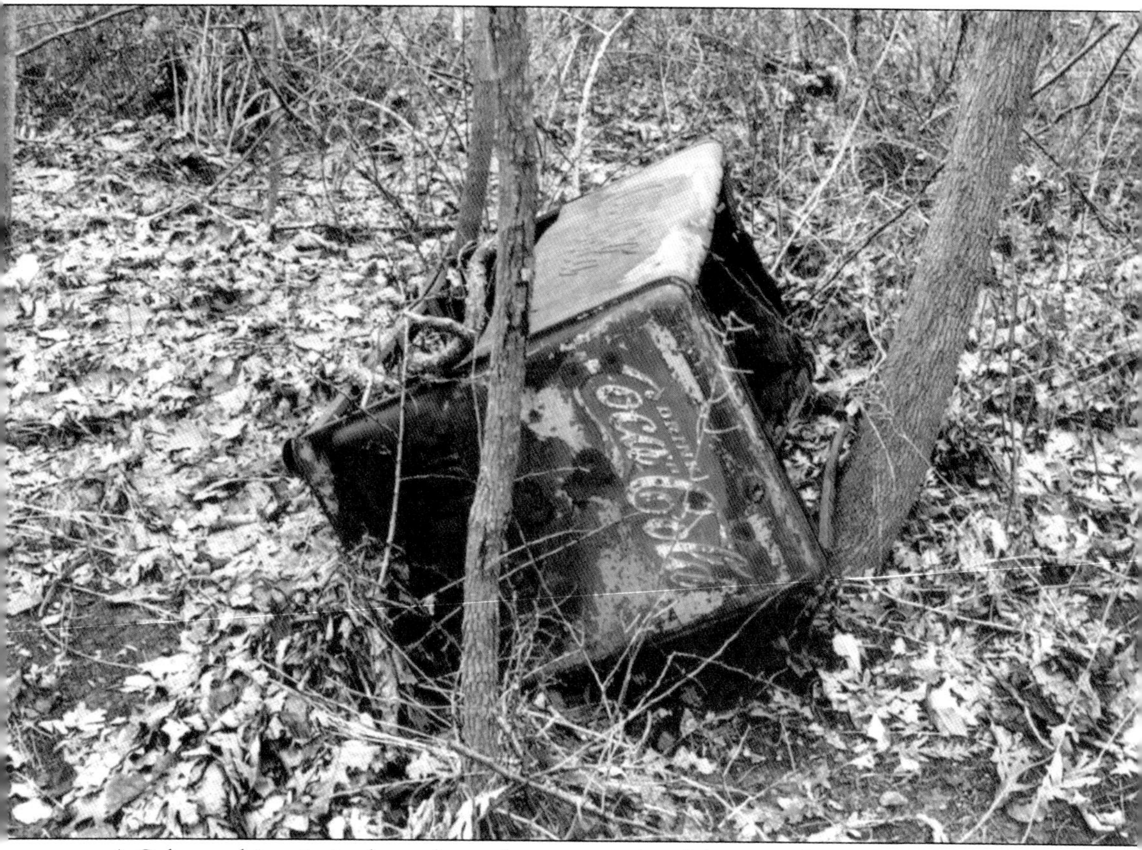

A Coke machine sits in the park woods as a reminder of days gone by.